D0857478

My Dear Wife and Children

Civil War Letters
from a 2nd Minnesota Volunteer

Nick K. Adams

Strategic Book Publishing and Rights Co.

Strategic Book Publishing and Rights Co., LLC
USA | Singapore
www.sbpra.com

For information about special discounts for bulk purchases, please contact Strategic Book Publishing and Rights Co., LLC. Special Sales, at bookorder@sbpra.net.

ISBN: 978-1-62857-966-6

Dedication

To my wonderful sister, Louise Kathleen Steuben, who insisted I do this, and was my constant supporter and counselor throughout the creation process.

Table of Contents

Preface 7

Introduction 9

The Letters 19

Beginnings—Fort Snelling, Minnesota to Lebanon, Kentucky 19

Army Life at Lebanon Junction and Lebanon, Kentucky 30

In Pursuit of Gen. Zollicoffer, Lebanon to Mill Springs,
Kentucky 63

Gathering of Forces Near Nashville, Tennessee 77

Gen. Buell's Army of the Ohio Marches South to Join Gen.
Grant at Shiloh, Tennessee 102

The Advance Upon and Occupation of Corinth, Mississippi 112

Guarding the Bridge at Cane Creek, Alabama 139

Chasing Gen. Bragg From Florence, Alabama to Louisville,
Kentucky 154

Chasing Gen. Bragg Out of Kentucky—Louisville to Bowling
Green 178

Guarding South Tunnel and Cunningham's Ford, Gallatin,
Tennessee 193

In and Around Gallatin, Tennessee 214

In and Around Camp Steadman, Triune, Tennessee 241

The Tullahoma Campaign to Winchester, Tennessee 289

On Toward Chattanooga, Tennessee and Chickamauga
Creek, Georgia 319

Endings—Chattanooga, Tennessee, to Spring Valley,
Minnesota 340

Epilogue 344

Appendixes 346

Appendix 1 – Significant Family 346

Appendix 2 – Significant Friends 348

Appendix 3 – Resources 351

Preface

It is deeply satisfying to know you are a part of history through the stories and artifacts passed down by your family. You feel connected. But, when that historical connection falls within as pivotal an event as the American Civil War, the satisfaction can be even greater. Such is the case with me.

I well remember the overwhelming awe I experienced when I received, and read for the first time, copies of one hundred letters written from September 1861 to September 1863 by my great-great-grandfather, Corporal David Brainard Griffin. Sent to the young family he had left on their southeastern Minnesota prairie homestead while he joined President Lincoln's struggle to maintain the Union, they describe in great detail the daily life and thoughts of a common soldier in the Western Theater during that period. They also meaningfully convey the heart of a farmer, husband, and father, separated from the place and people so beloved by and dependent on him: his personal loneliness, his concern for their well-being, and his constant hope for a speedy return.

As a child, I learned from my mother, his great-granddaughter, only his name, his Minnesota origin, and the fact that he had been killed at the Battle of Chickamauga. I never knew that she was aware of the trove of preserved letters somewhere in the extended family, though her own father had undoubtedly read them when they were circulated by his mother. Then, about twenty-five years ago, my mother borrowed them from her cousin, copied them with her permission, and they were presented to me. My life and teaching career were immediately changed.

During the last dozen years of my elementary school teaching career, I used them to introduce my students to that conflict on a significantly more personal level than any textbook could provide. Upon retiring, I told my distant grandfather's story from his letters in my first novel, *The Uncivil War: Battle in the Classroom.* Now in this volume, I present a careful transcription of the letters to make them available to a wider audience and am also using their content in a second novel, recreating the lives of David Brainard Griffin's family during his absence.

My grateful thanks, therefore, go to my maternal great-great-grandmother, Philinda Minerva Griffin, for preserving the letters; to my mother's cousin, Mildred Boyer, for allowing them to be copied; to my sister, Louise Steuben, for providing me with my copy of the originals; to the numerous other family members, Civil War enthusiasts, and former students who encouraged the work you now hold; to my painstaking primary editor and fellow Civil War enthusiast, Betty Pessagno; to KJ of www.kalpart.com for her creation of the maps based on contemporary resources provided by the David Rumsey Historical Map Collection; and to the wonderful staff at Strategic Publishing for all their invaluable help through the process. Finally, my dear wife, Carolyn, deserves special appreciation for her unending support of my obsession with these 150-year-old family matters.

As you read his letters, please share my personal connection to the American Civil War!

Introduction

The Family

David Brainard and Philinda Minerva Griffin arrived in Fillmore County, Minnesota, in 1857, a year before that state officially joined the Union. Two daughters came with them, Alice Jane and Ida May; a son, whom they named Edgar Lincoln, was later born to them in Minnesota.

These pioneers had begun their migration from long-established family farms in Connecticut and Vermont in 1853, a year after they were married. Alice Jane was born to them in Illinois in 1854 and Ida May (my great-grandmother) in Iowa two years later.

Interestingly, Brainard and Minerva, premarriage, shared the same Griffin name through a common descent from their great-grandparents Samuel Griffing and Mercy Bailey. Brainard and Minerva (both usually went by their middle names as was typical of that time) each came from large families, and numerous brothers and sisters from both sides are referred to throughout the correspondence. They also had a large number of acquaintances, including Minerva's neighbors and local compatriots with Brainard in the war. I have footnoted these connections at their first mention in his letters and provided additional information for many of them in the Index of Significant Family and Friends. Minerva's parents, Almon and Polly, followed them to Minnesota, accompanied by their son, Allen, and their eldest daughter's orphaned children, Eliza and Helen Churchill; they purchased a farm close by. Another of Minerva's siblings, Mary Durand, settled with her husband, Emery, in Spring Valley in the northwest corner of Fillmore County. These six appear regularly in the letters.

A single-room shack—repeatedly referred to in the letters as their "shanty"—along with a small barn and the few typical nineteenth-century farm structures that provided shelter for animals and storage for equipment and various supplies, comprised their home on a quarter of Section 15 of Beaver Township. Brainard was still *opening* new prairie land each year to add a few more acres for growing wheat, hay, oats, sorghum, and corn, a process Minerva continued with hired help after he left for the war. A horse for transportation, a Jersey cow for milk and calves, and a pair of young oxen for pulling and plowing were their large animals in addition to several pigs, chickens, and feeder steers for meat, eggs, and ready cash or trade. (Having personally walked parts of the homestead, I noted several remaining acres of hardwoods, a meandering stream, and a slight bluff close to the place where their shanty likely stood.)

This was the bucolic setting Brainard left behind when he began his journey to Fort Snelling, near St. Paul, to enlist on September 23, 1861. And, it was to this place that all his hopes and dreams, and most of his letters, were directed, right up to the morning the bullet struck him down beside a Georgia creek more than a thousand miles away on September 19, 1863. Throughout all the days, weeks, and months of marching, waiting, and fighting, mostly back and forth across the states of Kentucky and Tennessee, it was the thought of finally being able to return home that kept him going, faithful to his family and to his country. But this expectation, like that of so many, many others, was sacrificed in that terrible period we call the American Civil War.

The Letters

During his two years of service in Company F of Minnesota's 2nd Regiment of Volunteers within the Union Army, Brainard wrote his family nearly every week—at least one hundred letters in all. Most were in ink on unlined paper purchased at two cents a sheet from local stores or his camp's sutlery and mailed for an additional three cents (although some he sent with postage to be paid by Minerva). A few were in pencil when ink was not available. Following the Battle of Mill Springs, Brainard even mentions writing on paper he had retrieved from a rebel's tent, abandoned by its retreating owner. He most often wrote sitting on the ground with a board or his knapsack in his lap for a writing surface, but he also described himself as writing while standing at the tailgate of a supply wagon or beside a barrel head as well as by candlelight in his tent at night. He seems to be remarkably literate for a mid-nineteenth-century farmer. I have included a few samples of the originals in this work so that the reader can share my amazement at the high quality of his penmanship under those less-than-ideal circumstances.

Because of the nature of nineteenth-century warfare, which required constant movement, temporary shelter, and little if any storage, Brainard was not able to keep the letters he received from his wife and daughters as well as other family members and friends. But, most of the letters he wrote home have references to what those letters contained: information and questions about the farm and family, their social activities and problems, and the occasional small remembrances they sent. Mail call, for both incoming and outgoing mail, seems to have been once or twice a week. Sometimes, delays in delivery, as when his regiment was on a long march, caused writers on both ends of the correspondence to ask the same questions in subsequent letters, but normal transit times, at least from Minnesota to his regiment, ranged from four to ten days. Apparently, a few letters, sent both ways, were not received at all—perhaps lost in all the confusion of war.

The letters are presented in sets, according to date and place of writing, and include copies of actual letterheads Brainard used. Each set begins with a brief overview of its contents, along with a map of the area for that set.

The Regiment[I]

A mere two months following the formation and deployment of the 1st Minnesota Regiment of Volunteers in support of the Union at the beginning of the American Civil War, a second regiment was authorized and activated in June 1861. The ten new companies were temporarily divided among four Minnesota forts for drill and

---

[I] This is a summary of the information provided by Col. Judson Bishop in his "Story of a Regiment." The details summarized here are greatly amplified and personalized in the Griffin letters that will follow.

instruction, but on September 20, they were ordered assembled at Fort Snelling. This was accomplished the following week.

Adding a few more recruits (including the young men from Fillmore County), the 2nd Minnesota Regiment of Volunteers departed on October 14 by boat, under the command of their newly appointed colonel, H. P. VanCleve, traveling down the Mississippi River as far as LaCrosse, Wisconsin. From there, they were taken by train through Chicago and Pittsburgh, intending to travel on to Washington City. Their orders were changed, however, and instead, they were loaded onto three small steamboats for a four-day trip down the Ohio River to Louisville, Kentucky. Assigned to the forces of Gen. William Tecumseh Sherman, they were deployed thirty miles south at Lebanon Junction to begin guard duties and continue their military drilling.

Three weeks later, Gen. Don Carlos Buell assumed command, reorganizing his newly combined forces as the Army of the Ohio. The First Division, led by Gen. George H. Thomas, consisted of three brigades, with the 2nd Minnesota, one of four regiments assigned to the Third Brigade, Col. Robert L. McCook, commanding. After being relieved of their guard duties by the arrival of the new 3rd Minnesota in early December, the 2nd was finally able to relocate to Gen. Thomas's headquarters thirty miles further south and join the 9th and 35th Ohio regiments, with whom they would continuously serve, under Gen. Thomas, for the next three years.

With the first day of 1862, the 2nd Minnesota began its first military campaign, as Thomas's First Division started chasing down the command of Confederate States of America (CSA) Gen. George B. Crittenden. The forces finally met in battle eighteen days later at Mill Springs, Kentucky, centering on the encampment of CSA Gen. Felix Zollicoffer, who was killed during the fight. The result of their initial engagement, with the 2nd Minnesota playing a significant role in the day's struggle, was a complete Union victory.

After spending another month in the vicinity, they began a fifteen-day march—on most days in rain or snow—back to Louisville. There, they boarded the steamer *Jacob Straud* and proceeded down the Ohio to the Cumberland, then up the

Cumberland to Nashville, Tennessee, passing the newly captured Fort Donelson along the way. Following a three-week encampment outside Nashville, during which time Gen. Buell's entire Army of the Ohio was gathered, the five divisions began their ordered march down to Pittsburg Landing on the Tennessee River to combine forces with those of Gen. Ulysses S. Grant in the planned assault on the Confederate stronghold at the significant railroad junction of Corinth, Mississippi. Because of their recently fought battle, Gen. Thomas's division (including the 2nd Minnesota) was allowed to travel last in the line. The march was hindered by nearly constant rain that created almost impassable roads and flooded river crossings. Thus it was that, while Buell's three earliest divisions departing Nashville (Nelson, McCook, and Crittenden) arrived in time to make the difference on the second day of the Battle of Shiloh, the last to arrive only heard the rumbling of the fighting from a distance and arrived two days after the Confederates began their withdrawal back to Corinth. As a result, the 2nd Minnesota, with other regiments of Wood's and Thomas's divisions, were assigned to gather many of the more than sixteen thousand wounded and to bury the nearly four thousand dead from both sides still scattered across the battlefield, a grisly task Griffin does not relate to his family.

Gen. Hallack finally ordered the reorganized and reinforced armies of Grant and Buell to advance upon Corinth. As a result of rain and mud, nearly daily skirmishes, and frequent entrenching activities, the twenty-mile march became a five-week affair, by which time the Confederate Command decided to abandon Corinth.

Thomas's division soon began an eastward movement along the Memphis & Charleston Railroad, repairing and guarding it as far as Tuscumbia, Alabama, then continued east to Athens before crossing northeast toward Winchester, Tennessee, trailing Gen. Bragg's movement in the direction of Nashville. It was on the way to Winchester that the 2nd Minnesota's brigade commander, Gen. Robert L. McCook, was killed in a guerrilla attack, and in retaliation, the local countryside was severely punished by his enraged regiments. Col. Ferdinand Van Derveer was assigned that command.

By the time the division arrived at Nashville, Bragg was already racing for Louisville. Marching more than one hundred miles in seven days, without tents or baggage, the Federals passed through Bowling Green and reached the rear guard of the Army of Tennessee just below Cave City. By then, heading straight for the Ohio River and finishing the race by boat, the division was finally able to pass the Confederate forces and reach Louisville and the rest of Buell's command ahead of Bragg.

After a lengthy period of rest and reorganization into three corps, Buell finally initiated a push against Bragg's forces. The single major engagement was the October 8, 1862, Battle of Perryville, in which the 2nd Minnesota was only peripherally involved. It was basically a draw, and dissatisfaction with Buell's leadership resulted in his replacement by Gen. William S. Rosecrans and another reorganization, this time into the Army of the Cumberland, though the 2nd Minnesota remained under 3rd Corps Commander George Thomas.

As Bragg withdrew south again, his federal counterparts, including the 2nd Minnesota, retraced their previous northward march, passing again through Bowling Green on their way to Nashville. The retreating Confederates had blocked a railroad tunnel just above that city, and after helping transfer supplies for Nashville onto wagons, the 2nd Minnesota spent another week clearing the tunnel debris in order to reopen the line. They occupied several camps in the area for the eight weeks that followed, guarding, drilling, foraging, and skirmishing. From there, they also heard the distant rumbling of the year-end Battle of Stones River at Murfreesboro, thirty miles below Nashville.

Restarting their southward trek, the 2nd Minnesota spent the next month near Concord Church, below Nashville, coincidentally on the farm of the colonel of the 20th Tennessee Regiment, who had directly faced them at Mill Springs. An adventure there by Company H earned them two Special Complimentary Orders. Moving further south to Triune in early March, the 2nd Minnesota was involved in a series of small engagements with Confederate cavalry and infantry units while setting up a permanent fortified camp for the entire division. This was home for the next three months of drilling and guard duty, and it was there that the 2nd Minnesota finally traded their muskets for Enfield rifles, their wall tents for the new two-man shelter tents, and Gen. John Brannan for Gen. John Schofield as their new brigade commander.

From late June to early July, under constant rain and amid frequent skirmishes with Bragg's retreating rebels, Thomas's corps continued its push through southern Tennessee, crossing Duck Creek, passing through the mountains surrounding evacuated Tullahoma, traversing the flooded Elk River with ropes, and finally settling in Winchester, where the men spent a month repairing the railroads and preparing for the next chapter of the campaign, for Bragg had ensconced himself in Chattanooga.

Two major obstacles stood between them and the rebel army: the rugged Cumberland Mountains and the broad Tennessee River on the other side. When they reached the river, Company F of the 2nd Minnesota was assigned the task of constructing log rafts on which their entire division would cross successfully. Then, the long, dry, dusty ridges of Raccoon and Lookout Mountains still separated Brannan's troops from the location Rosecrans had assigned Thomas's XIV Corps. They were to secure a position just south of Chattanooga in order to hinder any retreating movement by the Confederate Army. With news that his most forward division, led by Gen. James S. Negley, had been attacked in McLemore's Cove along Chickamauga Creek, Thomas ordered the rest of the corps to advance in their support as quickly as possible.

What followed were the disastrous Union defeat at Chickamauga and the successful breaking of the Confederate siege of Chattanooga, the city into which Rosecrans's defeated army had withdrawn. Neither these events nor those of the additional year and a half of military and political conflict remaining will concern us, however, for the author of the letters you are about to read, Corporal David Brainard Griffin, was killed in the opening minutes of the two-day battle at Chickamauga Creek.

The Edit

As I transcribed the letters, I made an editorial choice to leave them basically as Brainard wrote them. Today's reader will encounter numerous extra or missing commas and capital letters, long run-on sentences, as well as spelling and grammatical errors. The only change I made is where a capital letter follows a missing period, typically at the end of a writing line, which would indicate the start of a new sentence. There, I have inserted the period within straight brackets ([ ]). I included those words he struck out when he changed his mind about his spelling or word choice. On rare occasions, there is an unreadable word or two, and a torn corner on one page leaves a few phrases missing on both sides. In all those cases, I either made a contextual guess at the content or inserted a word space between straight brackets, and all of these instances are so noted. He also circled an occasional important word (perhaps for emphasis), and these I indicated within curved brackets ({ }). One double page of his writing was inadvertently not copied for me, so I had to rely on an earlier transcription, and that text is also so noted.

These are his words, presented without apology for his language or social opinions, for he was a man of his own time, not ours.

Final Thoughts

Nearly one hundred years have passed since my great-grandmother, Ida May Griffin LeFevre, penned the following letter to her children and their families, connecting them to their own history by circulating the packet of letters her mother had preserved. I quote the letter in its entirety because I am simply continuing and broadening what she started.

Corona Calif. Nov 21/16

Dear Children one & all,

I am going to send my Fathers letters to you, his grandchildren, to read, they are all, or nearly all together and numbered, as they came, except a few that were not dated. I have just finished reading them. I had to stop many times, during the reading, as it brought everything back to me, & I can more fully realize the discomforts & hardships that Poor Mother had to endure, & as you will see by his letters, how she kept many things from him, so to not worry him, & you can read to, the long dissaponiting weeks & months & years, that he stayed & would'nt give up, & go home, as so many did, & the hopeing & longing & craveing for his little family, & besides that his letters were as near correct as to the war news of the time, as he could make them, as he was always careful to write only what he knew to be correct, so we have cherished them, all these years, & now you are all grown, I want you to read them, the ones whose names he mentions so often in his letters, were all familiar to me, & many I knew personaly, the Jim Thornton he mentions, stood beside him when he was shot, & visited us after he came home at the close of the war, Mr Cutting, "Jerry" James Nichlos, George Spaulding (Charlie Spauldings brother) & many others were all well known to me. I will send them first to Alice, by express, as I am sending a few things to her, she can then send them to one of you boys, & he to the next & so on, the last can send them back to me. I hope that none of you will be called on to endure what he did, but if you are, I know you will not be found wanting, & if you are only called to the every day battle of life, I hope you will be true to your princeples, so that when your finale record is written, it will be a clean one, tho perhaps a common one. I want to keep the letters if possible, so the grandchildren may read them too, the letters with the clasp on, are from his Captain & some friends to Grandma, anouncing his death, read them last.

I would like the wives & husband of you all to read them,

Mother

And now, I invite you to follow the personal two-year journey of David Brainard Griffin, from Minnesota to Georgia, as he described it to those he left behind. His letters open a window for us to visualize and perhaps better understand the momentous events of which he was a part—the war that both changed and confirmed our nation!

The Letters

Beginnings—Fort Snelling, Minnesota to Lebanon, Kentucky

Letters 1–3 (September 30–October 24, 1861)

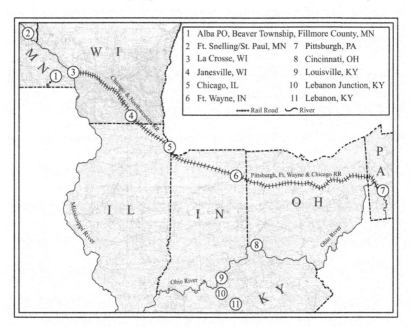

1	Alba PO, Beaver Township, Fillmore County, MN		
2	Ft. Snelling/St. Paul, MN	7	Pittsburgh, PA
3	La Crosse, WI	8	Cincinnati, OH
4	Janesville, WI	9	Louisville, KY
5	Chicago, IL	10	Lebanon Junction, KY
6	Ft. Wayne, IN	11	Lebanon, KY

Rail Road   River

David Brainard Griffin records for his family his travels from their Fillmore County homestead on the southeastern Minnesota prairie up to Fort Snelling outside of St. Paul for his enlistment and initial training. He also describes his clothing and equipment, their boat and train trip to Pittsburgh, and on to the first camp of the 2nd Minnesota Regiment of Volunteers.

2nd Regiment — MINNESOTA — Volunteers.

Letter Number 1

Fort Snelling, Sept 30, 1861

Dear Wife, I will write a few lines to you this evening, and let you know how I am, and what I have seen and done, I am well and have been well since I left home. I left Mr. Colby's[1] about one o'clock, got to Chatfield about ~~eight~~ nine o'clock, found the men there, started from there about eleven o'clock in an open wagon, it rained a little most all day, but still we had a very jolly time of it, we had to walk a good deal of the way, in the mud, we got to Winona about eleven o'clock the same night we expected the boat at 12 o'clock, but had to wait untill nine o'clock the next morning, so that we had a fine view of the river scenery, there was a good many high bluffs I tell you, and some very pretty places along the river, the wind blew very hard against us, so that we went very slow, and the river was very low, so that we ran upon a sand bar about 3 o'clock the next morning, and did not get of for about two hours, we got to St Paul about 9 o'clock ~~Friday~~ Saturday, I did not sleep any untill Friday night, and then they threw down some matreses upon the floor, and we all piled in there was thirty four of us, I did not sleep but about half of the time, that night. We took a good look of St Paul, there is some nice buildings there, we started then for Ft Snelling which is six miles from there, we

---

[1] Joseph Colby, a friend from nearby Spring Valley.

got here in time to see the Soldiers on dress prarade, and a nice sight it was, when I see them all, (500) in a body, dressed just alike, marching after a Brass Band, I just wished that "Nerva" could see them too, and when I thought of you, the tears came into my eyes, but I have not had much chance to feel downhearted since I came here, for there is something or other going on all the time. Sunday we all of us went up to the falls of Minnehaha, about two miles from here, that was a pretty sight, it is a stream about the sise of root river at Forrestville and where it falls is about 40 feet wide, and falls about 60 or 70 feet, and we can go right under the falls, when we stand below the falls and look at the water, it looks like a body of snow falling down[.] There is a good many Dutch volenteers in the regiment, but not many in our company, we were sworn in to the regiment to day, but we have not gone into the company yet, I was agoing along to day, and I see a man and woman in a wagon, and I thought that I knew the man, so I went up to them and asked him if his name was not Liman Russell, and he said that it was, he was glad to see me as well as I was to see him, I had not seen him for 12 years, he is a brother of Charles Russell[2], the boy that Grandfather Thompson[3] brought up, Charles lives about 6 miles from here if I do not see him here I shall go up and see him before we go away from here if I can. I must stop and go to Supper, we have enough to eat, and that, that is good enough for anybody to eat.

Oct 1st

As I could not write any last night, I will try to write some more to day, it rained all night and all the forenoon very hard, there was a frost yesterday morning here, tell Chipman[4] that there is some fifers here that will leave him in the shade, there was a Martial band played in our room last night and they made

---

[2] Charles F. Russell, a Ramsey County friend, Co. F, 3rd Minnesota Regiment of Volunteers.

[3] Ebenezer E. Thompson, Brainard Griffin's maternal grandfather.

[4] Mr. Chipman, a neighbor of the Griffins and Minerva's hired hand in Brainard's absence.

a good deal of noise there is everything agoing on here in the evening that you can think off, but it is all peaceable and in order.

We have just got our outfit, it consists in one overcoat, one dress coat, knapsack, canteen, haversack, two pair shirts, drawers, socks and one pair of shoes, one hat, & cap, we shall take our place in the tents tomorrow morning, Jery[5] is well and feels well, he is a writing to his wife now. James Thornton[6] is well, Minerva if you could see how the boys make fun of them that have enlisted in the fourth regiment, for the purpose of guarding the Forts this winter, you would rejoice with me that I was not with them for they call them evry thing that they can think of but patriotic and brave men, they call them "home cowards" ~~bloddy~~ bloody fourth's, petecoat guard, and all the names that you can think of, there was some of them told me this morning, that they would give five dollars if they could get into the 2d regment, but they cannot get out after they are sworn in very well, tell John Boynton[7] that there is not any show for him here, for each company does its own ~~clothin~~ cooking, they change about, first one and then an other, if you was here you would wonder how I can write atall for they are a dancing and singing, cutting hair smoking, talking, and at the door they are a playing on a drum and fife, but I do not mind them much but keep on a writing, we have just heard that the Chatfield boys will be here to night or to morrow morning, we expect to start from here some time next week, for Washington, so I cannot come ~~here~~ home before I go there, I will send you a paper to night with this letter[.] I stoped to Chatfield and had my name put down for the paper[8] it was not put down before, I will send you all the news that I can while I

---

[5] Jery/Jerry, Co. F, 2nd Minnesota, and his unnamed wife, are neighbors and best friends of the Griffins, but are never given a last name in the letters.

[6] James Thornton, a Fillmore Co. friend, Co. F, 2nd Minnesota.

[7] John and Sophrena Boynton, Beaver Township neighbors and holders of the mortgage to the Griffin farm.

[8] *The Chatfield Democrat*

can, I have not got my likeness taken yet. I will try to get it before I write again. I will write again before we go from here.

Now I have wrote you a good long letter this time, and I cannot think of much more to write to you this time, you must keep up good cheer, and not worry about me, for there is not a boy among the whole company that would see me suffer a bit while with them, and if you are taken care of as well as I am, we had not ought to complain, but while we are seperated we cannot help but think of oneanother, but we must be contented as it is. I will write to you as often as I can, and all the news that I can think of, you can write to me as often as you can and write how you all get along, tell Allen[9] that if he could see us here, he would wish that he was here with us, but tell him to help take care of the babys, that I have left behind me, and be as a father to them while I am gone, and if I do not come back again, I hope that he will be rewarded, if not in this world, in the world to come.

You must direct your letters to

D. B. Griffin,
Ft. Snelling, Minn,
Co. F. 2d Regiment, M.V.

and it will come to me whereever I am. Kiss the babys for me as often as you can, tell them that pa thinks of them pretty often and wishes that he could see them all, give my love to all of the folks, and take the largest part of it yourself, but now good bye, be a good girl and think of me, your friend and husband

D. B. Griffin

---

[9] Horation Allen Griffin, Minerva's younger brother, who works with his father on their nearby farm.

Letter Number 2

Ft. Snelling, Minn, Oct 12, 1861

My Dear Beloved Wife & children,

I will take my pen in hand once more, and address a few lines to you, and let you know how I am, and how I am a getting along[.] I am well, and as tough as a knot, I have enjoyed myself as well as could be expected, I get up in the morning by five o'clock. we sleep in tents, there is about 200 tents on the ground there is ten companies here of the 2nd Regiment, then the barracks are as full as they can be all the time, besides two large barns, of with the 3d and 4th regiments, and there is room for 1,000 in the Ft, or more, so you see that there is a few folks here, I have just come in from dress parade, and as I stood in front of them looking at the soldiers with a band of music on the march before them, the tears came into my eyes. I did wish that you could have been here to see them with me, imagine in your mind arow of soldiers 40 rods long and two rows of them, standing as strait as a line, and all dressd alike, with their bayonets glistening in the sun, then all faced one ~~ewa~~ way, withe a band of Music marching before them, and then about 3,000 people in front of them, you will have some idea how it looks, the Chatfield boys are all here, they are well, the Case boys[10] Cutting[11], Pete and all. Jehial Case was here three or fore days, he says that he thought that he should go down there and see you this fall, he thinks that he shall join us in Washington when his time is out as colporter, he was well[.]

As I was a saying, I get up at five, attend to the roll call at six, breakfast at seven, commence to drill at eight and drill untill 12, dinner at one, drill ~~at~~ from two, till five, then run around untill 9 o'clock when the roll is called and we go to bed, we have not been in the dress parade as yet but we shall often this, to day I have been on guard as sentinel, we are on guard 2 hours, then off four, it is not hard work. The 2d Regiment Starts

---

[10] Herman and Norman Case, friends from Chatfield, Co. A, 2nd Minnesota Regiment of Volunteers.

[11] Hiram B. Cutting, a friend from Chatfield, Co. A, 2nd Minnesota.

from here Monday morning at 6 o'clock, for Washington, so I expect that this will be the last letter that you will get from me untill I get there, and then I will write to you as soon as I can and as often. I have written one good long letter to you, and sent you a paper, and I will send you ~~a pap~~ three or four papers this time. I bought one of them and the rest of them was gave to me. I want that you should have something to ~~do~~ read while I can send it to you by paying the postage which is not much, and I want that you should write to me as often as you can because I begin to feel as though I should like to hear from home and the little ones, (kiss them for me) and may God bless and protect you all. It is now ten o'clock and I have got to go on guard at one o'clock and I will stop for to night and finish it up to morrow if I can, so good night.

Saturday, 2 o'clock P.M.

I have just got my dinner eat as there was a lot of boys got in here this noon from Chatfield I had to stop and see them, Ed. Rexford[12], Rundalls[13], and others, I got my picture taken this forenoon to send to you, and I should like to stand in some corner when you get it and see how you act, but I can guess, it is a very busy day with us, and I cannot find time to ~~you~~ write much more to you. I see Charles Russell every day, he is working in a stable here at the fort.

I want that you should get along about money as well as you can untill pay day and then I will send you all that I can, and get the shanty fixed up warm before winter, it has been very pleasant weather for a few days, there has not been but one frost here, write how you get along with the farm since you are the boss, write whether you get any letters or not and whether there has been any one of our folks there or not. Andrew Wallace[14] is well, look out and get your barrels made this fall before you butcher. Now do not want for any thing as long as you can get

[12] Edwin Rexford, a friend from Chatfield, Co. C, 3rd Minnesota.
[13] Ellicutt Rundell, of unknown Minnesota company and regiment.
[14] Andrew Wallace, from a neighboring farm family, rises to Sergeant in Co. F, 2nd Minnesota.

along without it. I do not know as I can get a chance to send my clothes home or not. I will if I can. I must stop for want of time I will write to you as soon as I can when I get to Washington, but I must bid you good bye, good bye, from your husband and friend

D.B. Griffin.

To Alice And Ida Griffin

Now I will write to you a little[.] Pa would give a good deal if he could see you here to day. I would show you the soldiers when they come out on dress prarade they look pretty I tell you. I see lots of little girls here every day, and little babies, kiss Edgar for me, wont you, there now pa is a crying, be good girls and help ma take care of him, and when he grows up to be a man he will be good to you, pa thinks of you a good many times every day, pa has not undressed him since he come away from home, he eats his dinners out doors, and sleeps on some hay in tents, ma will tell you what them are, pa has got a ~~bord bord~~ board bord in his lap to write on, and am a setting on the ground, now ain't that funny, now you must write to pa when ma does wont you, because pa does not know when he will see you again, now kiss one another for me and then kiss Ma for me, wont you, there now pa will have to stop and go to work, I have got to mend my trousers for they have not got any new ones here for me, you would laugh at me, wouldnt you to see me sewing my breeches but I make it go first rate I tell you, but good bye,

this to Alice J. and Ida M. Griffin from their father

David Brainerd Griffin

Letter Number 3

Lebanan Junction, Kentucky   Oct 24th 1861

Dear Beloved Wife,

I seat myself down on the ground, in my tent with a board in front of me to write upon, in order to write a few lines to you, and let you know where we are and how I am a getting along, you will see by the heading of this letter where I am, I am well as usual, I have not been sick any yet, nor there is not much sickness in the camp. I suppose that you would like to know how I came here. Well we started from Ft Snelling on Monday morning at 6 o'clock, went to the city of St Paul, Marched though the streets on to the boats, we had a fine ride on the river, got to La Cross about 12 o'clock at night, we got abord of the cars and started for ~~the~~ Chicago, we was cheered all along on the road, at Janesville the citizens brought us a good dinner into the cars, we got into Chicago about 11 o'clock P. M. we all marched into the Wigwam and stayed there two days waiting for orders. I saw Orlando Kellogg and Wife, and Leander and Lucy[15] they were very glad to see me, and so was I to see them they were all well, and all the folks in Ganoe. Watson Freeman[16] has joined a Cavalry company to go to Missouri, they said that he was in Chicago then or was a coming in in a day or two but I did not see him. Roena Hawley was out there a week before, she was well, and all the rest of Uncle Rogers folks, Mr Kellogg said that he thought that he should go out to Uncle Rogers this fall. I tried to have him say that he would go up to Minnesota if he did but he could not tell.

We started from Chicago Thursday night for Washington on the Pittsburg Ft Wayne and Chicago rail road, we had a very pleasant ride, we got to Pittsburgh Friday night marched to the city hall and got our supper, then marched into another hall, stayed there untill the next day at noon, Secretary Cameron[17] was there, and we was ordered to go to Louisville Kentucky which was 617 miles from there, we marched on board of three boats and started amid the cheers and roar of the citizens of

---

[15] The Kelloggs are some of Brainard's mother's extended family, as are perhaps others mentioned here.

[16] Watson L. Freeman, a friend of the Griffin family while in Vermont and Illinois, Co. B, 8th Illinois Cavalry. Following the war, Mr. Freeman, his wife, and their children, settled first in Fredonia and then in Mantorville, Dodge Co., Minnesota.

[17] Union Secretary of War, Simon Cameron.

Pittsburg. I cannot describe the places along the Ohio River now, but if I live to come home, I will, and I hope that I shall, we were on the boats untill Tuesday noon every place that we come by they waved flags and handkerchiefs and shouted, and when we went past Cincinnati, it was one continual shout for about 6 miles, and there was no end to the flaags, and handkerchiefs. I forgot to tell you how I did on the rail road, when we stoped at the stations, the women shook hands with us, there was lots of pretty women too, there was one little babe in one place that I shook hands with, and then kissed it, and dont you think that I thought of home some, well I did, I think of you a great many times in a day, and many a time does a stray tear start from the eye, but I have not had much chance to get homesick as yet, but I am a getting off the track we got to Louisville Tuesday morning, there was four regments landed there that day, we came here that night which place is about 30 miles from there. Louisville is a pretty place, there is thousands of Niggers there, it is strong for the Union now, we are stationed along with the Ill. 19th regiment, it is the regiment that was on the rail road when the bridge broke down, in the town of Mitchel Indiana, you have probably seen the account of it in the papers, they have been in Missoury 2 or three months, but they have not been in any battles yet. There is some secessions here but they do not dare to say any thing, about 4 weeks ago there was a camp of them right where we are, they burnt a large bridge about $1 \frac{1}{2}$ miles from here, and cut the telagraph wires here, but they have retreated south from here, and there is a camp of them about 50 miles from here, in bowling Green. We cannot tell when we shall go from here, nor where we shall go to when we do go, there is a good many rumors in camp, but we cannot place any dependence on what we hear, you can tell more what is a going on than we can, for the papers are not allowed to say anything about the war here. I sent you a letter since I started with my picture in it, and I sent you three papers since I came here. I hope that I shall hear from you before long, for I am anxious to hear from you all, Jery is well and contented, and it is rather hard writing, for it is a hard seat and there is four fellows a playing cards in the tent, by one candle, I play cards some but there is no gambleing in the camp of any account. I read all the papers that I can get but I do not get many here, it is a getting most time to go to bed, and I must stop for to night, so good bye for to night. I will wright some tomorrow to the children if I can get any time, but good night Minerva may God bless and protect you now and forever

D. B. Griffin

Lebanan Junction   Oct. 25th 1861

My dear affectionate Children, Alice and Ida Griffin

As I have written a good lot to Ma, I will write a few lines to you. Pa is well this morning, and he hopes that his little girls are well too, and his little boy babe Edgar Lincoln also. I live right by the side of the rail road and there is a train of cars a going by now, they make a great noise when they go by last night they went by with a great lot of soldiers and twelve great big cannons to shoot the rebels with. Pa dont know but that he will have to go and help shoot them too. I have to go out every day and learn how to use a gun, we have a lot of music here every day, two brass bands and two martial bands, Ma will tell you what they are. Pa see lots of little black bab's, down at Louisville they are just as black as the ground, and their Ma's was great big black wimen with great thick lips and they all had a checkered handkerchief tied around their head, they were most all of them slaves, poor little things. Pa felt sorry for them. I cannot write much more this time for I have not got much room, you must have Ma write to me, for you. Now be good girls and mind Ma. I wish that I could see you this morning and talk with you and kiss you all, but I cannot so good bye, good bye. This is from your Father Brainerd Griffin. Minerva I want that you should write to me as often as you can and let me know how you get along, and how you (are), good bye. Direct your letters to D. B. Griffin, Co F, 2d Regiment Minn Vol, and it will come to me whereever I am good bye with a{kiss}

D. B. Griffin

Army Life at Lebanon Junction and Lebanon, Kentucky

Letters 4–16 (October 29–December 31, 1861)

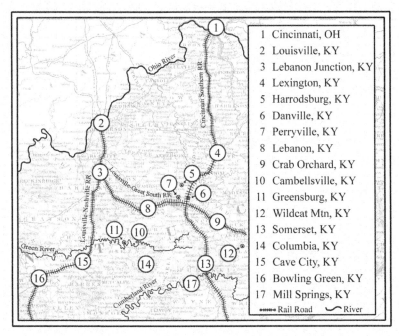

1	Cincinnati, OH
2	Louisville, KY
3	Lebanon Junction, KY
4	Lexington, KY
5	Harrodsburg, KY
6	Danville, KY
7	Perryville, KY
8	Lebanon, KY
9	Crab Orchard, KY
10	Cambellsville, KY
11	Greensburg, KY
12	Wildcat Mtn, KY
13	Somerset, KY
14	Columbia, KY
15	Cave City, KY
16	Bowling Green, KY
17	Mill Springs, KY

Rail Road ⌒ River

Brainard's letters continue to describe his new military life and his deep sense of separation from his family, partly relieved by the arrival of Minerva's first letter two months after he had left home. Snippets of war news, local skirmishes, weather conditions, and health reports abound, as well as very tender passages to his three young children. Here he receives his first pay and celebrates his first Thanksgiving in the Army. His biggest news is that he has been made Second Cook for his Company, which greatly changes his responsibilities. There are also numerous references to the work being done, and needing doing, as well as problems that have arisen back at the homestead in his absence.

Letter Number 4

Camp Anderson, Lebanon Ky   Oct 29, 1861

Dear affectionate wife and children,

I seat myself down once more to write a few lines to you I am as well as usual, with the exception of the teeth ache I had it all day yesterday and last night, but it has stoped now, but it is so sore that I can hardly eat anything, it is my back tooth, and I was on guard the sametime, so I feel pretty tired to day, there is not any sickness in camp of any account, and there is not any excitement as yet, there was a battle fought a week ago last Monday, about 30 miles from here at a place called Wildcat[1], in which the rebels were driven back, with a loss of near a thousand men our loss less than fifty killed and wounded, if they had (the rebels) won the day they would have marched on for Louisville, and if they had done so we should tried hard to have stoped them, but they did not, so we missed all of the fun this time, and we shall not probably have any skirmish while we stay here, and we are all anxious to get away from this place, for it is not a very healthy place to stay in, it is very wet heavy clay land all about here and the water is not very good either. The inhabitants are all, or pretty much all, old fashion "hoosiers," they bring in to camp apples, cider pies eggs vitles &c, there is some secession farmers about here that are now in the southern army, and their apples & potatoes, are free plunder for the soldiers when they can get out of the camp. I have not been out yet, but I have had all the apples that I wanted for a few days. I have got to go out on dress prarade now so I will wait untill evening. well I have been on dress parade and got my supper. I will tell you what I had for supper, we had boiled rice, applesauce, hominy, coffee and crackers, and sasafras tea, we have a plenty to eat such as it is, it is very pleasant weather here, there has been three or four frosts here but the days are quite warm yet, how is it there this fall, about frosts, how much sorghum have you made, how many potatoes was there, how does the hogs gain, how much did you get for wheat, and how much have you sold, how is Fathers folks[2] getting along with their payment, how does he and Gates[3] make out.

---

[1] October 21-22, 1862, CSA Gen. Felix Zollicoffer attacked, and was repulsed by, Union Gen. Albin F. Schoepf, who was blocking the Wilderness Road through the Cumberland Gap into Kentucky.

[2] Almon and Mary ("Polly") Griffin, Minerva's parents, who with their son and three of their daughter's orphaned children, moved from Vermont to a farm in nearby Section 16 after Brainard and Minerva had settled in Beaver Township.

[3] Mr. Thomas Gates, a neighbor and labor sharer, who by 1878 will have purchased the Almon Griffin farm following their deaths.

I wish that Allen would write to me if he will, you can let any one see my letters that wants to, I will try to write all that I can think of to you, and that is all that I can get time to write, too, and I will write to you as often as I can in order to let you know where I am, and I want that you should write to me as often as you can, for I am very anxious to hear from you all. I have not heard a word from home since I left there. I have sent three home and papers three times. I want to know whether you get them or not. I will send papers to you as often as I can get them, money is rather scarce with me. I try to get enough to pay postage[.] I left my clothes with Ed Rexford, he said that he would see that they was sent home, if anyone went down that way[.]

Jery is as well as usual, he is rather notional sometimes, if everything does not go just so he goes to doseing with pills or something else[.] James Thornton is well. So are all of the rest of the boys that we know any thing about, how does Mr. Chipman get along a farming of it this fall, does he get sick of taking care of you and the babyes, I hope that he will do well and feel at home if he can I wish that he would write to me as well as all the rest of the folks. Andrew Wallace is well you can tell his folks, you must look out and get your barrels from Mr. Wallace, in time to use them I cannot think of any thing ~~to~~ more to write to night, how does ~~Alice~~ Alice & Ida like it, to have me write to them. I would give most anything to see you all to night in the shanty, but we are a long ways apart, you in a shanty, and I in a tent with six men all strangers to me, but they are all friends to me I hope, but we have one thing to console us, in our seperation that the same being takes care of us all alike while on this earth, and if we are not permitted to see one others faces on this earth again, I hope that we shall all meet where parting will be at an end[.] Now be sure and write to me as soon as you can and write all the news that you can think of, this from your husband in ~~Ky~~ Kentucky, good night

David B. Griffin.

Letter Number 5

Camp Anderson, Lebanon Junction Ky.   Nov 11th 1861

My Dear Affectionate Wife,

I will write a lines to you to day, ~~in order~~ so that you ~~can~~ may know how I am, I am well and hearty yet, and anxiously looking for a letter from you every day. I have written six letters to you, but have not received one word from home yet. It would do me a great deal of good to hear from you and to know how you are a getting along, you must try to write once in a while, if not but a few words at a time, and have Fathers folks write too, and any one else that is a mind to. Jery is well at present he has not heard from home yet, Elicut Rundell is well he wrote a letter to Bonesteels folks today. We are all anxious to go from here as soon as ~~you~~ we can, and get into some place where there will be something to do all that the Regiment have's to do, is to guard the railroad each way from here for from two to four miles, and to keep a guard about the camp. I have been on guard three times since I came here, there is not much danger of any attact here, we do not know when we shall go, ~~to,~~ nor where we go to when we go from here, but we expect to go towards Nashville, as far as we can, the rebels are fortifying themselves at Bowling Green which is about sixty miles from here, and if we get into any battle this fall, it will probably be there, but we cannot tell any thing about it, but we all came for the purpose of fighting the rebels and we are anxious to commence as soon as we can with safety. Kentucky will probably be the battle ground this winter, you probably get some news from us through the Chatfield papers, we get a few papers in the camp to read, but I have not got any money to buy any with, if I had I would send some to you, we are expecting to get payed up to the 28 day of Oct. and when we do I will send all that I can to you, so that you can pay up the taxes and interest if you can, the debts must take care of themeselves untill you can get enough to pay them up, does anyone trouble you about paying them up. I hope not[.] I have not written to Vt. yet and I do not know as I shall, unless I hear from there. It is very pleasent weather here in the day time, but cool and damp nights, but we are pretty well supplied with clothes now[.] I have done my own washing and mending so far, but I have got my shirt and drawers out to wash to day. I get them washed for 5 cents apiece. I was pretty tired and we had to go off about 1 ½ miles this forenoon and get some straw for to put in our tents to sleep on, and so I thought that I would write a few lines to you, for we may be called upon any moment to march from here, but if we do I will write to you as soon as we stop again, but "<u>Minerva</u>," I want that you should write to me as often as you can, for we are far from each other and the only way that we have of conversing with ~~one~~ each other is on paper, and let us improve the time while we have the oppertunity, for you do not know how much good it would do me to get a good long letter from you, if you cannot write much at a time keep a writing a little every day untill you get a good long letter wrote, then direct it D. B. Grifin, Co. F 2nd Minn. Regiment ~~Co. F.~~ Louisville Ky. and they will come to me quicker than they would to send them to Snelling. I will write some to the children this evening good bye, this from your husband

D. B. Griffin, Minn.Vol.

Camp Anderson, Monday Evening, November eleventh, eighteen hundred and sixty one,

My Dear Children,

As I have wrote some to Mother and did not write any to you, I will write to you this evening. I am well, and I hope that you are well, for Pa, would not like to have his little children sick in Minnesota, and he be away down here in Kentucky, for I could not see them any then, how I would like to come up there this evening and go into the shanty and talk to his little ones, and laugh and play with them but no, instead of that, I am way down here in a tent, talking to them on a piece of paper, and instead of laughing and playing I am a crying you must not think that Pa cryes all of the time, for he does not. I enjoy my self first rate a most all of the time, but when I set down and commence to talk to you on a piece of paper, it makes me cry a little, and wish that he could talk to them at home, does little brother grow any these days, does he go alone any yet, does he talk any, you must be good to him, there is a little babe here in the camp, it is a little Dutch babe, he was born on the fourth day of July, they call him "Independence[.]" Pa goes and takes him and plays with him once in a while, but he is not as pretty as Edgar I guess, is he, kiss him for me, a good many times too, they have built up a fire out doors and they are a going to sing and dance and play on the flute, fiddle and tamborine. {'Alice,' good night,} {'Ida,' good night,} {'Edgar,' good night.}

Good morning Alice, Ida and Edgar,

I hope that you are all well this morning, and ma too, cant you kiss ma this morning right on the cheek for me all of you and then she must kiss all of you for me too. I hope that you are good girls, and mind Ma and Mr. Chipman, how is Mr. Chipman is he well this fall, how many potatoes did you pick up for him do you plague him any. I have had some beech nuts and some percimmons since I came here they are first rate. I have apples to eat most every day, it is quite warm this morning here, is it there, it is nine years this morning since Ma and Pa started from Vermont, you must keep still and let ma write a good long letter to me, and tell her what to write for you to, you must try and read his letters if you can, and write to him too[.]

I cannot think of much to write this morning. I have got to go and drill pretty soon, and I want to put this letter in the office so that it will start for Minnesota to day. Jery sets in a tent right opposite to me a writing a letter to his folks too, they are mounting guard now, and they are a playing with a brass band it is a pretty music. Pa has to go out on guard once in a while, he has to stand out all alone in the woods with a gun in his hands and keep watch of every thing that is a going on around me, and if I should see anybody and should tell them to halt three times and they should not stop, then I have got to shoot them if I can, but I hope that I shant have to shoot anyone, but I must stop so "good bye" one and all this from your father and best friend

David B. Griffin, to Alice, Ida and Edgar L. Griffin

Letter Number 6

Camp Anderson, Lebanon Junction, Kentucky   Nov 15th 61

Dear Wife

I am well to day, and in good spirits, there is not but one thing lacking to make me happy, and that is a good long letter from home with good news from you and about evry thing else. I think evry morning that when the mail comes in there will be a letter for me, but no. I have been away from home seven weeks and not one word from you yet, but I think that there will be one for me before long, but I will write to you whenever I get time, and feel like it, and I wish that you would write to me as often as you can, and get all of the folks to write to me that you can, if any one will write to me I will answer them, you cannot tell how anxious a soldier is to get a letter from his home, and friends. Jim Thornton got a letter from Ian Paul to day, he says that they were all well there when he wrote, but he says that Jo Colby was Married to Adelia Beldon, I think that he will have his arms full, perhaps he will get well and live along life, and have plenty of children. I expect to hear before long that Allen is married, but tell him not to wait untill he gets married before he writes to me, for if he does I am afraid that I shall have to wait untill the war is over, and I hope that it will be ended before the fourth of July, it is the opinion of all of us that we will be at home if alive, before that time and may God spare us untill that time. We expect to go from here next week, but where to, we do not know yet, but we shall probably go towards the enemy as far as it is safe to go at present, there is good news on our side from all quarters, you probably see about all the doings, that the army is adoing in the papers. I am a going to pay for a daily paper, for a month, and send it to you if I can, it will be cheaper than it will be to buy them evry day, and it gives all the news about the war that it can, there is some talk that we shall get our pay to morrow for the first month, if we do, I will send you a little money, in this letter, if not I will send some to you as soon as I do get it. I must stop writing for this time and get ready for dress prarade.

Evening.

It is quite cool this evening, but Tuesday and Wednesday was about as warm as it was any day last summer in Minnesota with the exception of two or three of the warmest. I was on guard Wednes. night, and a pretty night it was untill four o'clock in the morning when it commenced raining, and it rained hard, untill seven, and I had to stand out and take it, but did not get very wet nor catch cold, and it was showery all day yesterday but it is quite pleasant to day but quite cool, and to night the moon shines as bright as a full moon can. I sent you a letter on the twelfth in which I wrote to the children. I would like to know what they say about my writing to them, I would like to see them when you are a reading it to them, and I would like to see "Nerva" and the "boy baby" also, any time, but you are better off at home than you would be here, they are playing the tattoo, and I have got to "turn out" to roll call and then go to bed, so good night.

Sunday After noon, Nov 17th

As I had to go on guard duty yesterday and last night I did not finish writing, so I will write a little to you this afternoon. I do not feel first rate this afternoon, for I have been asleep most all day, it was quite cool last night, with a pretty hard frost, and it looks some as though it was a going to storm, there is not many sick in the camp now, but I am afraid that there will be if it comes on wet weather, there has not but one man died in the Regiment since we came here, he died with the Typhoid Fever, he belonged to Co I, he was not sick but a short time. Andrew Wallace is well and so are all the rest of the boys that we know anything about, we have not got payed of yet, but we are expecting to get it this week, and go on towards General

Buckner's[4] or Johnson's[5] Army, the Colonel of our Regiment says that he should not be surprised if we were all of us back in Minnesota in three months, from now. I hope that it will be so, God knows I do, but I think that we shall see some active service before we go home, if we do it is not at all ~~proble~~ probable that all of us will escape the bullets of the enemy, but I hope so. Co. F. is one of the best Co. that there is in the Regiment, our Capt. is a nice man, he is liked better as a man than Capt. Bishop[6] is, his name is Davis[7], most of the Officers are liked first rate.

Sunday Evening, here I am again a talking to you. I am alone this evening, all of the rest of the boys from this tent being on guard to night it is the first time that I have slep alone since I came away from home. I have been through camp this evening, the tents are all lit up and a good many of the boys are a singing songs. I have been a talking with the Case boys, they are full of their fun, and feel first rate. I would like to hear from you this evening. I want that you should tell me whether you get all of my letters or not, this makes eight that I have written to you. I will try and write one a week to you and you must write to me as often as you can, for I look anxiously for a letter from you because I want to know how you are, and how you get along this cold weather. I heard that they had had some snow in Minnesota, we have not seen any here yet, but they have a little snow here most every winter. I cannot think of any thing more to write this Evening, so I will stop and finish this letter to morrow, if I can get any time to write. I told you in my other

---

[4] CSA Gen. Simon Bolivar Buckner, newly drawn into the conflict by Kentucky's abandonment of its policy of neutrality. He will soon, unfortunately, be left in command at Fort Donelson, and will be required to accept Union Gen. Ulysses S. Grant's terms of "Unconditional Surrender."
[5] Either CSA Gen. Bushrod R. Johnson, or if his identification is wrong, CSA Gen. Albert Sidney Johnston, since both were in the surrounding area at that time.
[6] Judson W. Bishop, from Chatfield, who later became Colonel of the 2nd Minnesota Regiment of Volunteers and the author of their official history, *The Story of a Regiment.*
[7] John B. Davis, who later became Major of the 2nd Minnesota.

letter how to direct letters but for fear that you will not get it I will tell you again. D. B. Griffin, Company F. 2nd Regiment Minn. Volenteers, Louisville, Ky. I think that that is plain enough, so I must bid you all good night again and go to bed, "good night."

Monday morning Nov. 18th

I feel very much disappointed this morning for I thought shure that I should get a letter from you but no, no letter it is a foggy morning, there is some of the boys that have got a touch of the Ague. I hope that I shall not have it. I shall try to prevent it, there is not anything new to write about this morning that I know of[.] I shall endeavor to write to you as often as I can, you must not believe all the reports that you hear about us for you cannot tell anything about what you hear, but I do not intend to write anything but what is so, have you got any letters from Vermont, or from any other place, how does Grandpa and Grandma get along are they well, does Eliza[8] stay with you yet, who is agoing to keep the school this winter, has there any one enlisted about there since I came away, have any of you been sick, or any one else about there, how do you get along for wood, how much does the hogs weigh, and how many pigs do you keep, &c. I guess that you have heard enough of such stuff for this time. Now be sure and write to me as often as you can, and let me all the particulars about matters and things in general, and yourself in particular, give my respects to all the folks, and keep a good share of them yourself, kiss the babe's for me, tell them that pa would give a good deal if he could see them, and so I would too, and also to see "Nerva," this from your friend and husband

D. B. Griffin, M. V.

---

[8] Elizabeth Churchill, a twelve-year-old orphaned grandchild, living with Minerva's parents.

Letter Number 7

Head quarters, Camp Anderson, Lebanon Junction Ky, Nov. 22st 1861

My dear Companion and friend, I have just received your first letter written to me, and you had better believe that I was glad to hear from you all, and to hear that you were all well. I am well today, better than I expected to be a few days ago, for last Monday afternoon I had an ague chill, and a hard fever all night. Tuesday I got out of camp and found some crab apple trees, and I went to taking tea pretty thourough. Wednesday, I had to go to the doctors or else be obliged to go on duty he gave me some quinine to take with my tea. I pitched the quinine up to the tent and threw it in the fire. I stoped taking the tea last night and to day I feel as well as ever I did, and more so since I got a letter from you. I am glad that you get along with your work first rate. I dont see but that you and Mr. Chipman plan first rate as regards building and farming. I hope that you will get fixed up for winter so that you will be comfortable, and enjoy yourself as well ~~as well~~ as you can and not worry yourself about me, for I get along first rate, and I will write to you as often as I can, and you must go a visiting as often as you can, but I hope that you will look out and not get ~~out~~ lost upon the prairie any more. Andrew says that his folks have moved up into Wis. I hope that you got your pay of him, and of Coridon too for he is agoing east he says that Mr. Gilman bought them out, he will make a good neighbor. I do not think that you have lost anything there, not saying anything bad for Mr. Wallace.

We have not had any very cold weather as yet, a few frosty nights it has rained hard all of the forenoon, but it has stoped now (2 o'clock)[.] I am very glad to hear that Father and Gates made out to come to a settlement. I hope that he will get his pay from him now, if you do, I want that you should lett Mr. Gates alone in his deal, and be careful who you deal with, for you need all that you have got, or the value of it, if Father gets his pay of Gates, you had better ~~fig~~ let him have our share of it towards paying him up what we are owing him. We have not got payed off yet but we probably will in a few days. I have got enough money to pay the postage on this letter, and that is all, I have lent some out, but I can get enough to pay postage some how or other, I will send you a couple of envelopes already directed, I hope that after your letters get to coming to me they will come right along, and not be three or four weeks a coming here, do you get all of my letters, this is the ninth one. I cannot think of much to write this time, you say that you would be glad to see me. I do not believe that you would give any more to see me than I would to see you and the children. God bless their little hearts, and may you never repent it for letting me go and leave you. I have written to the children in the last letters all that I think of for now, tell them to dream away about their pa, for he hopes that some day he will come home and bring something home to them, the tent has been full all day but when I read your letter I could not keep back the tears, in spite of the crowd, I hope that you will get all of my letters, and answer as many of them as you can, it has commenced to rain again, you had more trout potatoes than I supposed that you would[.] I hope that you will secure them from frost this winter. I do not worry about you at all now for I think that you will get along first rate, I shall look for another letter from you all the time, untill I get one[.] I thought that I would send this off to day, but I am too late for the cars have got in so I will have to wait untill tomorrow, and perhaps I will write some more but I will bid you all good bye this time, this from your husband

D. B. Griffin

Saturday 23   I cannot think of any more to write to day, it is pretty cold to day but pleasant, with a south wind. I am well and all of the rest of the boys. Write as often as you can, good bye Nerva, babe, and all,

D. B. G.

Letter Number 8

Lebanan Junction, Ky, Nov. 26th 1861

My Dear Affectionate Wife, and children, I will write a few lines to you this evening although I have not got any news to write to you. I am well, and in good spirits to day for we were all paid off yesterday, we were paid up to the 31st of Oct, my pay amounted to $14.30[.] I am agoing to borrow $15.00, and then send $25 to you in this letter, so that you can pay Mr. Boynton some interest money, pay him all that you can of it, without suffering for the want of it, it will be two months before I shall get any more to send to you, if I live and do not get wounded in any battle, and I do not know when we shall get the chance of drawing a bead apon a rebel, but things look as though we were not agoing to stay here a great while, for the Colonel[9] has ordered all the women in the regiment, home as soon as transportation can be had to take them home, the third regiment is camped about four miles from Louisville, I have not seen any of them yet. Jery got a letter from home to day, he is well, she wrote that she had not got any letters from him since we came south, but that you had got some from me. I hope that you will get all the letters that I write to you, and that you will answer all that you can of them, and tell me all that you can think of for I am glad to hear about any thing from home now it has been quite cool here for the last three or four days, but it is pleasant again to day, what kind of weather is it there this fall, cold or not[.] I am agoing to send you some of Leslie's pictorials along with this letter. I will direct it to Ida, for I think that it will please her first rate. I would like to be there and show them the pictures, don't you think I would Minerva, wall, I would now[.]

I think that they have got some very pretty dresses. I hope that they will both of them be good girls and mind their Ma, for I cannot tell when I shall come home to help her take care of them but I hope that it will soon be so that I can come, for I

---

[9] Col. Horatio P. Van Cleve, Regimental Commander for most of the 2nd Minnesota's first year.

want to see you all very much just now, I hope that I shall get a letter from you tomorrow or else before long, now if you get this letter safe with the money, I want that you should write just as soon as you get it, and let me know it. I have been washing this afternoon, I washed my shirt, drawers, and socks, you would laugh to see me. I have sent to Louisville for a pair of buckskin gloves, and some postage stamps. I wish that Father would look out for my town orders before taxpaying time. I do not know ~~know~~ how much it is. I wish that he would write to me and let me know how Gates performed when he caught him. I guess that he thought "Dam" as the Dutchman said. I guess that he felt like leading a class meeting about that time or as soon as he got home, you write about it. I cannot finish this to night for we have to go to bed at half past eight, and it is almost time, so I will stop, so good night "Nerva" and "babes."

Nov. 27th good morning "Nerva" and Edgar,

I guess that he is nine months old to day. I would like to see you all this morning, to morrow is thanksgiving day here, and also in Minnesota. I wish that I could be there and help you eat up the old "rooster[.]" It rained very hard last night with a good deal of thunder and lightning very heavy to, we have all kinds of weather here, it is raining some this morning. I have waited untill the mail has got in but no letter for me, you must excuse me this time and I will write often, there is no news of any importance this morning. I will send a paper to you now and then, do you get the Preston paper now who were the Jurymen from Beaver this fall tell Allen to write to me have you heard from Dan[10], or anyone else yet, but I will close with my best wishes to you and all the rest of the folks in Minn, and especially yourself and children

D. B. Griffin

---

[10] Almon Daniel Griffin, Minerva's younger brother still in Vermont.

Letter Number 9

Camp Anderson, Lebanan Junction Dec 2nd 1861

My dear Companion and Children,

I will again seat myself ~~down~~ for the purpose of writing a few lines to you. I am not as well as I was when I last wrote to you. I was on guard last friday night and it rained and snowed some and I caught a bad cold and I was quite unwell Saturday night and Sunday, but I feel a good deal better this morning. I manage to keep away from the doctors, it is quite cold this morning and it is a snowing quite hard there is about two inches of snow, it is the first that we have had to stay on any length of time, we have had a good deal of rain for the last week and the streams have risen very high, we were on guard last friday night at the bridge which stood in the place of the one that the rebels burnt before we came here, and the water in the river raised so fast, and the flood wood came down against it so, that it took part of it (the bridge) away it was a very high bridge, about 70 or 80 feet high I saw it fall it made a terrible crash we are camped upon very clayey land and it has rained so much that we are right in the mud, and we have no chance to dry the straw in our tents, so it is damp all of the time, there is about one hundred that is sick out if the regiment, there was a lieutenant of Com. C. buried yesterday, he has been sick some time with the thypoid fever[.] I am afraid that there will be more of us sick if we have to stay here all winter, but I do not think that we will have to stay here but where we shall go to from here we cannot tell, there is some talk of our going to Louisville to winter, if we do, there is not any probability of our ever being in any engagement during this war, for I think that it will be ended before spring, from all accounts, the rebels are getting discouraged in some places. I hope that it will end without the sheding of much blood, the Kentucky folks think that the Minnesota boys are very large men, they ask us if the women in Minnesota are as large accordingly as the men, there was some soldiers from a kentucky regiment here the other night, one of them asked me the question, and I told him that they were larger accordingly. I told him that I picked the smallest one in the family for my woman, and she weighed 170 lbs, you must excuse me for telling him so, but it made some fun for our boys, we have some first rate times. I must tell you what I had for thanksgiving, I had some baked chicken, pumpkin pie, apples and cider, bread and coffee. I have not had but one letter from you yet. I should think that you would write to me as often as once in four weeks, when I write to you every week, do you get them all this is the eleventh[.] I want that you should write to me and tell me whether you received the money that I sent to you, $25.00, and Leslie's papers to Ida, and if you did tell me what she said. I will get one and send to Alice next time, it is pretty cold writing, I have got on my overcoat ~~on~~, we have got no fire in the tent, how do you get along this cold weather do you manage to keep warm. Jery is well. I cannot write any more this time[.] I hope that I shall get a letter from you before I write again, I will write to you if there is any change in the regiment. Now be shure and write to me, this from your husband and friend in the war,

D. B. Griffin

Letter Number 10

Lebanon Ky Dec 10th 1861

Dear ~~and~~ affectionate wife and companion,

I seat myself down this evening to address a few lines to you. I am well to night, but pretty tired, as we have been pitching our tents, we are now in the village of Lebanon, which is 37 miles from where we have been camped, we had to move yesterday, we got here about 9 o'clock last night and we got off from the cars, and took our blankets and lay right down upon the ground[.] I slept first rate, it is very warm here at present, and the grass is as green as it is in the summer, the cattle feed upon it, we have had about 2 inches of snow, but it all went of the next day, and it has been quite warm ever since. I hear that you are a having a hard winter in Minn, I hope that you do not suffer with the cold any but I do not know for you do not write to me, or else I do not get them, for I have not received but just one letter from you[.] Jery has received three from his woman, and so I have heard that you were well. I got a letter from Watson Freeman last week, he is in Washington he belongs to the 8th Ill. Cavalry Co. he was well and also his folks, his folks told him where I was, I wrote him a good long letter. I sent three papers to Father yesterday and two to Mr. Boynton, I will send you some[.] I am now to work in the cook shop. I have been in about a week, I am the second cook[.] I get along first rate. I have got two meals for the whole company, I do not have to be on any other duty. I do not know whether I shall get any thing extra or not, but I washed for myself last Saturday, and some of the boys wanted that I should wash for them, and so I washed eleven pieces at 5 cts apiece, and on Sunday I washed 14 shirts, 7 pair of draws, and one coat and a pair of pants and some other pieces which came to $1.60, and helped get three meals besides did not I do first rate, my fingers got sore some. I think I can get enough to do, to keep me in spending money, all that I do to them is just to wash them out in two waters, and rinse them, they are most all woollen clothes. As regards what we are a going to do we cannot tell as yet, but the regiment has been assigned into a brigade, called General McCook's[11] brigade, there is five regiments in the brigade there is a great many regments camped around this place but how many I have not learned we some expect to make a grand advance towards the enemy's lines in a few days, but we cannot tell untill the orders come from head quarters, and when they do come, we dont wait long before we act according to the orders, but you must not worry about me at all, for I do not think that I shall be in any danger as long as I stay in the cook shop. I shall stay there as long as I can, for I do not think it is as hard upon me as it is to be on drill and guard duty we are in a healther place than we were at the Junction, the Minn 3d took our places or four companies of them. I saw old Mr.

---

[11] Union Gen. Robert L. McCook, 3rd Brigade Commander under Union Gen. George H. Thomas in the Army of the Ohio.

Stevens and son, the rest of the Fillmore Co. boys stoped about 11 miles so I did not see them at all, they will not be ~~apet~~ likley to be called into action this winter, and it is the opinion of every one that the war will be ended by spring, if we make an advance upon them this winter you probably learn more about the war than what we do, for we do not get any papers only the Louisville Paper, if you get a good county paper, I wish that you would send one to me (this sheet is not large enough is it.) but I will stop for to night, good night

D. B. Griffin

Letter Number 11

Wednesday evening, Dec. 11th 1861

As I did not send off my letter to day, I will try to write a few lines to you this evening. I am well, but pretty tired, for I have been a washing dishes almost all day, it is some cooler to night than it was last night, but it has been very pleasent all day so that the Ladies walk out with their sunbonnets on, and set at the window with it up[.] I dream every little while of being at home and seeing you and the little ones, but when I wake up, I find that it is nothing but a dream. I hope that it will soon be so that I <u>can</u> <u>see</u> you all, but I have enlisted for the war, and I am bound to see the end of it if I live, and you can tell as well as I can when that will bee. I hope that it will not last long, but whether it does or not, I wish that I could hear from you a little oftener than I have[.] I know it is hard work for you to write, but if you knew how anxious I watch the mails every day, you would send a few words to me often, if you did not write any more that to tell me how you all get along and what kind of weather you are a having &c. I am anxious to hear whether you received the $25.00 that I sent to you. Jery's wife said that you had got my picture, how did you like the looks of it, did the children know that it was mine, are the children well all of the time this winter, I would like to pull their ears a little this evening and give them a kiss too, wont you do it for me,

"Nerva." I cannot write any more this time but I will write often, wont you, {yes}[.] I do not expect that we shall be here more than a week or so, there is about 12,000 troops here in all, and there is 8,000 more on the road here, so you can see that the North is bound to do something before long if the South does not back down. I am to chilly to write any more, so I will bid you good night and go to bed. I have got to sleep alone to night. I have not taken my clothes of but just when I change them, but two or three times, now write soon and which is the wish of your best friend and companion,

D. B. Griffin.
Direct the same as I gave you directions before
2nd Minn Regment Vol. Via Louisvil. Ky.
2nd Reg. Minn. Vol. Co. F.
Via Louisville, Ky.

Letter Number 12

Lebanan Ky   Dec 15 1861

Dear and affectionate Wife,

I received a letter from you last night, (it was only four days coming from Mc. Gregors[12]) and you better believe that I was glad to hear from you all once more and to hear fro that you were all well, it is the second one that I have had from you. I am glad that you are getting along first rate, where do you get your wood, and do you have enough of it, if you were here to day you would not want any wood for it is as warm and pleasant as it is in June, in Minn. I am seting out doors, and writing on the head of a barrel and my hands sweat so that I wipe them every few moments and since I set here I heard a golden robin sing. I have not got much news to write to you to day for I wrote a letter to you a day or two ago, but I must tell you of a little skirmish that the teamsters got into when they came up here, they went up to a man's house in the edge of the evening to see if they could not get some fodder for their teams, the

---

[12] Probably McGregor, Iowa, SE of Beaver Township, on the Mississippi River.

man told them to get off from his premises or he would shoot them, they went back to the waggon's and Lieut Havens[13] of Chatfield gave them a revolver and told them to go up and get some, they went up, and they offered to pay him for some fodder, he told them that here was the kind of fodder that he would give them and fired a double barrell shot gun at them, there was four buck shot hit one of the men, two in his left arm, one in his right, and one in his side, but not dangerous, they took the man prisoner, he is a brother to the Jackson that shot Col Ellsworth[14], they shot at him three times but it being dark did not hit him, it is a pity that they did not shoot him dead, on the spot, we are only 60 miles from the enemy's army, there was about 12,000 started from here two or three days ago, but when we go I cannot tell, nor any one else, we had a lot of ladies here last night to see us get supper they said that it looked so odd to see men a cooking, we were a baking pancakes, they called them batter cakes, the cook[15] told them that the Indian's called them slapjac's, it made them laugh. I went to house of one of them to day to get a slice of bread to toast for myself she gave me three or four, and she said she would gave me more, but they had only a part of a cone loaf in the house, now you will want to know what I wanted it for, well I will tell you. I had a very high fever most all night last night, and when the fever left me I comenced vomiting, and I drank a lot of water, and it phisicked me a considerable. I went to the doctors this morning and he told me that I did not need any medicine, just keep still to day, so I have been a bed most all day. I feel a good deal better this afternoon. I think that I

---

[13] Charles H. Haven, a Chatfield friend, Co. A, 2nd Minnesota Regiment of Volunteers. Lt. Haven will die aboard *The Jacob Straud* the last week of February 1862, while the regiment is in transition to Nashville, Tennessee (letter number 27).

[14] Union Col. Elmer Ephraim Ellsworth, killed in May 1861 by the Alexandria, Virginia innkeeper James W. Jackson, when Ellsworth and his New York Zouaves took down the inn's offending Confederate flag that was visible from the White House across the Potomac River.

[15] His name is Louis Allers, and he remained with Co. F until his term of enlistment ended on July 7, 1864.

shall get along if I am ~~carfful~~ carefull. I have a good bed to sleep on now and a plenty of blankets over us. I am in a tent with the cook, there was two of the men that I tented with married men, they lived west of St Paul, have you ever got any of the papers that I sent to you, and how many of the letters have you got, this is the ~~12~~ 13 th and have you got the one with the money in. I liked to forget to tell you that I had my teeth pulled yesterday, one tooth and two prongs, it did not hurt much and I am glad that they are out, I don't think that I shall jump when I am eating any more for a while. I cannot think of much more to write this time. I should like to be at home and see you and the children, especialy my boy. I should like to hear him call pa, pa, but I shall have to wait untill the war is over, and then if I am alive you will see me as soon as I can get home, unless we are released nearenough to Vt so that I can afford to go there, you must not worry at all about me for we are all of us taken good care of, but I must stop so good night, Nerva D. B. Griffin

kiss all of the babes for me and here is one for you { ___ } I ciskissed it ~~with~~

Letter Number 13

Lebanon Ky. Dec. 16th 1861

My Dear Children,

I thought that I would write a few lines to you to day. I put one in the office for ma this morning, but I guess that ma won't care if I write to you this time. I feel pretty well to day, it is real pleasent weather, it is cool nights, just enough so that there is a little jack frost in the morning[.] Now I am agoing to talk with you a little while. Oh! how I would like to see you all to day, the longer I am away from you, the more I think of you, and many, many a time does my nose tickle and the tears (tear drop) roll down my cheeks, but I hope that it will not be a great many months before we shall all see each other again, and if pa does get home alive and well, he dont think that he will ever go away and leave his little girls, and his little "boy," a great while at a time as long as he lives[.]

I dont suppose that you would know me now if you should see me, for I have got my hair cut short, and I have not cut of my "mus'nt touchit" since I came from home, nor I don't think I shall again untill I get home again. I guess that great grandpa would laugh at me then would'nt he. I sha'nt care for that, does Grandpa come down to see you any this winter, and do you go up there any. I hope that you are both good girls and mind ma, you must have ma tell me what you want to tell me. I dont care what it is if you will tell her something to write to pa, both of you, and then tell me what little Edgar Lincoln says for himself, this winter he dont slide down hill any does he, you tell him that he had better wait untill next winter. I went over to a house close by here and there was a little boy babe 7 months old it made me think of little Edgar, the little nigger girls tote him around, there is "right smart of niggers about here, all slaves, ~~how~~ would you like to be a slave and be sold from your ma and pa and never see them again, no I guess not. I think that you would rather let your pa go away from home a little while, there is a good many slaves in here every day, they are all black folks there was two little black boys in our "kitchen" today and the way they did play, I tell you, now I must tell you how our "kitchen" looks, well we have got a shed boarded up on three sides, and covered, and two crotches drove down in front, and a pole acrost them ~~at~~ to hang the kittles on and then we fixed up a table in the shape of an L the length of two bords one way and one the other, and then when we get our table set, we holler out, "grab pile, Co. F." and then the way the boys all scamper for the table, we have about 70 now, there is about 30 of the company in the hospital, but there is not so many getting sick here as there was at the other place we were at we have been here a week to night, it is a pretty place the whole village is nearer than you are to Granpa's, there is two or three meeting houses, there is a nigger meeting every Sunday and Sunday Eve, if we stay here next Sunday, I am a going to go and hear one, if I can get away. I have been to supper, now I ~~had~~ must tell you what I had for supper, I had a cup of "tea" (there dont tell ma) and a piece of johnny cake and butter, and I broke two eggs into a cup of hot water and boiled them, and ate them, dont you wish you was here to eat with me. I do now, but still you are better of along with your Ma. Alice, I sent Ida one or four in one of Leslies papers, when they come around again I will buy one and send it to you, so you must wait for the next one will be just as prety as that. I will send the letters to you for I want that you should learn to read my letters and then learn to write a letter to pa, now you will try to wont you. I have got this sheet so full that I shall have to write some on this one, how much lard did ma have this winter, what did you have good to eat on thanksgiving day. Now Alice I tell you what to do, you have ma get a good supper on the 13th day of January[16], and then you get uncle Allen to come down there and eat my share of it, and I will get as good a supper as I can here or wherever I will be at that time, and set down and eat it and think of you, and like enough drop a tear or two. I should'nt dare to promise that I ~~shoul~~ would not, for if you knew how many times the tears had started since I got ma's letter, you would think it was a great many, but I hope that they will soon turn into tears of joy, and we shall be able to see one another face to face, and set down to the same table, and eat out of the same dishes. I think that we should all of us be happy then, if we ever could be on this earth, may God, who ruleth all things, grant that it may so be, but it is a getting rather rate, and I want to write a few lines to ma, so I guess that I will let you go to bed while I write to her, so good night Alice, "kiss" good night Ida, "kiss" good night Edgar, "double kiss" because you must both kiss him for me, and kiss ma too, this from your Father who is in the American Army, in the State of Ky.

David Brainerd Griffin

---

[16] That would be his 31st birthday and their 10th wedding anniversary.

To Alice Jane, Ida May, and Edgar Lincoln Griffin

Monday evening Dec 16th 1861

I thought that I would write a few lines to you as there is a little room left for me, after writing so much nonsence to the children, but I thought if it pleased them so to have me write to them, I would write to them. Now about Mr. Holman's[17] keeping that skillet, I had had enough deal with them to have known better than to left a single article out of my hands that belonged to me, when Mr. Holman and I settled up that day that he was a stacking his hay, we talked all over about the stove and boiler and other things, as we had done two or three times before. I told him that I had not got that skillet from Lydia Ann's he said not a word against it, and we agreed on a settlement, and I gave him two pigs as the book will show and then, there was a difference of something like a dollar or two between us. I had not charged them any thing for putting up the fence, nor for drawing the hay, and Mr. Holman said that between him and myself we would call it even, and I told him that I did not want he should lose one cent by my dealing with Lewis or Mrs. Abbott through him. I told him if they would not allow it to him, that I would pay it to him when I came home, he said that he would not say anything to Mrs. Abbott about it, and probably it would be all right with Lewis, if not he would say anything about it untill I came back, and that if I never came back that you should not be troubled with it at all, so you can see how long his word lasts good. If it ever comes handy for you to let him see this you may, and I dont hardly think that he will deny any of it, for it is all just as we talked, but enough about that, did Mr. Wallace pay you, if not let me know how much it is, and I guess that Andrew will pay it to me here, the boys are all well except George Spaulding[18] he has got a fever[.] Jery got a letter from his woman yesterday she says that she

---

[17] Mr. Holman, a neighbor with whom Brainard had arranged to trade his labor and some livestock for a wood stove, to be installed in the shanty for cooking and heating after he left.

[18] George S. Spaulding, a Fillmore Co. friend, Co. A, 2nd Minnesota Regiment of Volunteers.

got the money he sent to her. I hope that I shall get one from you before long, telling me the same thing for I shall feel uneasy untill I hear from it, write to me as often as as you can and write all the news that you can hear of about there, did Norm write to you, if so what was it about, I must close for the mail will soon close. I did not quite finish writing last night, so I wrote part of this this morning Tuesday Dec 17th it is still very pleasant, I must bid you all good bye again, to "Nerva," "kiss" "kiss" "kiss"

D. B. Griffin.

Letter Number 14

Lebanan Ky. Dec. 20th 1861

Dear Wife, and Children, as I have got a few moments to spare this afternoon I thought that I would commence a letter to you. I feel as well as ever I did in my life. I have got all over my sick spell that I wrote about in my last letter and I feel better than I did before. I received a letter from you yesterday, written about the 10th [.] I was glad to hear from you again, as you must know by the way I have been a writing to you in my letters before, this makes three that I have got from you. I am glad to hear that you are all well, and that you have got the shanty fixed up so as to be comfortable this winter, and that you have got a good lot of Pork and Lard laid down. I should like to be there and help you fry "nutcakes" and eat some of them too, we fry some ourselves every little while and good one's too, it takes a good many to go around, we were a frying some the other day and there was a number of ladies come along and asked us what they were, they did not know what a "doughnut" was, we live tip top lately, one of our Lieutenant's bought enough oysters last Wednesday for the whole company to have a good Oyster Supper, and to day we have had a regular old Yankee dinner, "less see" we had some boiled fresh beef, and some baked beef, some boiled pork and cabbage some sweet potatoes boiled, some boiled onions, and cold slaugh and some

55

good bakers bread and butter, there was that not a good dinner, our company lives the best of any company in the regiment, the reason is because we have got the best cook, he has worked a good deal at the business in the cities, in coffee houses, we draw the same rations that the other companies do, but we save enough in cooking to ~~by~~ buy a good many things from the farmers, ~~with,~~ and it has been such warm weather here since we came here, that we could not ask to be any better cared for than we are now, as I have written and sent two letters to you this week, I have not got any news of any importance to tell you, we are camped upon a dry side hill, close to a creek, and a good well and spring of water, there is a company of Artillery about $\frac{1}{4}$ of a mile from here. I can see them drill, they have been over here twice and drilled they have six horses on each cannon, and a rider on each nigh horse and six men to handle the cannon, they go through the motions of loading and fireing very fast, and when they wheel or go from one place to another they go upon the full run. The cannan are all six of them brass pieces, part of them rifled and part smooth, some for throwing shell they shot at a target the other day two miles off. I do not know whether they hit it or not, but I know that they came very near it for I could see the ball strike the side hill close to the target, there is also a regiment of Infantry (the same that we are) camped upon the other side of us, they drill right in sight of us every day and then there is a number of regiments further off, our regiment drills twice a day, company drill in the forenoon, and Batalion drill in the afternoon, and then dress prarade just at sundown, they are just falling in line to go on dress prarade, and I must stop so as to have supper ready when they come in.

Evening.

We have been to supper and I have got the dishes washed, we did not get anything but bread and coffee, and cold meat. I must tell you how the "cook and myself" were serenaded last night, you see that the Colonel's tent is right behind our tent about one rod, so after we were nicely asleep, the Brass Band came to give the Colonel a Serenade, and they had to stand within a few feet of my head, and the first thing that I heard was a big blast from the whole Band, they played for about a half of an hour, it sounded beautiful, it was very pleasant and still, after they got through. I thanked them kindly, and bid them good night, and the boys have laughed a good deal to day about our being Serenaded. I got an other letter from Watson yesterday, he was well and seemed to be enjoying himself first rate he is 10 or 12 miles from Washington and about 3 from Alexandria, on Virginia soil. Jery, is to work with us this week in the cook house, there is a man picked out every week to help us in the kitchen the rest of the boys are all well except George Spaulding, he is quite sick yet, you must not believe all of the stories that you hear about us untill you hear for certain, we cannot tell any thing about when we shall go away from here we may go in a day or two, and we may not go in as many weeks or even months. I wished that I had been there when Mr. Holman asked $1.50 for the use of the stove. I think that he is a fine specimen of a "good" christian, to try to take the advantage of a woman, after every thing was settled up as he and I settled, and talked the matter all over about the stove, and then after I go away try to get a <u>dollar and a half</u> out of you, I think <u>that, that</u> is the worst kind of <u>develish</u> hipocracy, if he does not let you have it, the skillett, if I live to get home again, he will pay for it, and dearly too, but dont you bother much about it, for you cannot but just show him or tell him what I say when you get a chance, we have not got but a little piece of candle left and I must fix up our bed and go to bed, so I must bid you all good night again. I will try and finish up this letter in the morning, if I do not, it will not go out untill Monday morning. I cannot write much about the children this time for I wrote a good long letter to them a day or two ago. I should be glad to see them all as well as they would to see me. I think of you all a great many times a day, but I hope that we shall all live to see oneanother again and enjoy each other's society a good many years yet, but God's will be done. I do not know as I can think of much more to write if I should wait untill morning. I am very anxious to hear if you get that money or not. I have got a paper to send to Alice, and I will send it along with this letter and I want that you should tell me whether you get any papers or not, kiss our babe's for me often, good night <u>Nerva</u> good night all, this from your husband and friend in Ky.

D. B. Griffin

To Mrs Minerva Griffin
  Alba P.O.
    Fillmore Co.
    Minnesota

Letter Number 15

Lebanan, Ky Dec. 27th 1861

My Dear Companion and Friends in Minn.

I will address you in that way for I see by your letters, that all the friends read my letters, and I wish that they would feel interested enough in them to write a few lines to me in return. I am well and hearty to night. I do not think that I am a growing poor any for I was weighed to night, and I weighed 165 $\frac{1}{2}$. I think that it agrees with me to be in the cook shop, at any rate I get enough to eat, but as for that they all get enough, we get three meals a day. I received a letter from you to day dated the 20th at Forestville, and I was glad to hear from you all, and to hear that you were all well, and that you had received the money which I sent to you. I had worried some about it, for fear that you would not get it, but I shall feel easy now. I was glad to learn that you have had some good visits. I hope that you will continue to have them, although I am not one in your midst, you think that you have pleasenter weather there than we do here, you will see by my letters that it is not so, we have had a little rain since I wrote to you last, which makes it a little muddy through the day, it has frose a little for the last night or two, and I think it will freeze quite hard to night, but it is quite pleasant through the day time, we have not had any snow but once, and then not but an inch or two and that went off the next day. Gen. Buell[19] was here this week, and had a review of the troops in this place. I have heard that he said that the Brigade in which we are in, was the best Brigade in Ky and that is saying a good deal, for there is a good many troops in Ky. at the present time, we cannot tell yet when we shall go away from here, but it is not probably that we shall go untill after New Year's day, for we are to be mustered for our pay on the 31st of this month and then Uncle Sam will owe me $26.00 but we do not know when we shall get our pay, but I do not think that I can send home much money next time, unless you need some bad. I wish that you would write how you get along for things in the house and for clothes, if you need any thing, just let me know, for I can borrow some money of most any one of the boys after pay day. I am glad that Ida got her papers, as I said before I should like to be there to show the pictures to her. I have sent some to Alice, and I directed a letter to her, to. I hope that they will be as well pleased, with them, as I thought they would when I sent them. I will send a letter or some papers to them once in a while, tell them that Pa hopes that some day he will come home, and then he will not have to write to them. I guess that Edgar is a great stout boy by the way he goes about. I hope that he will always be so, and be a good boy too, if he should live it would not be but a short time before he would be a great help to his Mother, and I hope to his Father too, may God protect him you say that you hope that you will see me in the Spring. I hope and pray that God will answer your prayers. I should like to have been there and gone over to the meeting with you, I am glad that you had a good meeting. I hope that you will go as often as you can get a chance, if you see Emery[20] tell him to write to me and let me know what there is agoing on in Spring Valley. I expect that Charles Phillips[21] will be discharged from service, and go home

---

[19] Union Gen. Don Carlos Buell, in command of the Army of the Ohio.
[20] William Emery Durand, husband of Minerva's sister, Mary Elizabeth, will soon join the 8th Minnesota Regiment of Volunteers, defending white settlers during the Sioux uprisings.
[21] Charles H. Phillips, a Beaver Township friend, instead transfers from Co. A, 2nd Minnesota, to a Federal Marine Regiment.

before long he is not sound, his kidneys are affected I believe[.] If he gets home I expect that you will hear some big yarns (<u>about</u> <u>war</u>) he tells some big yarns now, no one can believe him at all. It is agetting to be bed time, and I cannot think of much more to write this time. Jerry is well, there was one boy died from the company this week in Louisville, he has been sick some time, it is the first death that has been in the Company, there is one or two more that are very sick now. I am well now and I hope that I shall remain so, but I must bid you all good night and good bye too,

D. B. Griffin, to Nerva Griffin and the babes.

Letter Number 16

Lebanon Dec 31 1861

My Dear Wife and Companion,

As it is the last day of the year, and I received a letter from you to day, I thought that I would write a few lines to you this evening. I am glad that you are a getting along well, and that it is pleasent weather there, it is very pleasent weather here to night. I am in our tent this evening with my coat of and without any fire, and my hands sweat so that I can hardly hold my pen, but as we are expecting to go from here to morrow, I will try to write a few lines, it has been a very busy day in camp to day, we have been mustered for pay, and have been a fixing to move we do not know where we are a going to go, but we expect to go towards Sommerset where Zollicoffer[22] is the rebel General is, we shall probably see some fun before a great many weeks, but we cannot tell. I will write to you as soon as I can get a chance to. I am well to night, and feel first rate for me. I have been a scufflening and dancing all day, tell Alice that when I read where she said that "he grined, he did," I had to grin in earnest, tell her that I dream about her and all of you often. I hope that your sausages will keep good untill I come home, for I

---

[22] CSA Gen. Felix K. Zollicoffer, under the command of CSA Gen. George B. Crittenden.

should like to have a taste of them. I should like to know where you find room to keep all of your stuff in the shanty, or do not you keep it all there, has C got the calves broke yet tell him he must get them broke, and let Edgar drag for him in the spring has he got some drag teeth made yet, it will soon be time to sow wheat if it is as warm all of the time there, as it is here, but time slips away very fast, it does not seem as though it was three months since I left home, but it is so. I hope that I shall see you all again before many months. I wore my shirt and pants away with me. I mended them up and have wore them all most all of the time, I tore up the old shirt to day. Jerry has not had the Ague but a very little, he got a letter from his wife yesterday, and she sent him her likeness and the babes. I do not think that I shall have the ague, I intend to take as good care of myself as I can, the boys are a talking in the tent about our going home, they think that we shall be at home by the time that corn will want to be hoed. I hope so, to. I do not think that Charles Phillips has not had a to go on guard every other night at all, since we came here, or any where else. I expect that he will go home before long, and as I wrort before, you cannot believe anything, that he says, scarcely at all, you said that James Nichols[23] wrote that they had sour bread and bad meat. I never saw fatter beef in my life than we have had since we came here, and we have had very good bread most all of the time so that we have not got much to complain of as yet, but we cannot tell what we may have after this for we have got to march the rest of the time. I am still in the "cook shop" there is not any women agoing to go along with us and the boys want that I should do their washing for them. I do not know but what I shall turn out to be quite a "woman" yet. Jerry and I washed together yesterday, we only washed about 30 pieces, it has been a holaday week with the slaves and we have had a plenty of them in the camp every day, they appear to enjoy themselves well, but I must stop for I want to put this in the office to night, but I must wish you a happy New Year, and I

---

[23] James Nichols, a Beaver Township neighbor, Co. C, 3rd Minnesota Regiment of Volunteers.

think that you will have one, tell Alice to remember the dinner on the 13 th but you must let me go this time, so good bye Nerva

this from D. B. Griffin

In Pursuit of Gen. Zollicoffer, Lebanon to Mill Springs, Kentucky

Letters 17–21 (January 6–22, 1862)

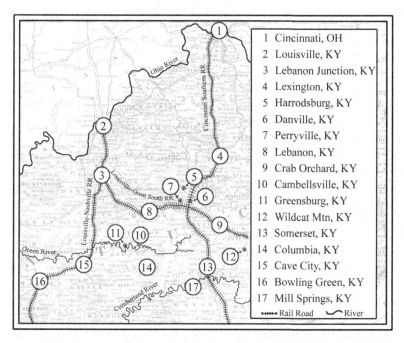

1	Cincinnati, OH
2	Louisville, KY
3	Lebanon Junction, KY
4	Lexington, KY
5	Harrodsburg, KY
6	Danville, KY
7	Perryville, KY
8	Lebanon, KY
9	Crab Orchard, KY
10	Cambellsville, KY
11	Greensburg, KY
12	Wildcat Mtn, KY
13	Somerset, KY
14	Columbia, KY
15	Cave City, KY
16	Bowling Green, KY
17	Mill Springs, KY
●━━━● Rail Road	⌣ River

The first four letters of this group recount the nearly daily movement of Brainard's regiment along with nine other regiments that have been gathered as a division of Gen. Don Carlos Buell's Army of the Ohio, seeking to engage the forces of the rebel Gen. Felix Zollicoffer. He includes many descriptions of the land and its inhabitants as the Union forces march through. Thoughts of his first impending battle raise questions of his survival. The fifth letter describes in graphic detail the events and outcome of the Battle of Mill Springs.

MAJ. GENERAL McCLELLAN.

Letter Number 17

Camelsville, Ky. Jan. 6 1862

My Dear Wife and friends,

I will try to write a few lines to you this evening. I am as well as usual this evening. We are here in a very muddy place about two miles from a place called Camelsville, and about 22 from Lebanan. We started on New years morning to march, where we did not know? but we supposed that it was for Bowling Green. We marched about 11 miles that day, through as hilly a country as ever I saw, but it was on a good road, we camped that night near a creek and got along first rate, the cook and I was up the next morning by two a'clock and had breakfast eat so that we were ready to start by sunrise the country was about the same thing as we passed the day before, the soil is of a redish clay, and the buildings and fences all, with a few exceptions, look old and worn out, there is a few rich slave owners along the road, and about them it looks more like living, but I have not seen any land in Ky. that I would exchange for mine, as far as the soil is concerned, we are camped right in the midst of the secesh, there is not but a very few union here, in Taylor Co. It has rained most all of the time since we have been here, but it has not rained hard enough to hender the boys from foraging a little on there own hook. Saturday we cooked 7 geese Sunday 12, and to day we have had about 30 geese, 10 Turkey, 4 hogs and a few chickens, brought in by our company, and there is two regiments camped here, 20 companies and I know that our company is not ahead any, some of the companies fetch in beef mutton pork honey &c, and the Col. of the Brigade, tells our officers to let the boys go, and get what they can, and if they get any thing from a union man he can pay him for it and if from a secesh, he had better keep still, that it was better for the boys to be a stiring around than to be a laying around in the mud. I have not been out at all, for they have keep me very busy in cleaning and cooking geese, or Ky. "pigeons" as we call them. I had to beg off to night, for they are a cooking and picking geese and turkeys this evening, we expect to start to morrow morning towards a place called Columbia, we do not get any news at all now about the war, the mails are not very regular here, I do not know when I shall get a chance to send this letter off, we are not but about 40 miles from the rebel army, but we are all afraid that we shall not ever be in any engagement but still we may be before long, it is not as sickly at present as it has been, there is some that are a coming down with the measels, Jery is well at present he does not have the ague any, there is none in the camp that has got the ague, there is some that have the jaundice but not very sick, and I hope that it will not be sickly, it is some cooler to night than what it has been it is freezing some. I hope that you will have good weather there this winter, and I hear that you are. I cannot write much more to night, and if I cannot get a chance to send this away before we stop again, I will write all about our march and all the news that I can hear about, you may not get as many letters from me as you have because I have not the chance to write when we are on the march, that I have in camp, but I will write as often as I can, and I hope that you will do the same, so good bye

this from your husband D. B. Griffin.

Letter Number 18

Camp near Columbia Jan. 9 '62

Well, Minerva, I will try to write a few more lines to you to night. I am well to night, it is quite warm to night but it is very muddy around the camp for it rained all night last night, as I wrote on the other sheet, we started on Tuesday Jan 7 and traveled, or marched, about 12 miles and camped about 3 o'clock on the land of a secesh we crossed Green river during the day, and it is rightly named, for the water looks very green and along the banks there is green trees and bushes of all kinds, it did not look much like the middle of winter. I saw some hemlock trees we passed a good deal of heavy timber, principally beech, I saw some large chestnut trees and black walnut trees under which lay bushels of nuts, we had a good road all of the way, the next morning the cook and myself got up about three o'clock and had our breakfast, and was ready to move by sunrise, we marched about 9 miles that day and we left the turnpike about 4 miles back, and since then the roads have been worse, the cook and I go along with the teams, and I do not have to carry my knapsack as they do in the ranks, it is carried in the waggon, there is 15 six mulesteams along with the regiment, and there is two regiments together now, and we are laying over to day, waiting for two or three regiments more to come up, and we cannot tell when we shall go from here we are camped on a man's land, who has a son in the secesh army, about 5 miles from a town called Columbia, and the land is completely covered with small stone around the camp. I have not seen but one school house since I came into Ky. the inhabitants are very ignorant, there is no enterprise among them, the man that lives near here, is a middle aged man and he has never taken a newspaper, there is some heavy slave owners upon the road, around them it looks better, generaly, large white houses and a number of nigger huts around them. I called in at one of them, and found out by asking him a good many yankee questions, that his name was Griffin, but I could not claim any relation with him, he had a nice place and a good many niggers. I received a letter from Mr. Chipman and Allen to day, and right glad was I to get one from them too. I hope that they will not stop now but keep writing to me, I cannot promise them that I will answer them, but I will try and write all of the news that I can hear of concerning the war, or any thing else that I can think of, we are within 25 miles of the rebel Gen. Zolicoffer we expect to march towards him when we start and we may see some fun before long, but it may not be such <u>fun</u> to a great many of us, and we cannot tell who it will be but I must close for to night, for it is after taps[.]

Friday morning Jan 10th,

I am well this morning and I had a good nights rest, we are not agoing to march to day, but we expect to march to morrow and we shall not stop, probably, untill we come in sight of a rebel flag or camp, and it is very likely that there will be some fighting before long. I cannot tell whether I shall be in the ranks or not, but if I am needed I shall not flinch a particle, but shoulder my gun, and fight even till the last drop of blood is shed. I have not the least desire to return home untill the war is ended, for I think that I am in a good cause, and that I am working for the good of my family and friends, as well as for my country, and if I die in the cause, I hope that my little family will never have to suffer for the want of the comforts of this world, while here, and at last if we should not meet again in this world, we shall all meet in <u>heaven</u>, which I do sincerely believe but I feel just as though we should all meet one ~~and~~ other here again, and before many months too, it is quite warm this morning the birds are singing and it feels like spring in Minnesota does. I do not think that we shall much cold weather this winter here, you must excuse my mistakes and bad writing, for I had to set down on a knapsack and take one on my knees, and write on that, last night, and to day I am standing up at the hind end of a wagon, and I have to stop every little while and see to the fire, and help cook, such is camp life, tell C. that he must have duke and dime broke first rate for I expect that I shall have to use them, some time and if they are spoilt in breaking he has got to take them himself, but I guess that they will be all right, tell him that I cannot get any time to answer him in perticular but that he must read your letters which will all be the same, to you all I hope Allen as well as the rest of you, I shall expect to hear in some of your letters that he is Married or is a going to be before long. Jerry gets a letter from his woman about every week[.] I guess that she worryes herself a good deal[.]

I hope that you do not for you need not to. I am getting fat every day, my appitite is good, and my vituals does not hurt me any[.] I weighed myself this morning. I weighed 169 dont you think that I am a pineing away[.] I think that I have written a good long letter this time, so I will draw it to a close[.] I hope that you will write as often as you can for we do not get any news now from that way only by letter, so good bye this time yours in haste

D. B. Griffin.

Letter Number 19

Camp, en route to Zolicoffer's Army, Jan. 14, 1862,

My Dear Wife and companion,

As I have a chance this evening to write a few lines to you, I will try. I am as well as usual this evening but very tired for we have been a cooking up rations for two days ahead, as we are a going to start on the march again to morrow morning, we started last Saturday morning and we marched that day and the next, and only made about 18 miles, and the roads were the worst, that I ever traveled in my life, it is very thinly settled, and the people are mostly poor and ignorant, they do not have any mail, and some of them do not know what a letter stamp is, we should feel thankfull that we were born in a civilized part of the world, some of them are very poor, and they are worse off than the slaves themselves, but enough of that, we have been in this place two days, a waiting for other regments to come up, there is now near us 8 regments of Infantry and one of Cavelry, and a company of Artillery ready to march and others behind us, we are within 15 miles of Zolicoffer's camp, we shall probably be very near to them when we camp again, we cannot tell what the intention of the regments is, so well as you do in Minnesota, for every thing is kept from us, and we do not get any papers now, and we shall not get any mail regular for some time again, and we shall have to watch our chance to send our letters off, we may be in a battle before I get a chance to send another one to you but you must not worry about me, if you should not hear from me for some time after you get this. I have got a chance to send this off tomorrow by one of the Captain's of the regment, it has been rather cool for the last two days, it snowed a very little, but not enough to whiten the ground, Jery is well, and all the rest of the boys, the Minnesota boys stand the soldering better than the Kentucky boys do, they die off quite fast in some of their regiments, we have not had many death in the regment, but there may be a great many men be killed before you get this letter, but you must trust in God for the chances of the future, and If I should through this war, and be permitted to return to the bosoms of my friends I think that we shall know how to prize one another's society for the rest of our lives, my earnest prayer is that I may be, and I believe that it will be answered, but I must bid you all good bye for this time[.] It was my birth day yesterday, and I thought of you all a great many times, and I know that you did of me also, I hope that I shall be at home on ~~the~~ my next birth day but I must stop for it is time to blow out the lights, may God bless you in this world, and at last may we all meet in heaven but good bye, again, this from you husband and friend forever,

D. B. Griffin

To Minerva Griffin

Letter Number 20

Camp near Zollicoffer's, Ky. Jan. 17th 1862

My Dear Wife and Companion,

As I have got a few moments this evening to myself, I will write a few lines to you, in order to let you know where we are, and how I am. I am well to night, and we are camped within 7 miles of the rebel army, we have been on the march for the last three days with the teams but the regiment laid still yesterday a waiting for the teams to come up, we started on Wednesday morning from where we were when I last wrote to you, and the regments went about 15 miles, but the teams did not get but about 8 miles the roads were so awful bad, and we had to work hard to git as far as we did with them, we stoped and camped in the woods where the land was worth five <u>cents</u> an acre and heavy timber at that, the regment were about 7 miles ahead they did not have any tents to sleep in, nor anything to eat, only what they got a forageing, and I think that they were not very backward about doing that, there was two regments together, the 9th Ohio, Dutch[1], and the 2th Minn, but we caught up with them last night just before dark, and they were glad to see us too, for they had not had any coffee to drink since Wednesday morning, we always get coffee twice a day, and the way "we" drink it is not slow. I do not suppose that would believe that your humble servant drank about one <u>quart</u> night and morning, but it is so. it I take a hard cracker, and crumb it into the coffee, and eat it without any milk, we have sugar a plenty. I do not drink any tea only when I am sick, and that is not often, for I have not been sick any since I wrote to Alice. I had like to forgot to tell you that I received a letter to day from you, and was glad to hear that you too were all well, and getting along first rate, and that were having some good visits with your neighbors. I hope that you will continue to do so, as long as you can, and try not to worry

---

[1] The 2nd Minnesota was paired with the German speaking 9th Ohio during all of Brainard's service. Their Colonel, Gustave Kammerling, was a very colorful, take charge, character.

any about me for I get along first rate[.] It seems ~~as though~~ by your writing that it had been a very dry fall and winter up there, for the increase of the population appears to be all "gals." I do not have time to talk much with the "girls" when I am in camp, but when I am on the road, I go ahead of the teams untill I see some of the Ky. "bells" and I stop and have a <u>fine talk</u> with them untill the teams come up, some of them are pretty <u>good</u> looking too, tell C. that if he was down here, he might find him a schoolmarm perhaps, for there is "a right smart chance of them, I reckon," and they all of them think a "heap" of the Minn. boys, but he would have to take them back there to live for he could not raise enough here to keep them, for some places that we have come by, they raise about 3 barrels of corn to the acre, and the ground is all coverd with great dead trees, that they have girdled, but I expect that if we should drive the rebels out of Ky, that we shall see better land south of the Cumberland river, but about the war there is now with us two regments of Infantry one of Cavalry and a battery of Artillery, when we all get together there will be about 20 thousand in all. I cannot tell when we are to make an attackt on the rebels, but I expect it will be before long now but we are afraid that they, the enemy, will not stand a battle at all, we heard that they are pretty well intrenched, if we cannot shell them out, we shall have to take them by Storm, and I think that we can whip them out, for we are determined to fight untill the last, for our country, and for ourselves, if we know long enough before we have a battle, that we are agoing to have one, I will write a few lines to you so that you will know it, and if I live through one I certainly will let you know as soon as I can, but it appears that I have not got all of your letters, for I have not got the one with Dan's Wife's letter in, but I guess that you have got the most of mine, but you must not worry if you should not get one every week from me, for the mails are very irregular here, tell Alice that I hope that she will learn fast this winter, so that when I come home she can read the papers to her pa. I hope that she will be a good girl, and mind what her teacher tells her, tell her that pa would like to see her and Ida and Edgar and all of you, and the folks in

Beaver, it is a getting late and I must stop for this time. I guess that you can read this if it is written with a lead pencel, you must overlook the mistakes and bad grammer for I have had to stop a number of times since I comenced it, and I have written it very fast for there is a chance to send it off tomorrow, you must not worry about the folks paying you that owe us, for I shall try to send you some money as soon as we are paid off, but good bye Nerva,

D. B. Griffin

Letter Number 21

Camp Hamilton Ky., Jan. 22nd, 1862

My Dear and affectionate Wife,

It is with a good deal of thankfullness towards my maker, that I am spared to write to you once more, I am very happy to inform you that I have passed through the long wished for, and long looked for battle, without even getting as much as a scratch[.] I hardly know how to commence, to give you a discription of the battle, for I have seen and heard so much for the last four days, and have thought of so much that I want to tell you, that I am afraid that I shall not begin to tell you the one half that I want to, but I will begin and do the best that I can, for I know that you will be anxious to hear from me now.

We had got the breakfast about ready last Sunday morning, (Jan 19th) when a messenger came into camp with the report that the enemy were advancing upon us with their whole force, and we soon heard the guns a cracking away at a fast rate, the regment was called into line and started towards the scene of action on a "double quick," they went up within one fourth of a mile of the enemy, when the 2nd Minnesota and the 9th Ohio, formed into a battle line, and awaited a few moments behind "Finney's" Battery, awaiting orders, while we stood there our battery sent a few shell into them with very good effect, and they answered us with us theirs but without any effect, for they shot to high, there was a cannon ball shot just over our heads, and struck the ground about thirty feet behind us, it came through the air with a whistle, and there was a good many heads that dodged, but your humble servant did not flinch, but before I say anything more about myself, I will tell you how I came to be in the battle, you may think that I do it, to praise myself, but it is not so, for I shall tell you the simple truth, as near as I can, I was getting breakfast with the other cook, when the company was called out, and our "Orderly Sergeant" told us that we need not go out, but when I heard the cracking of the guns, I could not stand it, I told Louis the cook, that I did not enlist to cook, but to fight, and he could do just as he pleased, but I should take my gun and go with the company, and so I threw off my overcoat, for it was raining quite hard at the time, and buckled my catrige belt around me, and bade the cook good bye and started. I ran about one mile and came up with the company after they formed into line, they were then ordered to the field, to which we started through a thick piece of woods, and came up to the enemy, just as the 10th Indiana were retreating, and the enemy were advancine on them with fixed bayonets, but the Minnesota boys came up to them with an Indian yell, and such a volley as there was pored upon them for about forty minutes was never before heard, when they, the enemy, gave way for us, we were so close to each other, that some of our boys pulled their guns out of their hands, there was nothing but a fence between us, but fortunate for our side they shot to high, there was only forty eight killed on our side, and 140 wounded, there was 12 killed and 23 wounded in the Minnesota 2nd, there was not a man wounded in Co. F., Co. A., the Co. from Chatfield were not in the battle at all, they were on picket duty, they feel quite bad to think that they missed the fight, the enemy had from 3 to 500 killed, and over 500 taken prisoners. We then gave them chase and followed them up for nine miles that day, they did not make a stand at all, as we passed over the battlefield, we passed by the dead and dying, lying in all shapes and formes, and the wounded calling for water, and begging of us not to kill them, we told them that no man should be hurt for they were amongst

73

friends, they were expecting to be killed they all carried a big knife about 18 inches long and 2 wide, I have got one of them to ~~bring~~ carry home with me if I go, their guns were a good many of them the old flint lock muskects, as they run they threw away every thing that they could, guns, blankets, knapsacks, haversack, coats, hats and every thing. Gen Zollicoffer was killed on the field and a number of their Officers killed and wounded, and taken prisoners, it was a perfect Bull Run, only the "Bull" run the other way, we came to a halt about one hour before sun down, ~~and~~ about one mile from their entrenchments, and our Artillery threw a number of shell into their camps, they answered by throwing a few shot, but they did not reach us. We had not eaten a mouthfull of anything all day, and we did not get any thing untill ten o'clock A. M.

The next morning, we threw a few shell, but got no answer from them[.] So we formed into line of battle, and marched inside of the intrenchments, which we found entirely deserted of men, but they had not taken anything with them, we captured about 2,000 horses and mules, 150 wagons, 13 cannon, 10,000 stand of arms, 1,000 tents, and thousands of dollars worth of clothing and provisions, there was about 600 log huts besides the tents, they were strongly fortified with breastworks, on all sides, and if they had made a stand it would took a long time to have driven them out, but they went out with such haste, that hundreds of them were drownded in attempting to cross the river, ~~as near~~ as near as we can get information from the prisoners they had about 15,000 men, of which about 8,000 came out ~~to~~ against us. We had not over 1,500 in action at any one time. Our boys had a great time in pilageing the tents, they found clothing of all kinds and quality, watches, jewelry, swoards, knives, pistols, daguerreotypes, letters, keepsakes, and most anything that you can think of, but we could not fetch a great deal with us, for we had no way to carry it, I got me a nice grey coat, which belonged to a Lieutenent in the secesh army, which I have got done up, and have put it into a trunk that Norman Case, got and is agoing to send it home, by express, I have directed it to you to be left in the care of Mr. Lyman Case[2], so if you should get a chance to send up there after it, you will find it, to Mr. Case's I will have Norman tell his folks to send it down to the Valley, if he should get a chance to, I also got an india rubber overcoat, an undercoat, a pair of White blankets, a shirt and one pair of socks, in all worth about $20.00, so you see that I am pretty well fixed up for winter, but I do not think that we shall have much of a winter here this year, for it has been quite warm all of the time, but very wet, for the last two weeks, and the roads are awful, to travel upon, we expect to go to Somerset to morrow, and wait there for further orders, and we may have to stay there some time, and perhaps we will not go from there at all, for it may be that the war will be ended in a short time, for we get good news from all sides of us, but how true they are we cannot tell you will most likely see in the papers, the accounts of the different battles, we hear that the enemy at Bowling Green, is defeated and badly cut up, I hope that it is so, and if the boys do as well on the Potomac as we have done in Ky, the War will be at an end, or in a short time for the army that they had here is so badly scatered, that they will hardly form into regments again, one regment that came out against us only had twelve men when they got back into their camp again[.]

Minerva, I have been in the most successful battle that has been fought in this campaign, and, I shot off my gun ten times at the enemy, and we stood almost face to face, but yet I cannot realize, nor does it seem to me that I have been in a battle at all, I did not feel the least excited, in the world, nor did I even think that I was in any danger, and such is the case with most of the boys, but still I have seen enough, I have no desire to be in another battle, but still if our country calls me I am ready to go, in any place[.] Our officers were all very cool through all of the battle, the Col of the Brigade had his horse shot from under him, and was slightly wounded in the leg, Col. Fry[3], the man that rode up to Gen. Zollicoffer and shot him

---

[2] Lyman Case, of Chatfield, is the father of Herman and Norman Case.
[3] Union Col. Speed Smith Fry, 4th Kentucky Volunteer Infantry Regiment, 2nd Brigade of the 1st Division of the Army of the Ohio.

through the breast with a pistol, had his horse shot from under him, but was not hurt himself, there is a good deal more that I could think of if I was there to talk with you, but as it is now near 12 o'clock, and I have got to be up early in the morning and fix to go to Somerset, I will draw to a close, I have writen this letter since dark. Jery has wrote a long letter to his woman, to day, this paper I got in a rebels tent. There is not a great deal of sickness in the camp at the present time, I am well as usual and am still getting fleshy I was weighed this evening and I weighed 170 lbs strong. I hope that you are all well and doing well, you must write to me as often as you can, for I am glad to hear from you as often as I can, and I hope that it will not be many months more before we shall all meet again, and if we do, we shall know how to prise oneanother, I must close, for want of time, and room, so I will bid you all good bye, and may God bless you all.

D. B. Griffin, to P. M. Griffin.

Gathering of Forces Near Nashville, Tennessee

Letters 22–29 (January 29–March 19, 1862)

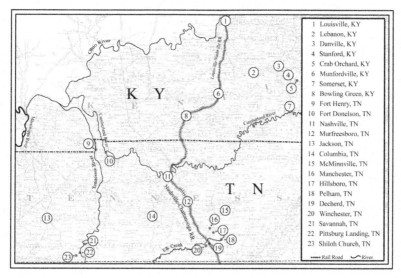

1	Louisville, KY
2	Lebanon, KY
3	Danville, KY
4	Stanford, KY
5	Crab Orchard, KY
6	Munfordville, KY
7	Somerset, KY
8	Bowling Green, KY
9	Fort Henry, TN
10	Fort Donelson, TN
11	Nashville, TN
12	Murfreesboro, TN
13	Jackson, TN
14	Columbia, TN
15	McMinnville, TN
16	Manchester, TN
17	Hillsboro, TN
18	Pelham, TN
19	Decherd, TN
20	Winchester, TN
21	Savannah, TN
22	Pittsburg Landing, TN
23	Shiloh Church, TN

These eight letters tell of the 2nd Minnesota's movements following Mill Springs. Initially, the regiment headed south toward Tennessee, but problems with supplies getting through, caused by significant rains, forced them to go back to Lebanon before starting again for Tennessee. Nashville was their goal, where they camped for almost a month. Brainard tells of washing clothes for some of the men to earn money, and instead of sending his pay home, he sets up a direct payment plan for the family's support. He records the news of Gen. Grant's capture of Forts Henry and Donelson. Information about his health and that of their friends along with other aspects of camp life fills the letters. His confidence in a quick end to the conflict is evident throughout.

Letter Number 22

Camp Cumberland Ky. Jan. 29th 1862

My Dear Companion,

I will endeaver to write a few lines to you this evening, and let you know how I am, where I am and what we are about. We are camped upon the Cumberland river, five miles south of Somerset, and within 25 miles of the Tennesee line, for which State we will probably start for in a few days, but for what point in it, I do not know, probably Knoxville or Nashville, we were two days acoming from the camp in which I wrote my last letter, about 13 miles, we had some awful hills to climb, and some to go down, but we got through all safe. I am as well as usual, and am still in the cook room, Jery is well, and he and I have been a washing this week, we washed 140 pieces, we have not washed much for some time and the clothes were very dirty, and so we had a hard washing, we will have another big washing to do to morrow if it does not rain, it has rained a good deal, here this winter, it is raining this evening, you need not be afraid of my doing to much, for when I am to work I feel first rate, I received a letter from you the 27th which was mailed in Forestville the 17th, I am sorry that you have such cold weather in Minn, and that you have not got a good house to live in, I hope that you will not suffer on account of the cold weather, it will soon be spring, and then you will get along first rate, it is more like spring here now, than winter, for the larks and bluebirds are a singing all day, I have been all day in my shirt sleeves[.] I have not wore any vest this winter, nor any neckerchief. I suppose that you hear and read all sorts of reports about the battle of Logans crossroads, in which I was in, and of which I gave you a description in my last letter, I sent a small sheet in which there was a partial description, but which is not all correct, the Tenn. Reg. (union) was not in the fight at all, there was no battery taken from us, and all such like, if you see or hear any thing that you do not understand, you need not be afraid to ask me any questions and I will do the best I can towards telling you, what I know about it, we are all very anxious to hear what the army on the Potomac is adoing about these days, but we will have to wait patiently, for all our news, when I wrote to you before I do not know as I mentioned anything in it about Dan, but I ought to, I will try and get time to write a letter to him before long, I hope that we shall all live to get home and see each other again, I cannot say how it will be about our going to Vt. I think if I live to get home, that, I shall try to get us a house to live comfortable in, but there will be time enough to talk about that when I get there, and how soon that will be, you can tell just as well as I[.] Sergeant Bailey[1] starts for Minn. to morrow, I hope if you will see him, and then he can tell you all about us here in the South, Jery got a letter last night dated the 11th and one to night dated the 18th so you see that our letters do not go either way very prompt, if there is any one there that wants to join the 2 Reg now will be the time, for Mr Bailey is going back to get recruits he says that if he should go down that way he will go and see you, I will try and send you five dollars, we have not received

---

[1] Although Sergeant Bailey is often mentioned in the letters, his first name, personal connection, and company membership are not established. He will die upon returning to the regiment (letter 34).

our pay yet, but we are expecting it before long, I have signed the allotment roll, so that you will receive $20.00 every two months in a check, through the State Treasurer, you will get the first about the middle of March, I have not got anything to do with it now, and no risk to run in sending it home, you did not tell me whether Alice got her papers and letters, or not, tell her that Pa is glad that she can get to the head of her class so much, I hope that it will not be so cold but what she can go to school most all of the time this winter, and then when I come home, she can read to me out of some book or paper, tell Ida that she must study her book at home and catch up with Alice, and tell Edgar that he must study too, but I guess that he will study mischief. I think of you all a good many times a day, and wish that I could see you, I cannot think of much more to write to night and it is a getting late and I have to get up early in the morning. I will stop for to night, and go to bed, there is four of us in our tent the Orderly Sergent, his clerk, the cook and myself. I have some straw, my overcoat and blanket under me, and three blankets over me, I sleep first rate, I do not take of my pants nor socks, but I am a getting sleepy and I will stop so good night "Nerva" and "babes."

Thursday morning Jan 30th,

 Good morning "Nerva" I am well this morning, and I hope that you are the same, it rained hard all night, and as I lay in bed and heard it fall upon our tent, it made me think of home, how much it sounded like falling upon the rooff of our shanty, I expect it snows there instead of raining, it is some cooler here this morning, the wind is in the North, there is a cave here by our camp which goes under ground about forty rods, I have not been to the end of it but some of the boys have, we have to go into it about 60 feet to get our water, ~~it opens~~ where we go in it is just about large enough for one man to enter at a time, and it grows larger and higher as you go down untill we get down to the spring where it's ten feet wide and 20 feet or more high, it is not much of a cusity, the land about here is a little better than the most of the land has been, over which we have passed, but it is not very good, there is a good many slaves around here but we do not see many of them, there is not any contraband's in our camp yet. I cannot think of much to write this morning, when you write please write about all of the folks around there, what they are all up to this winter, has Mr. Holman give you the skillett yet. I expect that it is pretty hard times there for money now, I want that you should keep enough by you to get along without pinching yourself to much, I can get along without using much myself, and I will send you all that I can spare, besides what you get there, I will send five dollars to you in this letter, and you must answer it as soon as you get it and let me know if the money gets there all right, perhaps I can send you some more after the boys pay us up for washing. I will if I can. I want that you should keep yourselves [unreadable] good and warm if you can, but I must stop for the mail will soon leave, as ink is scarce I have finished this with a pencel. I "reckon" that you can read "right smart" of it, I shall get to be quite a "hoosier" if I stay down here all summer, but I am in hopes that I shall not have to[.]

Give my best respects to all of the folks, and tell them that I would like to get a letter from any one, you can let them read my letters, which will be the same to them as though I wrote to them, but I must bid you all good bye again, this from your absent friend and Companion in Ky.

D. B. Griffin

To Minerva, Alice, Ida and Edgar Griffin in Minnesota

Feb 1st

P.S.   Saturday Morning, I have delayed sending this for I thought that I could get 5 dollars to send to you but I have been unable to get a $20.00 bill changed, so I will not send it this time, but I will send you some in a few days. I am well this morning. It rained all night and it rains hard.

Letter Number 23

Camp Cumberland Ky. Feb., 9th 1862

My Dear Beloved and kind Companion,

I seat myself down this evening for the purpose of addressing a few lines to you. I am as well as usual this evening, but some tired, for we have been prety busy to day, for we have got to march again to morrow, we have got to go back to Lebanon again, but where we are agoing to go from there we do not know, there has been a great deal of rain here, and the roads are awfull bad, so that government is unable to get supplies through to us, but we have not suffered any for the want of any thing to eat as yet. I have not had a letter from you for some time, and I am a looking for one every day, for I want to know how you get along this cold weather, for I see by the papers, that it has been very cold in Minnesota this winter. It has not been very cold here with us, as yet, it has been quite pleasent to day, but quite cool, we have had some very heavy thunder showers, and it looks a good deal like spring, the birds sing, and the frogs peep, and the wild ducks are a flying about just as they are in Minn. in April or May. I hope that we shall not have any wet, or cold weather while we are on the march, for it is very unpleasent to be a marching while it rains, it is about eighty miles from here to Lebanon, it will probably take us eight or ten days to go through, and unless we should stop upon the road for a few days, I shall not get any chance to write to you untill we get through, we are not agoing back on the same road that we came here on. Elicut Rundall has come out of the Hospital he has been very sick with the fever, he lay three weeks without knowing anything at all, but he has come through safe, and he looks as well now as I ever saw him. We get good news now from the army in other parts of Ky. and if we succeed in Liberating Ky., and scatter their army, it may be that Peace will be declared in a few months, at the most, I hope that the time will soon come when we shall learn war no more, when we shall be at peace with the whole world.

We still continue to hear reports of the battle of Mill Spring or, of some other name. I do not know as they have decided upon any name for it as yet, but we do not see many reports that are correct in all of the particulars. I saw to day, in Harpers Weekly, a picture of the battle, and the battle field, but we could not see anything in it which looked like the place, or like the battle but still I do not know as I could describe it upon paper, if I were to try, but if I should live to get home, I think that I can "talk," and tell you how it was, and how it looked, at the time of the battle, and afterwards too, but I will not attempt it now. I have not much news to write this time we heard that they had taken out, several hundred bodies, from the river, that were drowned, while attempting to cross, at the time of the retreat, it is possible that it is so, for they were in somewhat of a hurry to get across just about that time, and there was only one small ferry boat to carry them across. We heard that fort Henry, on the Tennessee river, had been taken with thirty pieces of cannon, besides taking a good many prisoners[2], and also that they had cut off the supplies of the rebels, ~~from~~ in Bowling Green, if it is so, their army will have to make a break, or surrender before long. I hope so anyhow, but it is not of any use for me to write, or think any thing about coming home, for, we shall not know long before hand, when we get our discharge, but you need not look for me untill the war is ended, I must close for this time for it is a getting late, and I have got to get up early in the morning. Jery is well. I dream of home very often lately, and of the dear ones that I have left behind. I hope that it will not be long before I shall see you all. Kiss the children, especialy Edgar Lincoln, for me, he will be one year old, by the time you get this, it does not seem so, does it, but time flies, and now I will bid you all good night, and go to

---

[2] On February 6, 1862, CSA Gen. Lloyd Tilghman surrendered Fort Henry on the Tennessee River to the combined land forces of Union Gen. Ulysses S. Grant and naval forces under USN Flag Officer Andrew H. Foote, after sending most of his 2,500-man garrison cross country to nearby Fort Donelson on the Cumberland River.

bed, so Good night "<u>Nerva</u>" good night <u>Alice</u>, good night <u>Ida</u>, and good night "<u>Edgar Lincoln</u>..."

D. B. Griffin.

Letter Number 24

Camp near Lebanon Ky., Feb.20th 1862

My Dear Wife and Children, relatives and friends,

I am well this evening and I thought that I would improve the evening in writing a few lines to you, we have at last got back to Lebanon, and we have camped about one mile east of the vilage. We started from the Cumberland river a week ago last Monday, we went only 6 or 7 miles that day, when we camped in an old orchard, we got up the next morning, when lo and behold it was a snowing very nice, it kept a snowing untill about 10 o'clock, when it ceased, and the boys had a regular pitched battle with snow balls, we all enjoyed the sport first rate, we did not march any that day, started the next morning in the mud, and we had an awful hard road to go, for the next 30 miles, when we come onto a turnpike which was good untill we got within 5 miles of this place, we passed through some of the most God forsaken country that I have ever seen, you can buy just as much of it as you are a mind to, for two cents and a half an acre, but I should rather give fifty dollars an acre for land in Minnesota and undertake to pay for it, for the longer a man stayes upon it the worse of he is, but after we came upon the pike we came out upon some handsome country, it is what is called the blue grass country, they have large farms, and nice building as I ever see any where[.] We came through three large villages, Crab Orchard, Sanford and Danville which were very pretty places, we got here last Tuesday night, and yesterday it rained the hardest that it has any time this winter, all day long which makes it very wet and muddy around the camp, while we were upon the road I went off from the road, through the woods about two miles and found a family there consisting of a man, three <u>girls</u> and two little boys, they said that I was the first soldier that had ever been there. I went in, and the old man had the girls go to work and get a supper for me, which they did, it consisted of a piece of corn dodger, a piece of cold pork, some boiled eggs some butter, and some sour milk, it was the first meal of victuals that I have eaten in a house since I left Minnesota. I think that I should have relished a meal of victuals at a table in <u>our</u> shanty, with you and the children there some better than I did that one, and I think that if we all live it will not be many months before I shall be there, for we are getting good news from the war every day, we have taken forts Henry and Donelson[3] on the Tennesee river together with a good deal of property and 15,000 prisoners besides a number of their Generals, I cannot give their names now, for I have not got any papers by me. I expect that you will see all about it in your papers, to day we hear that the Govenor of Tennessee has ordered his men to lay down their arms, and not fight any more against the United States[4] so you see that the ball that we set in motion at the battle of Logan's cross road has continued to roll on, and I hope that it will not get checked untill it rolls into the Gulf of Mexico, they say that the stars and stripes are now waving in every state in the union. I hope that they will never be taken down, we do not get any news from the Potomac which is of any interest. We expect to go from here in a day or two, to some point on the Louisville and Nashvill rail road. The boys were all of then making calculations to day, when we should get our discharge and go back to Minnesota. We cannot see what there is, (if every thing turns out to be true,) now to hinder the union men from gaining the

---

[3] During February 12-16, 1862, CSA Commanding Generals John B. Floyd and Gideon J. Pillow abandoned Fort Donelson, taking about 2,000 men and the cavalry forces of CSA Col. Nathan Bedford Forrest to Nashville. This left CSA Gen. Simon B. Buckner to surrender it and about 15,000 defenders to Grant and Foote, as had occurred at Fort Henry the week before.

[4] Isham G. Harris was governor at that time, but he led Tennessee out of the Union in 1861, then actively recruited men to fight for the Confederacy. Forced to flee Tennessee when Union control was established in Nashville, he spent the rest of the war serving as aide-de-camp on the staffs of several CSA generals.

day, and of Peace being declared before the first of April at most, but soldiers are not supposed to know anything in time of war, so we cannot tell. Jerry is well at present, he got a letter from Ed. Rexford a few days ago, he was well and all of the rest of the boys in the third Reg. they were sorry that they did not go up to Snelling with us, it is not very likely that they will ever be in any battle, nor either will the second. Jim Thornton is well, Norman Case is in the Hospital sick with a fever, we left him at Somerset, I do not know how sick he is, Homan is well, Peter is a driving one of the Brigade Teams, I have not seen him for some time, Elicut is quite well again George Spaulding is so as to be around some, but is rather slim yet, they say that there is about 1600 sick soldiers in Lebanon. I stand the marching very well for I do not have to carry any thing, but I have to get up in the morning and help get breakfast ready, I then I help load up the waggon, and stay along with the waggon through the day, and some of the time I drive the mules, they are drove with one line, and some of the time I get upon the top of the waggon and ride, and as soon as we get into camp I help unload, and bring water for our coffee, and boil meat for the company to take along with them the next day, some days I have more to do than others but I do not think that I am a pineing away, for I was weighed to day, and I weighed 173 lbs. which is the most that I ever weighed in my life.

I received a letter from you the night that we got here, and was glad to learn that you were all well with the exception of your eyes. I hope that you will not hurt them by working evenings, you wrote that you heard that we had all of us been taken prisoners, but that we managed to get away the same night. Now I saw Andrew and he says that he has not written to Mrs. Bender. I told you before that you must not believe anything that you heard, untill you was convinced of the truth of the reports. I expect that you have got my letter which gave a description of our battle. I hope that you get all of my letters, for I do not get all of yours, I know. I have written a letter to Dan but I have not got any answer yet. I have not written any letters to Vt yet, nor I do not intend to, for a while, you say that Peters[5] has writen a letter to me, I have not got any from him yet, but I hope that I shall you tell Mr Kingsley that if he waits untill I make a speech that he will not come to see me very soon. I hope that he is a good prophet, and that I shall be at home in May. I have not sent any papers to you since I went away from here, and now I have not got any money to buy any with, we have not got our pay yet, nor do we know when we will get any, so I cannot tell when I shall send any to you, you will be very likely to get what I allotted to you by the middle of March. All that we are allowed to carry with us is one over coat, one dress coat, one blouse, one hat and cap, two pair of pants two pair of shirts, two pair of stockings, two pair of drawers, and one blanket, but I cary along more than that, for I put some things into the waggon. I would rather that you would not send Edgars likeness to me, for I should be afraid that it would not get through safe. I hope that I shall live to get home and then I can see his little picture, without looking through a glass. I was glad to hear that you had enough orders to pay all of the taxes. You need not be afraid of my learning to use tobacco, nor of getting to be a "rowdy" any more than I am already. I was telling one of the boys to night how old I was, he said that he did not think that I was as old as that, ~~for I was~~ because I was always so full of my fun, I told him that I never had seen the place yet where I turned from my boyhood to be a sober old man, if I was there I do not think that you could tell which could play the hardest, I or the children, tell Ida not to tip Edgar off from his sled and crack his "crown" for him, I hope that Alice and Eliza will learn enough to pay them for going to school this cold winter, what books do they study. I cannot think of much more to write this time and it is getting quite late, I will draw this letter to a close hoping that I shall not have to write many more letters to you before I shall see you all again,

---

[5] Andrew Peters, the postmaster and general store keeper at Alba in Beaver Township, and a family friend.

"I'll suffer hardships, toils and pains,
   For the good times sure to come;
I'll battle long that I may gain
   My freedom and my home;
I will return, though foes may stand
   Disputing every step;
My own dear home, my native land,
   I'll win you yet"[6]

Give my respects to all of the friends and neighbors,

Good bye "Nerva" good bye to all, this from your husband

D. B. Griffin.

You must direct your letters the same that you have done all of the time, please write as often as you can.

Letter Number 25

Camp near Concord Church Tenn. Feb. 26

My Dear Wife, Children and friends,

As I have not got much to do to day, I thought that I would write a few lines to you. I am well to day, and have been since my last. I received a letter from you a few days ago, dated Feb. 10th and was glad to hear that you were well at that time, and had not got the meazles yet. I expect to hear in evry letter that the children have got them, but I hope that they will not have them hard, if they get them, but I see that you have had some cold weather this month, but one thing is certain you can not have a long winter. We have not had but a day of two of pleasent weather since I last wrote, Monday & Tuesday was pleasant[.] I was on guard Monday, ₫ and Tuesday I played base ball, all day. We had a good time of it to, there was some 5 or 6 games played at the same time, both by the Officers and men, and we all enjoyed ourselves very much, yesterday about eleven

---

[6] This is assumed to be a brief original poem written by Brainard for his family.

o'clock it commenced raining, and it rained very hard all the afternoon and night, and the creek is up a booming it has washed away the bridge here, so we cannot get to Nashville this morning, but they have put some men at work cutting timber, and they will not be long in getting another one up. I expect that I shall have to go and help some on it. It does not rain much this morning and the creek is falling fast. We have not had much excitement in camp of late, but it was reported last night, that Gen. Van Dorn[7] was out about ten miles from here, and we were ordered to fall in this morning with our arms and accoutrements, but as it rained all night, he did not come on, we intend to be ready for him if he should come, he is reported to have fifteen thousand men, our scouts brought in a few prisoners last night. It is also reported that the rebels are again in the eastern part of Ky. and are a making for Frankford and vicinity, if so it may be that we shall have to go back into Ky. again. I expect that you see in the papers what is agoing on, at the Potomac and at Vicksburgh, as well as we do. I will send you a Nashville paper in which you will find an account of the skirmish. We had an order read upon dress prarade from the Inspecter Gen, Complimenting the 2nd reg. very highly, as to their drill, dicipline and general looks as a regiment. You wanted that I should write whether I knew anything about Charles Phillips, he is in Louisville yet, and the boys that came from there a short time ago say that he was well when they came away, and had been all winter. I received the letter, with one it it from Eliza, I like to have them all write, Edgar, Ida and all. I should think that Fathers folks would write a few lines to me. I have not written to them, but them if he reads all of my letters, it is just as well for them, I do not have much paper, and what I do get costs two cents a sheet, and I have not got much money just now, but I have managed to get along so far, we have not got any pay yet nor it is not likely we will get any this month, but I can get along without it, but I should like to have some to send to you, but I see that wheat is pretty high in

---

[7] CSA Gen. Earl Van Dorn, at that time in command of the Western Theater.

Minn. this winter, and perhaps you will have some to sell, but keep enough of it

Afternoon,

Well I have had my dinner, I had some corn meal pan-cakes and molasses and some fried beef. It has set in to rain again and it rains hard with heavy thundering[.] I expect that instead of rain you get snow about these days[.] It is warm enough for things to grow, but it seems as though things do not grow so quick here as they do in the North. I saw some pigeons yesterday, and there has not been any time but what the robins and meadow larks are around just the same as they are up there in the summer, but I think that I had about as lief have some snow as to have all rain as we do here. You spoke about there being secret societies in Ill. and Ind. you will see a piece in the paper that I send to you, that speaks plain to them, it is a speech by Col Kimble at Indianapolis. I cannot think that they will amount to much, any traitor at the North should be <u>hung</u> "as high as Haman," and if they get their just deserts they will not go unpunished. You say that Edgar can tell who the President is, how old he is &c but can he tell who his <u>Father</u> is? I do not think that I should know who my <u>boy</u> was if I should see him any where away from home. Alice says her rings have not come yet. I have not got any shells yet to make them with. I could bye some rings but I had rather make them myself, and I think that you would rather I would. I am [very sorry that yo*]u do not have a good school for I was in hopes, [that the children woul*]d have a good chance to go to school this winter but [you and your sister M*]ary[8] must learn them all that you can. Please give Mr. Westfall what you can afford, [*] dollars for me. I am glad that you [don*]t have "Hell and damnnation" preached to you. I would like to hear him preach first rate, where does he hold his meetings, is there a good many Universalist in the Valley, do they have other meetings there. Where does Elder Warner preach now? One of our boys is

---

[8] Mary Elizabeth Griffin Durand, Minerva's younger sister, living in Spring Valley.

expecting to get his discharge this week and go home, he lives near Hamilton his name is Wesley Baldwin[9], he says that if he is able to go and see you, he will do so, he has been in the Hospitals a good deal, I am afraid that he never will get well. I he comes to see you he will tell you how we get along. Peter is well, and so is Cutting, Elicut, Jim Thornton and the Case boys. Captain Barnes[10] is as good a captain as there is in the reg, he went to Wis. last fall and was married since he came back he has not drank a drop of Liquor of any sort, he tends to his business and understands it to, but if there is any fun around he can have as much of it as any one, his shoulder straps does not raise him up so high, but what he can speak to a private as well as to an officer, do they get any letters from the third regiment in the Valley, if you hear from them let me know, where they are, and anything else that you can think of. I do not think of any thing more to write this time, but as the mail does not go out to night, I may think of something else to write before I send [this off to you. It has s*]toped raining now and I must stop and get [my dinner, I a*]m agoing to have some boiled beans and pork and [crac*]kers, don't you wish that you had some? We [*] them. I will close by bidding you all a [good bye once more, D. B. Griffin*]

Letter Number 26

Nashville Tenneesee March 4th 1862

My Dear Wife,

I expect that you think that I have stoped a writing to you but it is not so, since I wrote to you last, we have on the march, or else on the boat all of the time. We started from Lebanon on the 22, and were four days going to Louisvill, 80 miles, there was a good turnpike all of the way, but it rained hard all one

---

[9] Wesley Baldwin, from neighboring Hamilton County, Co. F, 2nd Minnesota Regiment of Volunteers.

[10] Charles H. Barnes, a Spring Valley friend, Co. A, 2nd Minnesota.

* Missing text from torn page corners.

day, which made it bad marching, the first night we camped in Dr. Jackson's door yard, the Officers took possession of the house (a very large nice one), and we of the things out of doors, such as chickens beacon hams, and feed for the teams, we used his door yard fence for fire wood, the next morning started on, we passed some of the handsomest places that I ever saw. I have not time to discribe them now, it was a good country all of the way to Louisville, especialy within a few miles of there, we arrived in Louisville Tuesday afternoon, and went on board of the boat that night, our regment was there presented with a very nice flag, by the ladies of Louisville, they had not any thing in Louisville to good for the Minn. 2t. I went into a house and got a got a good supper, and a Lady gave (me) a flag about 2 feet long. I have got it in my knapsack, we were on board the boat untill Thursday afternoon before we started. We then started down the river, we arrived, at the mouth of the Cumberland river, at Smithland Friday evening, started up the C. river the next morning arrived at Fort Donelson at dusk and started the next morning by day light, so I did not see any of the fortifications there but there was places on the river that they had fortified, which they, the rebels, left, the river was very high so that every thing is under water along on the shore, we arrived here Sunday evening and we are still upon the boat for what reason I cannot tell. I enjoyed the ride first rate, as I always do a ride on the water, we are on the rargest boat that runs on the Ohio river, it is called the Jacob Straud, it is three hundred and fifty seven feet long, it was loaded very heavy[.] I was all day yesterday about the city, it is a very nice place, to be seen if I could talk with you I could tell you what I see but I have neither time nor room to begin, now, the people were all very glad to see the Union troops march into Nashville. I have talked with a good many of them, every thing is very dear here, for instance a pair of boots that we could get for about four dollars, are worth from 20 to 30 dollars. We were paid of after we came on the boat. I will send you five dollars in this letter, also a five cent bill of the southern money, you will be very likely to get a 20 dollars check from St Paul, I hope that you will keep enough by yourself, for your own use, it is a hard matter to get postage stamps here, but I can send home money and let you pay the postage there. I do not know where we are a going to go from here, but we are a going to keep a moving untill the thing is settled, and I believe that Peace will be declared in less than 60 days, but there may be some hard fought battles first. I hope not, though. I got a letter from you the day we came on the boat and was glad to get it, it was mailed the 15th the braids that the children sent to me were in it. I cannot get any papers to send to them now, there was not any of Alices writing in it, as you said[.] Jery is well and did not get any of his ribs broken in the fight, either, there must be someone there that starts all of these reports in order to keep you in a stew, about us all of the time. I am well and in good spirits all of the time, and I hope that I shall be untill I get back home again, it has been quite cool for the last two days, but every thing looks like spring, the trees are budding out grass growing &c. I cannot write much this time, but will try to write as often as I can, and I hope that you will do the same, this from your ever affectionate husband,

D. B. Griffin.

Letter Number 27

Camp near Nashville Tennesee, March 7th 1862

My dear Wife and Companion,

As I have a few moments to spare this evening, I will improve them by writing a few lines to you. I am well, and am enjoying myself first rate. It has been quite cold for the last four days, we had a little snow, just enough to whiten the ground, but to day it has been very pleasant and the snow is all gone.

We have camped in a very pleasant grove, about three miles from Nashville there is a good many regments camped in sight of us, and there is about 75 thousand men in and around Nashville. I have seen more men since I came here, than I have any time before. I do not know whether we will go from here right away or not, but we will probably stay here a couple weeks, and if things continue to move on as they have commenced to, it will not be but a short time before our forces will be in command of Memphis the secesh army is composed of a set of miserable thiefves and cowards. We are within a half a mile of a bluff on the Cumberland river, on which the rebels had planted from fifteen to twenty cannon, and built up breast works of cotton and railroad iron, in such a manner that had they stood their ground, it would have been a hard battle to have drove them out, but no, as soon as fort Donelson was taken, they spiked the cannon, and some of them are "lounders," now I tell you, "64 pounders" weighs about 5 tons. I would not like to stand before one of them, and touch it off, for I think if one of the balls should hapen to hit a man, (which they would be pretty apt to do, if they came very near him), that they would make a hole through him, that would let daylight shine through, they had two magazines there, filled with powder and shell, and balls, they were covered over with railroad iron, they blowed them both up, and the way that it tore things up and threw the iron is a caution to small folks, and in Nashville Gen. Floyd[11] ran all the cannon that he could get out, upon the bridges, (a nice railroad bridge and a suspension bridge, that cost 150 thousand dollars, the railroad bridge cost 250 thousand) and then set fire to them both, against the wishes of the inhabitants, and burned them up, and then spiked the cannon in the place, about fifty more, and then ran off without fireing a gun. we are right in the midst of secessionist, and when we ask them where the men are that could whip five to one, they recon that that is played out, I think that by the time we have got done with them, they will think that the "mud sills" are "some pumpkins," and that the Black Republicans are as white as they are, and nearly as good in a fight too. We heard that Columbus was evacuated and that they had burned every thing that they could before leaving there, they are a little afraid of our Gunboats, I have seen four of them, they

---

[11] CSA Gen. John Buchanan Floyd, former U.S. Secretary of War, the Commander of Fort Donelson who fled to Nashville rather than surrender to Union Gen. Ulysses S. Grant.

are hard looking things to fight against, I tell you, we also heard that the Burnside[12] fleet was a coming towards Richmond but it is not confirmed as yet, you will be most likely to hear all about it before you get this letter, we do not get many papers now, in camp, we have not heard from the Potomac for some time, but we think that things are all a coming around about right.

I received a letter from you yesterday, and was glad to hear that you were all well, and that you had got my letters which I wrote after the battle, because they gave you a slight sketch of the battle, and you know that I was not hurt, I do not think that our regment will get into any other fight, but still it may. You and Allen may break up all the prairie that you are a mind to, but I hope that I shall be there to drive breaking team for you, you will hire me, if I come, wont you[.] I think that Allen had not better wait for me to come home and shoot the wolves, but take down his gun and shoot them himself[.] I am a learning to shoot at larger game, than prairie wolves. I am glad to hear that Dan is a doing well, and has got to be a Lieutenant in his Company, it shows that he is liked and that he learns the art of war readily, I do not crave any office yet, and it is not very likely that I shall get any in this war, there is not so many sick in the regment as there was, there has not been over five died out of our Co. Lieutenent Haven's[13] of Co. A died very sudden while on the boat[.] Mr. Cutting has gone to Chicago with his remains[.] C. Phillips has returned to the Co. he did not get his discharge as was expected, Norman Case is still in the hospital, the rest of the boys are as well as usual. We have not heard anything from the trunk we sent home yet, you may hear from it before we do, I done the coat up and directed it to you, in the care of Lyman Case, I hope that you will get it, you spoke of getting Edgars likeness taken and send it to me, I should like well to see him if not anything more than his likeness, but as it

---

[12] Union Gen. Ambrose E. Burnside, under the command of Union Gen. George B. McClellan.

[13] Charles H. Haven, a Chatfield friend, Co. A, 2nd Minnesota Regiment of Volunteers, aboard *The Jacob Straud*.

is so uncertain about the mail in this part of the country, that I should not advise you to send it, although you can do as you think best, if you should, you must get your's and his both taken on one plate, it will not cost any more to send it, nor to get it taken, I should like to see the little Cherub a runing around the house, and cutting up his pranks, tell Grandpa and Grandma[14] that I should like to go into there room some of these long winter evening, and have a good visit with them, I am glad that they are both well this winter, how do they like the Minn. winters, have they got a good warm room to stay in, is Father and Mother and the rest of them well all of the time, I have not slept cold a night this winter, for I have got three blankets and the cook has one, and we get some hay, straw, or cedar boughs and lay on the ground, then spread down our rubber coats, and over coats, and one blanket under us, and three blankets over us, we take our knapsacks for our pillows then we take off our boots and blouse, and tumble in, there to lay and dream of home, and the scenes attached to them untill reville in the morning, I do not expect that I could go to sleep in a good bed now if I had a chance, but I think that I should try to pretty hard, if I got a chance to try it, but you need not worry about me for you know that I can sleep upon the soft side of a board or rail as well as on a <u>feather[.]</u> I sent you a letter two days ago, in which I enclosed a five dollar bill, if you get it all safe you must let me know, and also if you get the money from St Paul, if you get it, be sure and keep enough of it, so you can have enough to get your clothes and your groceries with. I must draw this letter to a close for it is getting very late, I did not think that I should get as much wrote as I have when I commenced, it is a good deal better soil here than in Ky tell Alice that Pa could not hardly keep the tears back, when he came to her <u>letter</u>. Pa was glad that she could write so much to

---

[14] Since Minerva's parents are mentioned in the next sentence, this must be his maternal grandfather, Ebenezer E. Thompson (mentioned in letter 1) and step-grandmother, Mercy (Cole) Thompson, as they alone of that generation are both still alive at that date. The unanswered question is their location: the context (both here and in letters 6 and 13) implies that they are in Minnesota, close enough to visit.

him, if I should be gone all summer she will get so that she can write a good long letter to Pa. Pa hopes that he will come home and help her make some flower beds, and fetch her home some flower seeds too and Ida some too they must both be good girls and mind their mother kiss them all for me. It is getting rather chilly in the tent and I must stop, so good night Nerva and babies, from

D. B. Griffin.

Direct your letters the same as you have all the time before

Letter Number 28

Camp near Nashville Tenn March 13th 1862

My Dear Wife and Children,

As I had a few minutes to spare this evening, I thought that I would set down and write a few lines to you, so that you may know how I am and what I am a doing, &c. I am well and as hearty as a buck. I think that soldiering agrees with me first rate, for I keep fat upon hard bread and coffee, with a little bacon and rice, which is the most of my living we have beef, bakers bread, and potatoes once in a while. I have been a frying some doughnuts this afternoon, it takes about a bushel to go around, we give them three apiece, they go like "hot cakes" I tell you after not having any for some time, we cannot save fat enough when we are on the march to fry them in, we have had some desecated vegetables, for making soup with, it makes good soup, we have a pretty easy time in the cook shop now, when it is pleasent weather, and it has been pleasent most of the time since we came here, there is thousands of rabits here and the boys have fine times in catching them, the land that we are on belongs to a great stock grower, his name is Cochran or some such name, he got the premium on some of his cattle at the world's fair, he has got a park with twelve deer in it, they look handsome too, there is so many regments around here that the fifes and drums, and brass bands, are playing from day light untill nine o'clock at night. We have not received any marching orders yet but we have to be ready to march at a moment's warning, we have received good news from the Potamac and Arkansas and all the other places of any importance. I have bought a Louisville paper to day, which has got all the news in that that I have heard, I will send it to you and if I can get some more of them as good as that is I will send them to you. I got a letter from Rundell, in the 3d regment, the boys are all well, they wish that they had joined this regment now for they have got tired of guarding bridges, but I heard yesterday that they had received marching orders, if so they may come here[.] I should like to see them. Jery is well, he has been a washing for the boys some since we came here, I have not washed any but my own clothes. I have collected what little there is was coming to us, and with that and my pay, I had enough left, after paying up my debts, to send you five dollars, and I had three dollars left, and to day the Captain called me into the his tent and gave me ten dollars for doing extra duty as cook, he asked me if that was enough, and I told him that I did not ask anything, but if the Company gave me any thing that I would take it and be very thankfull for it, and that I should send it all to my family, so I will send it to you in this letter, the company have had to settle up with us for the clothing that we had drawn up to the first of March. I have drawn $29.92 worth which is about twelve dollars more than was my due at $3.50 per month. I expect that it will be taken out of my next payment, if so you will not get so much from the State Treasurer but I hope that I can save enough to make it good to you, now if you get it be sure and keep enough for your own use, and to get some drag teeth, and if Mr. Chipman wants some to use let him have some, for I think that you will owe him some for building you a house to live in. I think that I shall be home in about two months from now if alive and well, but still it is not any thing but guess work, but we cannot see what the rebels are agoing to do, we heard to night that Gen. Grant[15],

---

[15] Union Gen. Ulysses S. Grant, commanding the Army of West Tennessee (supported by Union Gen. Don Carlos Buell's Army of the Ohio), preparing

was in Alabama with his part of the Army, if so we will soon march through Tenn. and on through to New Orleans, and drive them the rebels into the Gulf of Mexico if necessary.

I cannot think of much to write now. I hope that you will get the paper, do you take the Tribune this year. I have not received any letters from any one in Minn, but from you, except the one that Allen and Mr Chipman wrote. I would like to have some of the folks write to me and let me know how the town meeting comes off, who have got into "Office" &c. I will close for this time for it is time to go to bed, now write as often as you can, for whenever I get a letter from you, it does me a great deal of good. I will write as often as I can so that you may know where I am, and how I am. I hope that I shall soon be where I shall not have to talk to you upon paper, don't you? give my best respects to all of our folks, and accept these few lines, from your husband and companion in the Union Army in Tennessee, <u>Good night</u>,

D. B. Griffin

Letter Number 29

Camp near Nashville Tennessee March 19th 1862

My Dear Wife and Children, Friends &c,

As I have got a few moments to spare this afternoon and as we are expecting to start on the march southward tomorrow, I thought that I would write a few lines to you. I am as well as usual to day, and am still in the "cook shop" we have had quite pleasent weather since I last wrote to you, untill to day. Last night we got orders to march this morning at seven o'clock, so we went to work and cooked up the rations for to day, and it was eight o'clock before we got through, and we got up this

---

to confront the gathered western forces of CSA Gens. Polk, Bragg, Hardee and Breckinridge under the command of CSA Gen. Albert Sidney Johnston (with CSA Gen. P. G. T. Beauregard his second in command) at Corinth, Mississippi.

morning at four, and we had to get breakfast, in a heavy thunder shower, and it did not stop untill ten o'clock, so we did not have to start to day, but it is quite likely that we shall start in the morning. I cannot tell where for, but I think that we shall go towards Jackson Tenn. We do not get a great deal of war news, but what we do get is of the right kind. Our Captain said that he thought that the war would be closed by the 19th of April, others think that it will take two months or more, as for myself I do not care how quick it ends, for I am anxious to go home and see you all once more, and I hope that I shall live to do so. I have learned that my coat arrived in Chatfield safe, but I did not learn how much my share of the expenses would be, if you should get a chance to send for it, you will find it to Mr. Case's, and you must send some money along to pay the charges on it. It will not be over a dollar I guess and I would not take 15 for it. Jery and I boxed up some of our clothes yesterday and sent them home by express. I sent my overcoat and dress coat, it cost me 60 cts for both of them. I did not need them with me for I have got blankets enough to sleep upon and I think that I shall get home before cold weather again[.] Jery has wrote to Mr. Colby to get them, there was two more boys put in some with us, and they were directed to Fillmore, so you need not worry about them if you should not get them untill I get home, which I feel confident of doing before many months[.] I have written two letters to you since I received any from you, in the first one I sent five dollars ~~with~~ and the next one I sent ten, now you must write and tell me whether you received it or not, as soon as you get this, if you have not written before. I went down to Nashville last Sunday and I had a good look of the city there is a good many nice dwelling houses, and the State house and State's prison are very large nice buildings, but it is said that about one half of the inhabitants of Nashville are Lewd Women, so you must know that there is some sunken, low, and nasty places in the city, we are not allowed to send off any papers now or else I would send Eliza one of Leslies papers. I have got one, with the picture of the battle of Logans cross roads, and ft Henry and a good many other pictures[.] I will send it as soon as I can, I cannot write any more this time for I have not got time but I will write to you as soon as we stop again, you must write as often as you can if not but a few words at a time, for I like to get a letter from <u>Home</u> accept these few lines from your husband and friend

D. B. Griffin.

Gen. Buell's Army of the Ohio Marches South to Join Gen. Grant at Shiloh, Tennessee

Letters 30–33 (March 25–April 20, 1862)

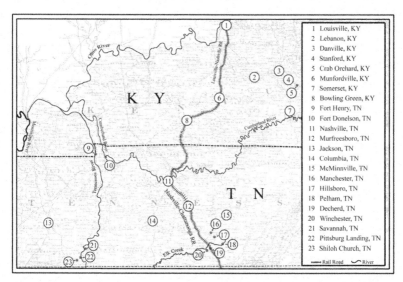

1 Louisville, KY
2 Lebanon, KY
3 Danville, KY
4 Stanford, KY
5 Crab Orchard, KY
6 Munfordville, KY
7 Somerset, KY
8 Bowling Green, KY
9 Fort Henry, TN
10 Fort Donelson, TN
11 Nashville, TN
12 Murfreesboro, TN
13 Jackson, TN
14 Columbia, TN
15 McMinnville, TN
16 Manchester, TN
17 Hillsboro, TN
18 Pelham, TN
19 Decherd, TN
20 Winchester, TN
21 Savannah, TN
22 Pittsburg Landing, TN
23 Shiloh Church, TN

Rail Road   River

The army is ordered south, with Gen. George Thomas's Division (including the 2nd Minnesota) in the rear. As they move further into "the slave working region," the first escaped slaves, referred to as *contrabands*, are added to each regiment. The continuing correspondences between camp and home highlight the differences in weather conditions and communicate their separate activities, health conditions, and extended family news. Because of rain-soaked roads, his division arrives too late to participate in the Battle of Shiloh, but the Confederate Army has only retreated the twenty miles back to fortified Corinth, Mississippi.

Letter Number 30

Camp near Spring Hill Tenn. March 25 1862

My Dear Beloved Wife and Children,

I will try to write a few lines to you this evening, and let you know that I am well, and feel first rate for I think, if all the reports we have heard for the last two days are true, that it will not be many weeks before I shall be in Minnesota, and if that would not cause a fellow to feel first rate, I do not know what would, particularly if he had a loved Wife and children there, to go home to. Now I will tell you what we hear or a part of it, we hear that Richmond is surrounded, with Jef. Davis[1] and his Cabinet in there, and that Memphis and New Orleans, were ours and several other small places in Tenn and Alabama, if they are all true, I cannot see what there is to keep us in the service a great while longer. We are camped about thirty miles from Nashvile on the Columbia road, waiting further orders, from head quarters, for things have taken such a turn within a few days that there is no telling what to do, but I hope by another week I can write and tell you what we are agoing to do.

---

[1] CSA President Jefferson Davis, former U.S. Senator and Secretary of War.

I have not had but one letter from you since we came into Tenn, it has been ten days since the regment got any mail untill to day and there was no letter for me. We are right in the heart of the secession country, and in the slave working region, we have got some contrabang's in the regment, there is one in our company, he tells some pretty hard storyes. I have talked with a good many slaves, they are all in the fields, men and women a plowing, it is very late for this country, there is not any corn planted yet, the peach trees are all in blossom. It is a nice country, every thing looks better than it did in Ky, the soil is rich, plenty of fruit, and grain, but the curse of Slavery spoils it all. I will not write any more to night.

Wednesday morning 26

I will try to write a little more this morning. I am well this morning and all the other boys that you know. I suppose that you have got sleighing yet there, it does not seem to me as though it was six months since I left home, but so it is, I hope that I shall see you all within two months. I have not received any letter from Dan yet, the Third Minn Reg. is in Nashville. I have not heard from any of them yet, if you have not sent your likenesses yet, I would not send them at all, for the mail is so irregular down here, that I might not get ~~any~~ them. I cannot think of any thing more to write just now, so I will wait untill evening, and perhaps I shall hear of something cheering, or get a letter from you when the mail gets in I hope that I will, so I will stop.

Evening.

There was not any mail to day, we have had a pleasent day, and there has been a good deal excitement in camp this afternoon on account of the treatment the men in the 18 regulars get, they had two men tied up to trees, they tie there hands and then raise them up over their heads and tie them to a limb and make them stand on their toes for three or four hours at a time, so to day the boys in the 9th Ohio went and cut the rope two or three times, when the Officers tried to stop them they knocked one or two of them down, and hooted at and groaned at them all the afternoon, our men are all down on the Officers of the regulars, and so are all of their own men[.] I have not heard any news to day, so I have not anything to write about, and as the evenings are short I will stop and bid you all good night, once more, these few lines from your husband and father

D. B. Griffin to P. M., A. J., I. M., & E. L. Griffin

Letter Number 31

Camp near Spring Hill Tenn, March 28th 1862

My Dear Wife,

I will take this oppertunity to write a few lines to you, it is after bed time, and I have been to bed, but we received orders after I got to bed, to march early tomorrow morning, and as I did not know when I should get a chance to write to you again, I thought that I would get up and write a little to night. I am as well as usual. I was cheered up last night after I got to bed, by getting three letters from Minn, one from you, one from Father and one from Peters, and you better believe I got up and lit a candle and read them all. I was glad to hear from you all, and to hear that you were all well, but I cannot help thinking what a hard winter you have had. I think that you have had to fight with a harder enemy than I have, to wit, the cold weather, I hope that you will not suffer so another winter, it is quite warm here at present, instead of my fingers being ~~being~~ cold, my hand sweats so that it bothers me to write. I am glad that you have written some to uncle Harrison, I hope that you will receive an answer from him, so you can hear from my folks once more. I sent a letter to you yesterday so I have not got any news to tell you to night. I do not know which way we are agoing to march from here, but it will be South somewhere. I hope that we will keep a going untill we get the rebels cornered up in some of the Southern swamps, where the musquitoes will torment them day and night untill they will give up the Ship, and go home to learn war no more[.] I made out to read Alice's letter, and am glad that she can write as good as that, I can remember when I could not write as well.

I think that you will not have to write to any one to get the money, for your name and address was put down in a book for that purpose, if you get any you must let me know, and also when you receive any from me. Now Minerva I want to caution you to be shure and keep enough by yourself so that you will not want for anything. I think that Edgar is has got to be quite a large boy, but I should think that Mrs. Boynton's was a larger one. Why did not Sophrona fetch over her <u>boy</u> to brag on, you must try to go and see them all, if you do not untill I come home, we will go and see them all around, and I hope that I shall be there in a few weeks, or months at the most, you must not worry about me for I shall fare first rate as long as I am well, and I hope that I shall not get sick. Jerry is has not been verry well for a couple of days but I think that he will get along, he is a little bit <u>old maidish</u>, like myself, when he does not feel well. C. Barnes has got to be first Lieutenent in his Company, he is liked first rate[.] Norman Case has not come out of the Hospital yet the rest of the boys are well as far as I know, tell Mr Peters that I feel very gratefull for his short letter. I hope that he will keep on writing to me, but he must not look for any letters from me, but he can read yours, which will be just the same, and Father also, give my best respects to all of the folks about there, tell them all to write to me as often as they can, I will send this off in the morning if I can, and will will write to you as often as I can, whenever we stop long enough to get fixed up. I must stop for it is getting quite late and I have got to get up early in the morning so good night Nerva, kiss the children for me.

D. B. Griffin

Letter Number 32

In Camp near Columbia Tenn. March 31st 1862

My Dear Companion and Wife,

As the letter that I wrote three days ago has not yet gone out, I will write a few more lines to day and send with it. I am well to day with the exception of a bad cold, but I do not think that it will result in anything serious, my lungs are some sore and I am quite hoarse, otherways I feel well. I have not much news to write to you this time, but as I promised to write to you as often as I could I will try to. We started on Saturday from Spring Hill and marched about ten miles through a very pleasant country and past some very pleasant country seats, amongst them was one that formally belonged to Gen. Pillow[2], but now belongs to Uncle Sam, there is a great many such places, and the further south we go the more we shall find. It has been very pleasant weather for some time, the trees are looking quite green, the peach trees are in full bloom and there is thousands of them all over the country, in the fields as well as in orchards. I wish that they would grow as well in Minn. We are camped in a very pleasant place besides a large piece of timber, and in front of our Co. tents is a beautiful family burying ground, it is all full of cedar trees and rose bushes &c the family is buried inside and the blacks on the outside, the slaves are leaving their masters evry day, there was a man in camp this morning a looking for one, he did not get much satisfaction from us, some of the boys told him that he wished that every d—n one of the niggers and all them that owned them were dead, for them were the very ones that coused this war, the man sat on his horse a few moments, then turned and rode off. I expect that he felt some better, most all of the White mem around here have gone in the rebel army, but the soldiers are not alowed to harm any one, nor any thing. I cannot tell when we shall start from here, but probably by to morrow. we expected to moved on this morning, but we did not, the

---

[2] CSA Gen. Gideon J. Pillow, who also fled from Fort Donelson with Gen. Floyd.

bridge is not quite done, the rebels burned the old one down in there retreat, that is the way that they do ~~every~~ evry where, most evry thing is very high here, but I hope that we shall soon set things to right but it may be a long time yet, we may have some hard fighting to do yet, but we are confident that we can clean them out in a couple of months.

April the 1st

I did not get a chance to finish this letter yesterday and I am glad of it, for to day I received a letter from you dated Forestville March 25th. I wish that I could get all of your letters as quick. I should think that you have had a rather tough time of it with the snow. I hope that you will not lose any thing, by my coming away, and I think that I shall be at home before another winter. I had a letter from you and Father a few days ago and one from Peters, and was glad to hear from them, you say that Lewis Abbott has got home I wonder if he has brought much <u>Gold</u> home with him. If you see Mary again before I do tell her that she has got even with Emery now and she had better say quit now, what does she call her girl, tell her to call her <u>Doratha</u> or <u>Peggy</u> I do not care which <u>that is</u> if she wants that I should <u>name</u> her, how do the folks like the looks of my Secesh Coat do they think that it is worth sending home, Jery got a letter to day from his wife she had received the money which he sent to her. I am anxious to hear whether you have received the money that I sent to you, $15.00 we did not go to day as we expected, but we expect to go to morrow, there has been about 15,000 soldiers past here to day, we are a looking for the third Reg. but it has not got along yet, tell the folks there that I do not want the town clerks office, let some one have it that will not go to the war, and I should not advise any one to come now for it is quite warm weather here, the folks have commenced planting corn, they do not plant the cotton seed untill the middle of this month. I feel better to day of my cold, I am very ~~hoarse~~ hoarse, but I can speak loud yet, to day my nose has bled several times, so I think that I shall get along. I wish that you had some of our warm weather in Minn. just now. Elicut Rundell is well, and is a gaining all of the time, they are agoing to leave all of the men behind that are not able to march 20 miles a day, so we are agoing to drive the rebels if there is any such thing, if we have to fight for it, and for one I am willing to fight till death, before I give up. Minerva be carefull with your eyes do not hurt them by working evenings. I expect to tan up as black as a mullatto, if I stay down here all summer, but I do not expect to. I long to be with you all, and when I do get home again I think that I shall stay there but I do not want my discharge untill the end of the war. I cannot think of any more to write this time, we do not have a chance to send ~~of~~ our letters off only as the mails are ordered by the Gen. I will try to write to you often, and hope that you will do the same, tell the children that I think of them a great many times a day, and dream about you all very often, tell them good bye for me, too. I must stop now and help get supper (or coffee) good bye Nerva, once more I hope that I shall soon quit writing good bye and be where I shall not leave you so long again.

D. B. Griffin

Letter Number 33

Camp near Pittsburg landing April 20th 1862

My Dear Wife,

I guess that you will think that I have forgotten you entirely because I have not written to you before, but I have not you may be shure. I have not had a chance to send one off, if I had got one written, so I will write a few lines to you to night. I am well to night, and have been all of the time except a hard cold, we have had a hard tramp since I wrote to you last. I had a long letter written to you, in which I had given you a description of our journey and of a good many of my adventures on the road &c. I had sealed it up and put it in my pocket, and was agoing to send it out to day, but I lost it out and I could not find it. I am very sorry for I had taken a good deal of ~~panes~~ trouble to be very particular in my descriptions of the country &c but I hope that it will not be many months, if I am alive, before I shall see you, and then I can tell you all, we are camped upon the ground where the battle was fought, it was a hard fought battle[3], as you probably have seen the accounts before this time, ~~also~~ I will not try to describe it now, our regiment was not in the battle, it has been a very rainy spring, the roads are very bad, we cannot tell where we are a going to next. I hope that this war will soon end, so that we can go home to our friends and families. I saw Emery's brother the other day in the 14th Wis. reg, he looks some like Emery, he was in the battle[.] I have not received any letter from you for over three weeks, every thing is as green here as summer, what kind of weather have you there, it rained hard all day yesterday and to day, and it is not very pleasent getting the meals out in the rain. I am wet all of the time and go to bed in my wet clothes. Jery is not very well just now he has blistered his side for a pain in it, &c. I shall not write much this time for it is ~~is~~ wet and it is getting dark. I am in hopes that it will clear off before long for I am sick of the mud, give my respects to all of the folks. I will try to write more next time, I do not feel like writing to night, for I am mad at myself for loosing that letter. Minerva I think of you often and think how hard it is for you to get along through the cold weather. I hope that you will receive your reward sooner or later and I hope that I shall be permitted to see you before another winter. I do not think we shall be at home before the fourth of July now. I expect that we shall have a few more battles before we quit, our regiment and the ninth Ohio were out on picket night before last, they drove in the rebel pickets, and the reports are that they are evacuating Corinth, but we

---

[3] The Battle of Shiloh, April 6-7, 1862, in which the forces of CSA Gen. Albert Sidney Johnston nearly overwhelmed those of Union Gen. Ulysses S. Grant, but for the mortal wounding of Johnston. With the timely arrival of Union Gen. Buell's army, CSA Gen. Pierre Gustave Toutant Beauregard was compelled to lead the Confederate retreat to fortified Corinth, Mississippi.

do not know for sure. I must close this short letter for the want of any more to write about, so good bye, this from your husband in Tenn,

D. B. Griffin

To My Nerva and the babies

God bless you all.

The Advance Upon and Occupation of Corinth, Mississippi

Letters 34–42 (April 25–June 15, 1862)

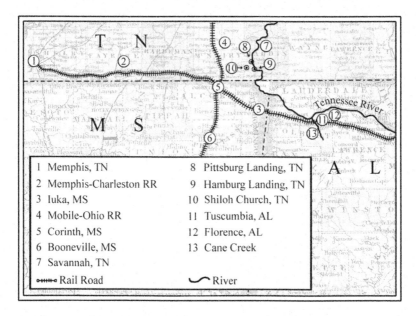

1 Memphis, TN	8 Pittsburg Landing, TN
2 Memphis-Charleston RR	9 Hamburg Landing, TN
3 Iuka, MS	10 Shiloh Church, TN
4 Mobile-Ohio RR	11 Tuscumbia, AL
5 Corinth, MS	12 Florence, AL
6 Booneville, MS	13 Cane Creek
7 Savannah, TN	
◦┼┼┼◦ Rail Road	⌒ River

The incessant rains continue, restricting the movement of the now-combined Union Armies to only a few miles on the days they attempt to advance toward Corinth. Occasional engagements with Confederate pickets or other small forces occur along the way, but rumors of the South's evacuation of Corinth lift the Union's spirits. Those rumors prove true, and they are able to occupy Corinth without a fight. In these letters, Brainard often reflects on the war and its destruction of the South, on slavery and the slaves he encounters, and on his separation from home and family. He also creates a very poignant scene of daily life in camp and asks many questions about the people at home and Minerva's management of the farm.

Columbia, Columbia, to glory arise,
The queen of the world and the child of the skies;
Thy genius commands thee, with rapture behold,
While ages on ages thy splendors unfold.

Letter Number 34

Camp near Pittsburgh Landing Tenn. Apr. 25/62

Dear Wife and friends,

I will try to write a few lines to you this afternoon. I am well and as tough as usual, we have moved our camp some five miles towards Corinth where the rebels are fortified, it is about seven miles to their intrenchments, our fources went out yesterday and routed a camp of two or three thousand men, driving them in, and taking a few prisoners and a gun or two, besides some conversary stores and other things, there was no one killed, on either side. We are expecting an advance movement before many days, but some think that the rebels will not fight very hard, again, but I do not know, it may be a hard fought battle, but we are confident of success, there is a strong force here now, I suppose there is from 150 to 175 thousand men, around here or somewhere in the vicinity, it has been very wet here which has put us back some in marching, and it has also been a great help to government in transporting troops and provisions. We are camped in the timber on a side hill, it is very gravely, but it is some dryer than it was at the other place, it has been a raining all day, but we have got a cover over our fire which is a great help to us when it rains. I do not know as I shall stay in the kitchen much longer after this month, there is so many gone out of the company that I am needed in the ranks, when the company is on duty. We have heard that Sergeant Bailye died on his way back here. Jery is about the same as usual, he wants to get his discharge, and go home. I hope that he will for if a person gets unwell and discontented he had better get his discharge if he can, for they will not get well very fast, if they should get well at all, but I hope that I shall not get sick.

I sent a letter to you three days ago, and I received one from you the same day. I was glad to hear from you all, and to hear that you were all well, and that the snow was a leaving you. I hope that it is all gone, and that it is warm weather there by this time, for I think that you have had a cold time of it this ~~time~~ winter. I was glad to hear that you had got all of the money that I had sent to you, I do not know when you will get the $20.00 from St Paul, but I think that you will get it before long, if you do not get it before the next pay-day I shall stop the allottment, and send it to you myself, we received our pay to day. I got six dollars. Uncle Sam will owe me $26.00 the last day of this month, I do not have to spend any money only just for what paper, ink, envelops, and postage money I want, and sometimes I get my boots fixed up a little and such like, I have enough to eat and wear, and drink. I expect that I shall be a regular coffee drinker by the time I get home, so you must learn how to make it, if I go without it in the morning I have a hard headache before night. I expect that you will laugh at me now. I am glad that you have been over to see Jery's wife, it was Dan Paul's wife that wrote that she was growing poor, and not you. I think that if Capt. Thrasher has got a boy, it is because he has got some kind friend living near him, for I think that he is to old now to learn ~~young~~ new tricks, and I should think that it would be a "darned" new trick for him to make a raise of a boy, or anything else. I expect that I have got some letters lately that I have not sayed anything about for I lost the letter that mentioned about my getting a number of letters. I wrote to you that I thought Allen had better shoot the wolves off himself, and not wait for me to come home to do it. I do not know as I shall fetch any gun home with me, for they belong to U. S.

I have never been into a regular hospital, they have almost every thing to eat that they need, they have cots and hammocks to lay upon, but in a camp hospital, (or tent) they do not have the same conveniences nor necessary care that they do in a hospital. I have not any desire to go into a hospital, but still I cannot tell how soon I may be taken sick, but I hope that if I am sick I can go home and be amongst my own folks. I am not a gaining in flesh now. I weighed 165 lbs in my shirt sleeves, I have not shaved me yet, but I have got my hair cut off short, you must not set any time for me to come home, for we cannot tell how long this war will last. I hear this afternoon that the rebels are evacuating Corrinth. It would not be anything strange for them to do. I believe that they intend to keep us a "tagging" after them, and if they see a chance to pitch into a few of us, they will try to drive us, but it will be of no use the union will carry the day sooner or later, it is seven months to the day since I left my little home and family, and as you say it has been a long time, will it be seven more months before I shall see them again, God forbid, but still many a one has left their home and friends, never to return again. I will send you five dollars in this letter, and I wish that I could send you a V. evry time I write to you, I shall have enough left to stand me through, how did the cattle come out this spring, tell Alice that I could read her letter first rate, I have got it in my wallet, I should like to see you all to night. I dreamed of seeing you all last night, and talking with you about my adventures, but when I woke up, I found myself in a tent away down in Tenn, close to the rebels and close to the State line of Miss, we have not been troubled with any misquetoes yet. I cannot think of any more to write to night so good night Nerva, good night baby's and all.

Saturday morning.

I am well this morning, it has cleared up and the sun shines out very warm, I hope that it will stay out. We are a going to advance in a day or two[.] I have got a chance to send this letter of this morning. I have not got any news to tell you this morning, kiss all of the baby's for me, tell them that pa wants to see them real much, and all the rest of you to, now write as often as you can. I shall get them some time, do not forget me, nor worry about me. Now I will bid you all good bye again, this from your husband

D. B. Griffin

to <u>Nerva</u> and the children

good bye, good bye

Letter Number 35

Camp Near Pittsburgh Landing, Tenn. Apr 28/62

Dear Wife and Companion,

I will try to write a few lines to you this afternoon, and let you know how I am, and what little news there is. I am well to day, and hope that these few lines will find you all enjoying good health, it takes a letter so long to go from here, and to get and answer back from you again, that I do not know what to write to you about. Jery has gone off to the Hospital to day. I do not know as I have got enough sympathy for him, but I did not think that he was very sick, he has made himself sick by fretting himself about home, and his wife keeps writing to him to try to get his discharge and come home, and he is a trying to get one, the doctor says that his Lungs are affected, but I think that he will get well again if he can get home, and stay with his woman, but I do not think that he would give any more to see his woman, than I would to see mine, but I shall not make myself sick by fretting about you, you know that I do not let anything worry me, for I do not believe that a man was made to make for the purpose of making himself (and every one around him) miserable, by fretting and borrowing trouble. I know that you cannot get along as well without me, as you could with me, but you must try to look on the bright side of this world, and let the dark side pass by, if you cannot get along and have things just as you would like to have them, you must try and put up with them just as they are. I do not think it will be a great many months before I shall be at home, if I live, and then we can tell how to prise each others society, so we will try to put up with a few hardships and privations, for a few months or days[.] Jery's wife wrote that you had lost all of your calves, and that father had 3 or 4 head of cattle, but you did not say anything about it in your letter of the tenth which I received last night, I was glad to hear from you and to hear that you were all well, but was sorry to learn that you had to battle with the snow yet. I was in hopes that the snow would stay off when it went off, did you have enough hay to feed your cattle after buying that of Chipman. I think that you cannot do any better than to buy some lumber if you can get it hauled and can pay for it in pork. I hope that I shall get home before next fall, so that I get a stable built for our cattle, and a good many other things besides, you need not worry about paying Mrs. Bly at all, for he has not settled with me for the reaping nor for the butter either[.] I do not know but what he has settled with some of the rest of them so you had better let it be as it is. I have found out the reason why you did not get the allotment, I thought that you would get it before we were payed, but it is not so, you will not get it untill after we are payed, so you will probably get it before long, we expect to get payed of again in a few days, the pay master is here yet, and to morrow is muster day, if you should not get a letter every week from me you must not think that I am sick, for the mail does not go out evry week. I do not think that I shall stay much longer in the cook shop, for I have got tired of it, it is five months since I came into it, and I have not drilled any nor stood upon guard untill night before last. I stood on guard two hours, so I think that I have got along first rate. I do not know how long before we shall get into a fight, there is a grand movement of troops to day, there was two rebel deserters came into camp to day, they say that they are nearly discouraged and if they get whipped out at Corrinth, that they will quit fighting, New Orleans is in our possession, it was taken on the 22nd I think, and they think that there is not any use of fighting any longer it is reported that Yorktown is taken, and if so I cannot see what they are a fighting for. I hope that the war will soon be ended, for we are all of us anxious to go home again, and see all of our friends and then we can talk with each other, and tell over our adventures and our hardships. I cannot think of much more to write to night and the mail is a going out before long, the boys in Co. A are well that we know, the 3d regiment is in Nashville yet, if we have a fight here, we will be apt to have it before many days, and I will let you know how it comes out, if I am alive and well, and I hope and pray that I shall be spared to meet my little family on earth, if not may we all be so happy as to meet in Heaven. Charles Barnes is got to be Captain of Co A, Capt Bishop is Major of the Reg, the Post Master is after the letters and I must stop, so good Bye Nerva, good bye Alice, good bye Ida, good bye Edgar, this ~~Father~~ from your Father and Husband in Tenn. May God bless and protect you all on this earth,

D. B. Griffin.

Letter Number 36

Camp Near Corinth May 6th 1862

My Dear Wife and Friends, as I have a few moments to spare this afternoon, I will write a few lines to you. I am as well as usual but very tired, for I have been to work in the mud and water this forenoon, a helping make a bridge for our teams to cross over. I have quit the cook shop, and was agoing to go with the company, but the evening before we started, (Saturday) I partly sprained my ankle so much that I could not walk, so I had to go with the team, and it commenced to rain, and made the roads so bad that we did not get up to the regment untill to day, my ankle is so that I worked in the mud and water as hard as any of them I guess, the boys were all glad to see us for we had all of the rations with us. We are expecting a grand move in a day or two and then if nothing more hapens to me, I intend to go with the boys untill the war is ended, if I live, and we are confident that there will not be many more battles fought before ~~we~~ it is ended. We cannot hear of any war news that is reliable, for evry thing is suppressed, there is a great many camp rumors, but we cannot put any trust in them, I hope that it will not be long before we are permitted to hear what is agoing on in the world, the boys are well. Norman Case has joined his company again, he is well. I have not heard from Jery since he went to the Hospital. I got a letter from W. Freeman. He has been sick all winter with the measels and fever but he is well again now he expected to go to Fortress Monroe he had not been in any engagement then (Feb 22) there had been a good deal of rain there as well as here, we are within 6 miles of the rebels intrenchments, now, I cannot think of much to write this time. I hope that I shall have a chance to write you some good news about the war in a few days, evry thing is very high, here, especially Whisky $6.00 a gallon, cheese 25cts a lb, ~~and~~ &c, but I do not trouble myself about buying anything for I have enough to eat, drink and wear, we have never had whiskey dealt out to us but four or five times, and then when we had been out in the rain or on a hard march. I must stop for supper is ready and the mail is agoing out right after supper, so I must bid you all good bye once more. I hope that the time will soon come when I can see you all again, and then I will quit saying good bye, but we mus wait and ~~trust in~~ hope[.]

Well good bye one and all, good Bye, yours in haste,

D. B. Griffin

to Nerva and the babys.

God bless and protect you

Camp on Meel Creek Tenn May 8th 62

My Dear Wife and Children, I will once more
try to write a few lines to you I am well to day
and feel first rate, never felt better, we have
all been out this forenoon on a general review
Gen Sherman reviewed all of his troops to
day and a splendid sight it was to. I donot
know how many there was but there was a
great many thousand of them, it is very
warm to day, the winter wheat is all headed
out and peaches are about half grown, but
wherever we go there is not anything done
towards spring work, I hardly know what
the people will do towards living this summer
if the war does not end soon, I think that
it will end in a short time, but there is
various ideas about it, we hear a great
many reports about the war in We, we heard
that McClellan had bagged the entire
rebel army at Elizabeth City, but he had
lost one of his arms and 16000 thousands
of his men, but it is uncertain as yet

As regards the prospects of a fight at
Corinth. I cannot say much about, we hear
that the rebels are a leaving there, but that is
uncertain, there was a good deal of heavy
cannonading in that direction all of the
forenoon, but what the results was we
have not yet learned, we have to be ready
to start at a moments warning with two
days ration in our haversacks, and 100 rounds
of cartriges, and our blankets, there is a
great many batteryes here there is one of six
guns, that will shoot seven miles, they take
look like a black log, it takes 10 or 14 yoke of
oxen to draw them, the roads have got
good again, I hope that we shall move soon
and decide this war as soon as possible
for I do want to go home before it gets
to be such hot weather, but I have stood
it as well as the best of them so far
and I intend to live through it and go
home again, I will not write any more
this time so good bye Nerva and the babys
this from your husband and father D. B. Griffin

Letter Number 37

Camp on Mud Creek Tenn May 8th 62

My Dear Wife and Children,

I will once more try to write a few lines to you[.] I am well to day and feel first rate, never felt better, we have all been out this forenoon on a general review. Gen. Sherman[1], reviewed all of his troops to day, and a splendid sight it was to. I do not know how many there was, but there was a great many thousand of them, it is very warm to day, the winter wheat is all headed out and peaches are about half grown, but wherever we go there is not anything done towards springs work. I hardly know what the people will do towards living this summer if the war does not end soon. I think that it will end, in a short time, but there is various ideas about it, we hear a great many reports about the war in Wa. we heard that McClellane[2] had bagged the entire rebel army at Elizabeth City, but he had lost one of his arms and 16,000 thousands of his men, but it is uncertain as yet[.]

As regards the prospects of a fight at Corrinth, I cannot say much about, we hear that the rebels are a leaving there, but that is uncertain, there was a good deal of heavy cannonading in that direction all of the forenoon, but what the results was we have not yet learned, we have to be ready to start at a moments warning, with two days ration in our haversacks, and 100 rounds of cartriges, and our blankets, there is a great many batteryes here there is one of six guns, that will shoot seven miles, they look like a black log, it takes 10 or 14 yoke of oxen to draw them, the roads have got good again, I hope that we shall move soon and decide this war as soon as possible for I do want to go home before it gets to be such hot weather, but I have stood it as well as the best of them so far and I intend to live through it and go home again. I will not write any more

---

[1] Union Gen. William Tecumseh Sherman, a Division Commander in Grant's Army of the Tennessee.

[2] Union Gen. George Brinton McClellan, twice Commander of the Army of the Potomac, and President Lincoln's 1864 Democratic Party challenger.

this time so good bye Nerva and the babys this from your husband and father

D. B. Griffin

Letter Number 38

Camp near Corinth Miss. May 14th 1862

Dear Wife and friends,

Once more I am permitted to write a few lines to you. I am well at the present time, and have been all of the time[.] We have camped in a beautiful piece of timber about five miles from Corinth the last strong hold of the rebels I hope, we have been expecting a fight to come of every day now for over a week, but for some reason unknown to us it has been delayed untill now, and we are just as ignorant of the time to day as we were two weeks ago, but we are advancing a little evry day or two, all of the news we get is of a cheering nature to us soldiers, we hear that the Miss river is opened all through, if so, there is not much of a chance for Beauregard[3] to get away from us by going on to the other side of the river, we have got a large army here now, (200,000) we have to move slow on account of the swamps which we have to make roads through, but I do not think the time is far distant when the stars and stripes will float triumphant over Corinth, and also over the whole south we are now in the state of Miss. it is a pretty piece of woods, quite large trees and no under brush, and as green as any pasture just rooling enough for the water to run off the soil is of a sandy loam. I think that it would be a good place for a farmers to make good farms but niggers drivers do not do it, they are very slovenish about evry thing, for one I do not want to live here as long as there is any slavery here, although I believe

---

[3] CSA Gen. Pierre Gustave Toutant Beauregard led the assault on Fort Sumter and provided most of the field command at 1st Manassas. He assumed command following the death of Gen. Johnston at Shiloh, led the Confederate troops back to Corinth, Mississippi, but eventually abandoned that important rail junction as well.

that it would be a good country to live in, there is any amount of fruit of all sorts I have seen some figs a growing out in the open air although is is quite a late spring I have seen some new potatoes, and some green peas, I have not seen a field of corn yet, but the wheat is out of the blow, it is very thin on the ground. I have not heard from you for some time, but I am a looking for a letter evry day. I have not heard any thing from Jery since he left the rest of the boys are as well as common. I wish that I could write something to you that you would be glad to hear, but I do not think of anything now, but I hope that it will not be many days before I can, you must write about all of the folks, how they get along with their springs work, and how you and C. gets along a farming together, how did the cattle come out this spring, did you have hay enough &c. I do not know but what I shall take the team to drive, there is some talk of it. I shall know in two or three days. I do not think of any more questions to ask now, but I could ask you a few if I was there, and could tell you of a good deal more than what I can write, if there was not any thing for a soldier to do but to stay in camp they would have an easy time of it. I wish that you could see us to day. I am sitting by the side of a tree in the shade while I can look around me upon all sides and see them, some under bough houses some under shade of the trees some a writing some reading some playing cards some sleeping some cooking some a washing their clothes and others a loitering about camp whilst I can hear the sound of the bugle and drum, ~~all is~~ such is camp life all is joy, but who knows how soon we may be called forth to the battle field, amid the roar of the cannon, and the muskets. I hope that it will soon cease, then we will learn war no more. I must draw to a close for the want of more room and the lack of anything to write about so I will bid you all good bye again

D. B. Griffin

kiss all of the babies for me Nerva.

Letter Number 39

Camp near Corrinth Miss. May 24th 1862

My Dear Wife and friends,

I will once more write a few lines to you. I am as well as usual this morning, and I hope that this will find you all well. I received two letters from you this week and was glad to hear from you all, and also to hear from my friends in Vt, and to hear that they were all well, I have not written as soon as I should on account of the expectation of a battle evry day, but there has not been any yet, only a few skirmishes with the pickets we have to go out on picket duty evry two or three days, we have built a good deal of breast works, and are well prepared for an attact if the rebels see fit to pitch in, we do not know why we do not attact them, but probably the Generals know the reason[.]

If you get all of my letters but the one which was in Nashville, I do not care, for it was a short one informing you of our start from there, there was not any thing in it of any account, I have paid the postage on all of them so far you need not send any more stamps, for if I get out of money, I can send them without paying for them, it was some mistake of the P. M. that that one did not go through. I was sorry to hear that C had left you, but I hope that it will all turn out for the best, if anyone should see fit to talk about it, just let them go ahead, and they will soon get tired of it. I hope that evry thing will be so shaped that I can be at home in a few months if alive, and well, I have not been sick any yet. Jery is at Hamburgh landing acting as nurse in the Hospital he is about well. George Spaulding is here he starts for home to day or tomorrow and I am agoing to send this letter home by him, and I will send you five dollars in it, you will most likely get the allotment before this. I do not fret myself at all about it for I think that it is safe enough, we have had some pretty hot weather, but it is wet and cool to day, there is a good deal of preperations made in expectation of the coming battle Minn. has sent a boat down in order to carry the sick and wounded home. I hope that I shall not have to go home in it, but it would not be anything unprobable, for I intend to pitch in with the rest of the boys, when the time comes, but I hope that I shall be one of the lucky ones to come off unscathed[.] I shall put my trust in him who is the ruler of all things, his will be done. I cannot write much this time, tell Alice that I am glad that she can write such <u>long</u> letters to me. I hope that I can see her and all the other babys before long, you know that I borrowed 50 cents of Eliza you must pay her some way.

you must write to me as often as you can. I went to the river last week I saw Emery brother he was well, he said that he had written Emery a letter, you do not write anything about him, write all of the news, give my best respects to all of our friends, and remember me, kiss the children for me. May God bless and protect you all, which is the wish of your dear Husband and Father,

D. B. Griffin
To P. M. Griffin
A. J., I. M., & E. L. Griffin

Letter Number 40

Camp beyond Corinth June 1st/62

My dear Wife and friends,

As I have got another oppertunnity to write a few lines, I will commence. I am well to day, and in good spirits for the stars and stripes are now waving over Corinth, we have taken the place without a strugle, the rebel army evacuated it last Friday morning, leaving almost evry thing behind them, they tried to burn evry thing up, but "scedadeled" so fast that there was a great deal of stuff saved from burning, our brigade was the first to go into their intrenchments, they met with no opposition except a few pickets, we took a few prisoners that were left behind[.]

We have all been prety busy the last week, in building intrenchments, standing out on picket &c[.] We were called out last Wednesday with arms, expecting an attact evry hour, we laid out all night. Thursday we were orderdered to the right about two miles, we went into camp, got our dinner, and started, we got to the place after a good deal of Military manouvering, and were set at work throwing up breastworks, we got done before dark, and again threw our blankets down and layed down for the night expecting to have an attact by day light the next morning but morning came, and we heard an awful explosion which we afterwards learned were cartrages in the building that were burnt. I was up at the time, but you had ought to have seen the men jump up, it was all still as it were, but in an instant thousands of men were upon their feet looking with an anxious look, wondering what under heaven was a coming, but our Gen. Robert McCook, did not wait a great while untill he had started two regment out to reconnoiter, we all waited anxiously expecting evry moment to hear the sound of muskets and the whiz of the bullets, but alas we were all happily disappointed, for soon we heard a shout, and the news soon went from one end of the camp to the other that "Bob" McCook was inside of the rebels breastworks, soon the order came to "right face, file left, march" we started with a light heart and a firm step for Corinth we went within $\frac{3}{4}$ of a mile of the vilage and halted, we had a grand time in runing around the rebels camps but there they had burnt up evry thing of any importance, we were soon ordered back to our camp where we arived about noon, we got our dinner and soon the order came for us to be ready to march in 20 minutes, we were ready and we started, we were on the road untill after midnight, when we were ordered to lay down untill daylight, we were ready in the morning to start but we did not get any orders to move, so we laid still, untill night, when we were ordered to pitch our tents and go to sleep. We do not know why but it is rumored in camp that Gen. Mitchel[4] has cut off their retreat, and caused them to fall back. I hope

---

[4] Union Gen. Robert T. Mitchell, serving under Gen. Buell in the Army of the Ohio.

that it is true, for I think that we can soon blot the whole army out, if they will make a stand where they are, for they can not hold out a great while longer on account of getting supplies. I got a memphis paper of the 28, there is not much war news in it for it is not allowed to be published, you thought that tea was very high there, "$1.50 per lb," but it is $10.00 per lb in Memphis, what do you think of that.   I saw the fourth reg yesterday there is not a great many boys in there that I know, Sam Shits Bishop and others from LeRoy, they are all well[.] I saw S. Lamb of the fifth reg. the 2nd is in Mitchels division. I hope we shall see that in a few days. We do not hear very good news from the East, Gen Banks[5] has been driven back. I think that there is a screw loose some where, but still we cannot tell, it may all turn out right after all, it is terible hot weather here now I tell you, but I think that we can stand it, if the southeners can, but I hope that we will not have to stay here a great while longer, but I dare not entertain a hope, for fear of a disappointment[.]

I sent a letter home last week by G Spaulding, and I put a five dollar bill in it, he said that he would go and see you and carry it to you. I hope that you will have a good visit with him, how does the crops look this summer, there is not any crops a growing here where the army goes, there is a plenty of fruit of evry kind, I have not heard from Jery this week, the boys are all well there is not as much sickness as there was some time ago. Minerva I would like to write to evry one seperate, but I can not get the time to do it, so you must let the folks read my letters and tell them to write to me, for I should be glad to hear from them all, I want to see you all very much "especialy you and the babys," when will the time come whem when we shall meet again. I think that I shall know how to appreciate the presence of women and children after the war. I think it would be good for the sore eyes, to see them around again, especialy a "yankee" woman, but we have got to wait with patience and trust in a kind providence for the future[.] I

---

[5] Union Gen. Nathaniel Prentiss Banks commanding the V Corps of McClellan's Army of the Potomac, as part of the Shenandoah Campaign.

cannot think of any thing more to write this time, so good bye one and all, I will try to write oftener after this. I have not ~~seen~~ had a letter from you for two weeks, the mails are quite irregular here as yet I do not know when this will go out, but I will have it ready to go at any time, there is not a half a dozen in the company but what have had more sickness than what I have, I can not say that I have been sick a day yet, and I hope that I shall be able to say so all of the time. I do not think I have ever enjoyed better health in my life I do not have the summer complaint at all, it is about all that ails any of them now, I will send you the markets prices of Memphis. Our Chaplain is agoing to start for Minnesota, and I will send this letter along by him, it rains a little just now, and dinner is ready. Well, we have been to dinner and I will tell you what =} we had we had some boiled pork and beans, some dumplins and molases, all of which belonged to the secesh. Now I will tell you what them marks mean up there, just as I got there some one spoke and said "how do you do Mr. Griffin[.]" I looked up and who should it be but James Nichols, if one should have risen from the dead, I should not have been any more surprised for the last letter that I got from you you said that he was sick, and you did not think he would ever be any better. I was very glad to see him as you must know, and also to hear from home, too, and to hear that you are all well and a doing well. I do not know when he will go to his Regiment, he is quite well at present, he will report himself to our head quarters, and stay with me untill he can get a chance to go to the Reg. I will close for this time but I may write some more before I send this away.

I cannot think of any more to write Jim and I have seen our Col, and he tells him to stay here untill he hears from the Col. of the 3d, he says that it would not be safe for him to try to find his regiment now, so he will stay with me for a while yet. I shall look for a letter from you all of the time untill I get one, you must excuse me from writing any more this time, so I will bid you all good bye once more good bye, good bye, from your husband and friend,

D. B. Griffin.

Letter Number 41

In Camp near Corinth June 11th 62

Dear Minerva and Children, and all the rest of the folks,

I have once more set myself down to write a few lines to you, so as to let you know how I am and what we are about. I am as well as usual, and so are the rest of the boys as far as heard from[.] We have been in pursuit of the enemy for the last week, but could not get near enough to them to get into an engagement, they have scattered in all directions, we went about 20 miles south of here, and stoped, at a place called Carolina Meeting house about three miles from Boonville, our Cavelry were so close to them at Booneville that they did not have time to remove about 20 car loads of provisions, and 3,000 stand of arms our men burnt them up and took some few prisoners, they retreated back a few miles not being able to hold the place untill our reinforcements came up, but when we got up there they had left there was a couple of contrabands came in the morning that we started back (yesterday) they say that they were (or what there is left of them), about thirty miles from there, and still agoing south as fast as they could, we have been ordered back, that is our Division, we are now here, but we expect to move from here in the morning, but in what direction we do not know, some say that we are agoing to Virginia others to Memphis so you see that I cannot tell, we are in a good country of land I think if it was worked as we work land, but there is not a great deal of stuff a growing now, and what little there, is about destroyed by the time both armies go over them, the wheat is already cut, but it is very light not more than five or six bushels to the acre, some few fields of corn looks well but generaly the corn is very late. I have seen some as high as my head. I have not seen any cotton a growing yet, people prefer to plant corn in the place of it, there has been a great many thousands of dollars worth of cotton burnt all around here, besides a great deal of other property. I do not know as I can tell you any news about the war, we have heard some of the news of the fight at Richmond but we do not know how it has terminated yet, we look very anxious for the result.

It is very hot and dry, water is very scarce through the country and what there is, is not very good, and the land is very clayey so when we are on the march there is a perfect cloud of dust all of the time, we have been gone from our tents one week, to day, laying some of the time in the dirt and some times in the woods so you must know that when we got here to day, we were not the cleanest set of men that you ever saw, but we have got washed up and doned our clean shirts, and look and feel some better[.] James Nichols has started for his regiment they are in Florence Ala., he was quite well when he left. Pete has heard from Dixon he stayed around there in Ill. awhile finely he cut up some caper or other, he did not know what, and he had to run away out of the country. I have seen some men from Cedar rapids, but I did not know any one that I saw there was a good many in the reg. (1250) that I knew but they were either taken prisoners, or had gone home. I heard from a good many of our old friends, Lydia B. is married and her man lives with uncle Jason, Mrs. Dunaway is maried again, both of them have got good men[.] Jo Holland was in the war in Missouri, he got wounded in the foot, and got his discharge, the Bryans live in the Rapids the railroad bridge croses the river on the dam, and the railroad runs on west, I cannot think of any thing else just now[.]

I received a letter from you day before yesterday, and was glad to hear from you all again, and from Mary to, tell her that I was very glad to hear a few words from her, I see by your letter that you are a getting along with the farming first rate, you must not let Edgar drive the breaking team too much this summer, I am glad that he is well and grows fast. I expect that he will be as smart as his "Daddy" by the time I get home. I do not expect that I should know him now, nor the other children either, but I could soon learn who they were if I could get there, which I hope will be before another winter, but things look rather dubious, but still we cannot tell what a day will bring fourth, we are all very anxious to have the war close so that we

131

can go home to our families and friends, I wish that you would tell me how many acres of Wheat, Oats and corn you have got in, I think that you will get the money from the Treasurer as soon as it gets there, so do not worry about it. We expect to get paid off again in a few days, and I shall stop the allotment then, and send the money by mail, you must tell me whether you get the money that I sent by Geo. Spaulding also five dollars some time before that[.]

I hardly know what you will do to get your hay cut, but I guess that there is someone around there that will put up enough for you if they can have the money for doing it, if Father will see if he can get some one to cut some for you, I will try and do as much for him some time if I should live long enough, if you do not get enough put up, you can sell off the cattle this fall if I am not there[.]

If Peters sends me some stamps you must pay him for them I have not got any yet, from him, I should like to have any one and all of the folks write to me but I cannot write to them unless we are in camp some where for a number of days. I am in hopes that we shall go where there is a plenty of good water, for it is bad getting along without it, fruit will soon be fit to use, blackberries are ripening peach trees are breaking down with their loads[.] I never saw the likes, I have seen a few fig trees but the boys keep the figs picked off[.] I believe that this would be a good country to live in if it was not for that curse to the American soil, African Slavery, here it exists in its worst form, they are poorly fed and clothed, and hard worked but they say that they do not have to work so hard this year as common, for it is not so hard to work in corn as it is cotton, if I was there I could tell you something of it.

I never found the letter that I lost, and I do not get any time to write it over now if I should ~~should~~ come home in any kind of time I can remember it all or enough of it. I guess that you can manage to read this, but it is not written very good for I am out under some bushes, and have to almost lay down to write, but I have made out to scrible off a few lines. I do not know when the mail will go out but I will have it ready, you must write as often as you can, and tell me what is agoing on there. I hope that the children will have a good school this summer. I did not send the flag home[.] I wish that I had, have you got the coats, what did it cost to get the secesh coat there, how I wish that you could look out of the window and see me acoming. I think that if you started to meet me, that I should meet you all of half way, unless you run faster than I can, but I must stop and bid you all good bye once more so good bye all

D. B. Griffin

Letter Number 42

Corinth Miss. June 15th 1862

My Dear beloved Wife,

I seat myself down this morning with a good will, to write a few lines to you all. I am as well as common this morning, we are a getting very hot weather just now. We have pitched our camp on a flat piece of timber land close to a fine creek, so we have plenty of water and good spring water to. We have cleaned out all of the underbrush and rubage, and fixed up shades around our tents, so we are as comfortable fixed as we can expect to be, we are not bothered any with the musqueitoes, but the house flies are very think during the day, we expect to stay here four or five weeks, we are about two and a half miles east of the village of Corinth on the Memphis and Charleston rail-road, the village is or was a very pleasant village, handsome houses and gardens, and has been a great business place, it is where the Ohio & Mobile and Memphis and C. rail-road cross each other, but when the rebels left it they burned all the houses of any importance and the citizens have nearly all of them left the place, but it is again assuming a busy appearance for the houses are being taken for head quarters of officers, and two or three companies of the Michigan Engineers and Mechanics are have been seett to work building cars and fixing up old ones, so that we will soon have a plenty of cars runing from here to Memphis in a few days as that city is in our possession as you must have heard before this time, we did not hear of it for certain untill yesterday so I expect that the whole of the Mississippi river is in the possession of our Army, which will cut off a great source of the southern armys supplies, but I do not think they will attempt another fight in the west, for the papers state that Beauregard has gone to Charleston with his army, but I know that they have not all gone there for I think that a good many of them have gone north as prisoners. I have seen and talked with a good many of them, it is reported that we have taken twenty thousand prisoners, besides any quantity of arms and ammunition, our men find newly made graves which upon being opened prove to be cannon and guns, instead of men. I have seen a good many of their guns mounted on their breastworks, which are nothing but an a black oak log with the end blackened with coal, but I have also seen some of their heaviest guns, we have got a round shot in camp that weighs 64 lbs, and I have seen a good many of our guns that will carry a ball seven miles, I should not like to have one of the bals hit me, but I do not expect that we shall ever have another chance to fire at them, or to let them fire at us, for I think, and so do others, that this regiment will never be in any more engagements with the rebels, there will probably be some hard fighting done in the east and south, but it is not probable that this Division, (Gen. Thomases[6]) will leave the state of Miss, untill the close of the war, and I believe that that long looked for time is not many months distant when we shall not be wanted to fight any more.

Minerva, you think that it is hard for you to get along without some one to look to, but if you had been with me when I have been around amongst some of the families which are left behind, you would have said that your lot was an easy one, just imagine yourself in the South with your little family of children, with scarcely clothes enough on to cover their nakedness your husband taken and tied hand and foot and carried into the army, and the last cow and mouthfull of provision taken from

---

[6] Union Gen. George Henry Thomas, Gen. Buell's second in command in the Army of the Ohio, and later a Division Commander in Union Gen. William Starke Rosecrans's Army of the Cumberland.

you, and not a mouthfull agrowing this summer, I have seen such, and have divided my rations with them, there is a good deal of want around here, they have subscribed a large sum in St Louis for the relief of the women and children around Corrinth[.] I feel thankfull that your lot is as good as it is, for you have a plenty to eat drink and wear, and are among kind friends who will not see you want for anything, that will make you comfortable and you can look forward to the time, if I am spared, when I will return to my home and family, when we can set down and talk over our past adventures, and trials, and our future prospects, and pleasures, my earnest prayer is that I may be spared to return, and live a long and happy life with you and the babes, and I think that our prayers will be answered, don't you think so, but I want to see the trouble between the north and south, so effectually wiped out, that it will never show itself again in my day, nor any body's else day, before I can go home contented, and then and not till then do I want to go home, unless I am taken sick.

I have not heard anything from Jery since my last letter, the other boys are all well at present, there is a great deal less sickness now in the army than there was one month ago, there is general health throughout the army, it is very hot yet[.]

We expect to get paid off in a day or two, and I shall try and stop my allotment, so that I can draw the whole of it myself, and send it to you through the mail. I think that it is about time that I should hear from the money that I have sent to you, five dollars about the first of May, and five by Geo. Spaulding. I will send you all that I can spare after I am paid I do not spend much for I think that you need it more than I do. I wish that you would recon up and see how much I have sent home, and let me know when you write again. If I should not get home in time I wish that you would keep enough money to buy a good plough, and hire the ploughing done if you can, besides getting the hay cut and put up in a stack, how have you got along with the fencing, and do the cattle bother you any this summer, or horses either, I hope that Gates folks will come to their sences, and all of you be as neighbors once more, do you have any meetings there this summer, &c. Oh! I want that you should tell me what girl Al goes to see this summer, tell him not to get married untill I come back for I want to be at the Wedding, is he breaking much this summer, and how does he stand it this summer and how does Hen.[7] make it go with the school marm, have you a good school, tell Hen. not to go to writing letters to the school marm, nor any one else, telling them to meet him at the corner of the fence, has Norman Gates commenced to go home with the school marm. I hope he will have better success the next time he goes home with any of the girls, has Adalaline got married yet or any one else around there, has any one got any new babies. How does Father and Mother stand it this hot weather, or is it not hot weather there. I never knew what it was to sweat much while I was there, but I sweat here in the tent so that it runs down the side of my face, it is still and the sun pores right strait down, when we were on the march I sweat so that my shirt was wet through and through, and that you know is more than I could ever do there and work as hard as I was a mind to. I feel well all the time none of the victuals which I eat ever rises on my stomach, as it used to there. I have not weighed myself for sometime but I do not think that I grow poor any yet, how is Grandpa and Grandmam, stand it this summer, I expect that Grandpa works in the garden as much as usual, how much of a garden have you got this summer, and how does it all look. I wish that I could go along with this letter, and get some good pie plant[8] pie, I have not had any good pie since I left home. I am afraid that if you keep that jar of sausoges untill I get home that they will be spoilt did the pork keep good, how much is it worth per pound, &c. I guess that I have asked you questions enough for once, so I will stop I wish that we could set down together as long as I have been in writing this letter I commenced about nine o'clock and have not got up only to eat my dinner and it is about three o'clock I

---

[7] Both Brainard and Minerva have brothers named Henry, but this is most likely Minerva's brother, Henry Tyler Griffin, as he moves to Beaver Township from Vermont to farm with his father and brother Allen.

[8] Rhubarb.

cannot write much more this time for if I should write evry thing this time I should not have anything to write about next time. I will stop and rest awhile now. I may think of something more to write about before I send this away.

Well I have been out to take a walk but it is so hot that I did not go a great ways. You wanted that I should write over the letter that I lost. I will write a little which was in it[.] I believe that I commenced it about the first of April, we got nicely fooled on that day, we were camped about 3/4 of a mile of from the road in a pretty green place by the side of a family burying ground, and where they had buried a good many blacks, but I must tell you how we were fooled, we were told that the third Minn. reg. was agoing to go by that day, so a great many of us went out to the road to see them but no, they did not go by at all, we went through some of as handsome country as I ever saw, and some large timber[.] I saw one tree measured, it measured 27 feet around up as high as the stump that would make it 9 feet through it was a white wood tree, I saw a great many other large ones but not any other ones so large as that, it run up 40 feet very large[.] I stoped at the house of Gen. Pillow, it was a nice house it cost 18,000 dollars I went all over it, he had left it in the charge of his negroes, one of them went with me through the house, and garden, the garden was a very nice one as was also the glass house, but there had been so many there, that they had picked off all of the flowers, while I was there a niece of Gen. Pillow's came there in a nice carriage with a driver and waiter, (blacks) she was dressed in very rich silk and was as handsome as a picture, her husband was taken prisoner at Ft Donelson and was then in Columbus Ohio he was a Major in the Southern army. She and I had a good long talk concerning the war, and the yankees she sayd that she had been made to believe that we were agoing to set there slaves free ravish the women and destroy all of their property, but she had become convinced that it was not our intention so to do, she was well pleased with the treatment her husband received in prison for she had received a letter from him[.] I cannot remember all, for I stayed and talked with her for nearly an hour. I went from there to the house of Gen Polk[9], an other secesh Gen. he is a cousin of the old President, his family was at home, but his gardener took me all over the garden, it was the prettiest laid out garden that I have ever seen, and as for his hot house a person could immagine himself in a garden of roses it is a very large one and it was in full bloom if you can imagine how it looked if you have ever seen a hot house, we went through some pretty vilages but there was not much of anything transpired except the daily tramp some of the time in the mud, and some of the time in the water, the most curious people were the blacks they would stand and stare at us with amazement, wondering where we all came from, one old black woman stoped me, and says she, "good lord a'mity where did you all come from, I did'nt know as there was so many folks in the world, 'pears like you had moulds to make 'de' men in." I told her that they was made in moulds, and asked her if she did not think that we had some pretty good looking moulds to she, says ('yes, 'yes, 'yes) she had a little mulatto girl by the side of her. I asked her what made that little girl fade out so, says she, "O her fadder was a white man," says I is that the way they all do, "yes," she says, "a heap of them do that way," &c. I went on thinking that I had heard enough, there is a great many other things that I could write if I had room, but I guess, that I will not say any more untill I get home, I guess that you will say that I have said enough, tell Alice and Ida and Edgar that their pa thinks of them a great many times in a day, and wishes that he could see them and have a fine play spell with them. I feel just like it to night, tell Hellen[10] and Eliza and Alice, that they must write a good long letter to me, and then I will answer it, give my love to all of them, and take a share of it yourself, from your husband in Miss, but in hopes that he soon will be in Minn,

D. B. Griffin

---

[9] CSA Gen. Bishop Leonidas Polk, who served under both CSA Gens. Albert Sidney Johnston and Braxton Bragg.

[10] Helen Churchill is the older orphaned grandchild living with Minerva's parents. The youngest grandchild, Horace, is never mentioned in the letters.

Guarding the Bridge at Cane Creek, Alabama

Letters 43–46 (June 30–July 20, 1862)

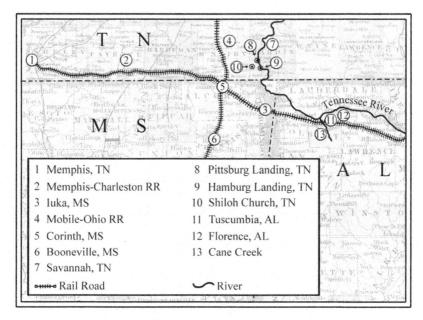

1 Memphis, TN
2 Memphis-Charleston RR
3 Iuka, MS
4 Mobile-Ohio RR
5 Corinth, MS
6 Booneville, MS
7 Savannah, TN
8 Pittsburg Landing, TN
9 Hamburg Landing, TN
10 Shiloh Church, TN
11 Tuscumbia, AL
12 Florence, AL
13 Cane Creek

●┼┼┼● Rail Road   ⌒ River

After pausing at the medical springs of Iuka, Alabama, two companies, F and C, draw guard duty of the railroad bridge across Cane Creek, a mile up from the Tennessee River. Their three-week stay is uneventful. Brainard playfully chides Minerva concerning the false news of his death circulating at home, then reflects on the "thousands of soldiers" already dead or with lives shattered, and expresses his desire to return home whole to his family. There are several passages regarding contact with slaves and slave owners, foraging for food and supplies, and responses to Minerva's letters.

LIBERTY—UNION.

Letter Number 43

Cane Creek Alabama, Monday, June 30th 1862

My Dear Wife, Children and Friends,

I will try once more to write a few lines to you all, and let you know how I am, where I am and what we are a doing. In the first place I will assure you that I am <u>alive</u> and well, if it were not so, I should not be here a writing to you to day. Nerva, it made me feel bad to hear that it had been told to you, and all the rest of the folks about there, that I, Brainerd Griffin, of the 2nd Minn. reg. vol, was "dead." I would'nt have cared anything about it, if you had not have heard so, for I had just as lives as not that a good many others would think so. I should like to have called in and seen some of you before you had heard to the contrary, would there not have been some stareing done. I hope that I shall haunt the one that started the report, if it was done intentionly. I never thought that I should live long enough to hear the report of my <u>death</u>. But I am glad for your sakes, and the little children. <u>God bless you all</u>, that it is as well with me as it <s>it</s> is to day, for I can say for one that I am well, and in camp, whilst thousands of our soldiers who started from their homes, with health and joy beaming in their faces, are now in their graves, or their constitutions shattered for life, and thousands more will be ere this war closes, I fear. I do not know how the war is a progressing now for we have not had any papers since the 20th[.] I received your letter three days ago but I have not had a chance to answer it before, for we have been on the march. I intended to write to you before this, but just as we had got evry thing fixed up at Corinth so that we could been comfortable, we received orders on Sunday morning a week ago to be ready to march at noon, we packed up and started for a place called I.U.Ka[1], in the eastern part of Miss. 22 miles from Corinth, we got there on Wednesday and went into camp here, stayed here untill Saturday, the country that we passed through was princapaly what we call pine plains there is a great deal of the pine taken off and it has grown up to bushes, it is quite hilly, and there is not any farms of any account. I.U.Ka is a pretty little place on the rail road, it is very widely known as a summer resort, here is a number of Medical Springs, which are beautifully fixed up, there is one large Hotel rigged up for the accommodation of boarders there is several other handsome buildings, but not a great many, here our Brigade was divided up into companies and sent off on the rail road, and other roads, to guard bridges. Com. F. & C. of our reg. was sent to guard a

---

[1] He may spell Iuka this odd way to help his readers pronounce it correctly.

bridge acrost Cane Creek in Ala, about 22 miles from there, and about eight miles from Tuscambia and ten from Florance. Our Reg. was payed off for the months of Mar. and April, Saturday forenoon, and we started from there about four o'clock, and traveled untill long after dark, and through an awful hilly country. Yesterday morning we started again before sunrise, and came through, we came past some large plantations, but they are mostly all planted to corn, instead of cotton[.] I saw one field of cotton, of over three hundred acres, it is sown in rows about two feet apart, the Stalk and leaves look more like buck wheat than anything else, there is some of the old crop left around here, but there was a great deal burnt about two weeks ago, there is some handsome residences through here, one ~~ownd~~ man by the name of Dickson who is in the secesh army, has a splendid one, he owns about 2,000 slaves. I have some great times a talking with the slaves, we are camped in a big plantation and the blacks, both male and female, are a hoeing to day, there is an overseer over them. I have not said much to them yet. I do not know but I shall get myself into a muss, but when I am with them, I shall free my mind to them, they think it strange that we do not have any servants to work our farms, and wait upon our wives and children, they call me "massa" when I speak to them. I can talk real nigger fashion, they think that I am a Southern man, they say that I do not talk like a Yankee, but I "recon" I can talk yankee if I get home again, but I can put in "a right smart sprinkle of hoosier" once in a while, just for fun[.] I was glad to hear that you was all well, and that you had got the letter that I sent by Geo. Spaulding, with the money. I took all of my pay from the paymaster this time, so there will not any go to St Paul, this time, if you get the twenty that is due you there, you need not look for any more from that way. I will send it to you in fives and then if a letter gets lost I shall not loose it all at once. We have just been mustered for another two months pay. I am in hopes that when we are mustered again, that we will be mustered out of the service, but we cannot tell yet[.] I hardly know what you will do this winter if I do not go home this fall but I think that the best way for you to do, will be to go ahead and get your hay cut, at least, and then if there is not any prospect of my getting home before winter, let out the place if you can, and if you cannot get the house fixed up so that you can live comfortable in it, you had better let out the cattle or sell them, and rent a house in the Valley or somewhere, where you can get your wood, and get it cut, &c. You must talk over the matter with Father's folks, and do the best that you can, it is different from what we expected when I came from home, then we all thought that I should get back home before this time, but it has turned out differently, and there is no telling when I shall go home, if I live, but we all live in hopes that we shall see Minn. this ~~home~~ fall, I will send home all of the money that I can spare and you must try to pay the interest on the land, and keep enough by you so that if you should need anything you can get it, as to the bargain between Chipman and myself it is, as near as I can remember, like this, I was to find team and seed and pay for thrashing my share one half that is "pay the machine" and board him, and he was to do the chors, and cut and get up the wood, I think that I told him if he would fix up a shed and bank up the house, that I would pay him what it was worth. I do not know anything about the worth of the shanty, you can settle that with him some way I recon, I hope that you will not have any trouble with any one, it has been very dry here for the last ~~two~~ four weeks, but we have had some showers lately the corn is tasselling and earing out here, some of the apples are getting ripe, peaches will commence to ripen in three weeks, we have all the Blackberies that we can eat, and the darkeys fetch in some buttermilk, eggs, corn dodgers, potatoes, and such like, so we live first rate just now. I will not write any more to night, the boys are all well now. I will send you five dollars in this letter and keep asending you some in evry letter, and I hope that you will get it all.

July 1st

It is quite cool and cloudy this morning. I am as well as usual, I have seen the homestead bill, but I do not think it gives the soldier any better chance than the settler[.] I had about as

143

lives pay for mine, as to take the benefit of the act, is there any one working Jery's place, Jery was well the last I heard from him, did you read any of his letters, if you did, you know how he writes to her, has G. Spaulding been over to see you yet, you must tell Alice that Pa thinks a good deal of her letters. I think that she improves in writing, does she have a good school this summer, tell Ida that she must write someto Pa too, Edgar will tell her what to write, I recon. I shall be gone away so long that I shall forget all about the little <u>boy baby</u>, he will be a great boy by the time I get back to you again, how much would I give if I could see you all this morning, money would not be of any value, it has began to rain a little and it looks as though it would be a rainy day. I cannot think of much to write now. I do not know when the mail will go out, we do not get it very regular here, but I will try to write as often as I can, if you get any letters from Vt let me know what the news is there, and all the news that you can get. I will send this letter without paying the postage, if you get all the money up to this time let me know in your next. I must close for this time so good bye "Nerva," good bye Alice, good bye Ida and good bye Edgar L. Griffin, from your husband and father in the Union Army in Alabama,

D. B. Griffin

Letter Number 44

Camp on Cane Creek Ala, July 8th 62

Dear Wife and friends,

I will once more try to write a few lines to you, and let you know that I am well, and enjoying myself first rate, we do not have much to do except guard duty, which is pretty heavy, we have to go on guard about evry third day. I came off guard this morning, we have not had anything to disturb us since we have been here, except once, we were called out night before last, in double quick time, one of the guards alarmed the camp by firing his gun, but we found out that it was not any thing attackting us but a few harmless cattle, so we laid down again, and slept as sound as ever untill morning, we spent the fourth just the same as we do evry other day, there was not any of us drunk, ~~for~~ but there was a good reason for it we could not get anything to drink, except coffee and water. I was on guard all day, how did you spend the 4th we enjoy ourselves first rate here, there is a plenty to eat and plenty to drink, and a good place to bathe in, the Tennessee river is about one mile from here, we go down there once in a while and have a good swim and bag a few fish, &c, we have a plenty of apples, potatoes, milk butter blackberries, and we occasionly draw a porker by the heels, as we do the potatoes by the tops, this morning we drew a fine beef creature out of the secesh woods the inhabitants around here are mostly all secesh, but they keep very quiet, they have about as much as they can tond to to keep watch of their niggers and their other property. It is very dry and hot here, the corn rolls their leaves up some during the day time, it is nearly all tasselled out. I have seen some cotton blows, they look just like a white morning glory, a field of it must look fine when it is all in the blow. I have not heard a great deal of war news of late, but the last that we heard was that Richmond was burned, but we have heard so many rumors about Richmond that we do not credit much that we hear, we have hard work to get any mail at all, I have not had any letter from you since my last. I sent you five dollars in that letter and I will send you another five with this one, you have probably got the twenty from St Paul before this time, for the boys have heard from theirs, I have not heard from J. Nichols since he left me, how does Mrs Nichols'es folks do now, they must have a pretty hard time of it being sick so much, I hope that you will not get sick nor either of the children. I do not know when I can send this off, and it is excessive hot this afternoon that I will stop writing now, and finish it when it is cooler. I have not heard from Jery yet, the rest of the boys are all well, as far as I know, we are nine miles from the rest of the regiment, they are in Tuscambia they say that it is quite a pretty little place.

July 9th, evening,

It has been a very hot day I tell you I am as well as usual to night, there was a mail came in to day, but not any letter from "Nerva" yet I look very anxious for one, for I like to hear from you all, and hear how you get along with the work on the farm, and how the crops come out, I hear that the crops look fine this summer, in Minn, we had some green corn in camp to day, we will have a plenty of it in a few days, but a good deal of the corn leaves roll up pretty close during the day, we get some ripe apples in camp but they are not as good one's as we have in the North, but there is any amount of them this year, and peaches without end, they are not ripe yet. We have heard that Richmond was in our possession but the most that we can learn is that McClallan has placed his army on a hight, that commands the City, but I expect that you learn how matters are before we ~~are~~ can get any thing here but we are all very anxious to have the war end, so that we can go to our homes, and I for one am as willing as any one to go home to my ~~families~~ little family and stay with them untill death shall part us, and live in peace the rest of our lives, for I have seen enough of war ~~for~~ to last me for a long time to come, as well as the effects of war. I have got a chance to send this letter off in the morning, but I cannot think of any thing to write to night that will be of any news to you. I shall close for to night, hopeing that I shall hear from you in a few days, I have got to be on guard again tomorrow. I must bid you all good bye, once more, good bye "Nerva" good bye "Alice" good bye "Ida" good bye "Edgar" from your husband and father in Alabama,

David B Griffin.
P. M. Griffin
A J. Griffin
I M. Griffin
Edgar Lincoln Griffin

Letter Number 45

Camp on Cane Creek, Ala. July 13th 62

My Dear Wife and Friends,

I thought that I would write a few lines to you to day, not that I have got any news to tell you, but to let you know how I am, and because I can send one off, to morrow. I am as well as usual to day, and am standing guard to day[.] It is hot enough to roast eggs I think to day, it is so hot in the middle of the day that the niggers have to stop work, we had a lot of niggers in our camp last night, one of them had a banjo, on which he tried to finger out a few tunes, and to accompany the music with a few verses of negro melody, some of them were after this fashion

"Ole Mrs. Gumbo she was big and fat"
"Her face was as black as my old hat"
"Get out de way"
~~And~~ And another one that ran in this wise, and sung in the tune of Old Dan Tucker, or some thing like it to wit,
"Old Gumbo came from Tennessee,"
"Biggest fool I ever seed,"
"He clim a tree to see his Lod."
"The limb it broke and he got a fall,"
"And he did'nt get to see his lod at all."
"Get out de way" &c,

but it was not of a very comical turn, they have to steal away from their master after night, and consequently, they fetch in some chickens and eggs, apples onions, &c, which they steal from their masters, they are not fed nor dressed well some of them appear to know about as much what is agoing on as the whites, they appear to know that there is something a going on that concerns them, one old nigger, over seventy years old, asked me if I thought that the darkies would ever be free this side of the grave, they hardly know what it is but freedom to them is something like heaven to us, they think that if they only knew that they could have it before they die they would be hapy, but they do not know how to obtain it. One bright looking darky told me, in answer to the inquiry if he was ever

147

paddled, he said that he was once, and that was because he went off one night to see his "wife" but was back again before morning, he said that he had had two wives, but his master forbid him to go and see them and he had to let them go, his voice quivered while he told me, about it, still the whites say that they have no feeling and no sense it is not so, give them the chance, and let them know that they are men like ourselves and there is a plenty of them that will out do their masters, but enough of this, there is some talk of our mooving south before a great while but we do not know for certain yet. I think by the accounts we get from Richmond, that they have had a hard fought battle, but we do not know the result of it yet, we have heard that the President has called for 300,000 more men, so I think that the North has no notion of being bluffed off. I wish that they would end it before winter, and I cannot see, how, if we keep the ground we have gained, the war will keep up more than three months longer, but we do not know how the thing will turn.

The mail came in to day, but no letter for me. I do want to hear from you, but I do not worry any about you, for I think that you are amongst friends, who will not see you suffer for the want of any help if you are sick. I heard that Jery was intending to go home, perhaps he is there by this time he can tell you some thing about our travels, have you seen G. Spaulding[.] I have got to go on guard now, and I will finish after I come off.

Well I have come off guard and eaten my supper, there is quite an excitement among the boys this evening, on account of one of the citizens stabing one of the nigger waiters in Co. C. he cut his shoulder prety bad , he will not be arrested to night, but the secesh devil ought to be shot and I dont think that we will be accountable for his life if we stay here long, he would not hesitate to shoot one of us for a moment if he caught us out in a by place. I have been to his house he is a hard master, he is the one that whipped one of his slaves with a battle board, for going off to see his wife, as which I have mentioned in another part of this letter. I will let you know what is done with him if

148

anything, it is very warm this evening, almost to warm to write, I will send you another five dollar note, in this letter, which will make the third one this month, or $15.00, let me know if you get them all. I suppose that Mr. Parch has got to be paid this fall, perhaps you had better turn out some of the stock to him for the pay, if there is no probability of my coming home this fall but then I would wait for a while yet before I did so.

I cannot think of any thing more to write to night for it is not but a few days since I wrote to you. I have not received any letter from Peters yet, nor any one else[.] I have not written to Mary yet, she can see the letters that I write to you and then she can write me the news from Spring Valleys, do you hear anything from Dan this summer? or anything more from Vt. I would not wonder if Henry[2] would come out to Minn, and take the benefit of the homestead bill. I wish that he and Mother[3] both would go out there. I understand that there is a good deal of emigration into Minnesota this summer, it will make the produse some higher I think. Well Now I will stop and seal up this letter "Nerva" kiss all of the <u>babies</u> for me, and tell them that Pa wants to see them all <u>very</u> bad, but he is where he can not see any babies but little <u>black</u> ~~black~~ babies, and "<u>Nerva</u>" <u>you</u> know that I do not want to <u>see you</u> any, <u>Oh no!</u>, I guess not. If I live to get home, I recon that I shall know how to prize the comforts of home, and my family, experience is a good school. I think now that I know what it is to have a home, and the comforts of one, and also what it is to be away from home and <u>near</u> and <u>dear</u> <u>friends</u>, but all that I can say will not better our condition any, so I will wait the will of a kind Father who doeth all things well, so I will bid you all good bye for this time, hoping that the war will soon terminate and that I will be able to join my family once more, so good bye all, "<u>Nerva</u>."

<u>D. B. Griffin</u>.

---

[2] This Henry is most likely Brainard's brother, Henry Franklin Griffin.
[3] Brainard's widowed mother, Hannah Kellogg Thompson Griffin. His father had died in 1857

Letter Number 46

Cane Creek Ala. Sunday July 20th 1862

My Dear Wife and Children,

I will once more try to address a few lines to you. I am well to day, and in good spirits, and I hope that you are in the same state of health and feeling. we are still a guarding the bridge, we were expecting an attack from the enemy a few days past, and Co. A. and Co. I. were sent down here to reinforce us, they were here three or four days, we went to work and made some breast works, and secured ourselves as well as we could, but we did not have any attack as yet and I do not think that we will have any while we are here, but it is reported this morning that we are agoing to be relieved in a few days, and are agoing to go on to Huntsville, some 75 or 80 miles from here. I do not know whether it is so or not, there has not anything happened worthy of note since I wrote before. We have got two prisoners here, they are charged with aiding the Southern army, by carrying provisions, and information to them, their family has just drove up to see them, they feel quite bad, we are a going to send them up to Tuscambia to day, there has not anything been done with the man that cut the niggers arm, he has gone off somewhere now, his niggers say that he has gone up into the mountains where the Secesh Cavelry are. We have had a nice shower this morning, we have had quite a number of showers the last week, and things look some better, we have a plenty of apples and peaches now, and the cornfields suffer severely, so you see that we are aliving high just at the present time, but we cannot tell how long it will last.

I received a letter from you last week dated the 15th June, and was glad to learn that you were all well, and doing well but I was sorry to see that you did not like to write to me how evry thing got along, there, you said that you did not like to tell me when the calves died for fear that I would worry about it, now Minerva, you know that nothing would be any more wellcome to me than to have you write every day occurrances on the place, and if evry creature on the place dies, it will not make me worry

150

at all iff you only get along and have your health and keep the children. I hope that you will not keep anything back when you write to me, but open your mind freely to me, just the same as you would if I was there, with you, you must try not to let any thing worry you. I know that you have a great many things to think of, and to see to, that you would not if I was there, but it cannot be remidied now, if I had suppossed that I should have ~~been~~ to be gone away one year from home, I should not have left you at all, but here I am bound down as tight as a slave, in U. S. service, where I intend to stay untill the war is ended, unless something turns up that I am not looking for. Jim Thornton received a letter from Mrs. Paul dated the 27th June, in which she says that Jery has got home. I expect that there was some rejoicing when he got home, I know that there would be some joy in the old shanty if I should step in some evening just as you had got ready to sit down to supper, I hope that It will happen so before another twelve month, I hope that Jery will get his health again now, tell him that he must write a letter to me as soon as he can and let me know how he managed to get his discharge, and whether he will get any bounty or not.

I expect that you have had a long talk with Jery about the war and the privaleges and deprivations of the service, if you see him tell him that the boys are all well and that we have been having a regular tare up, among the noncommissioned officers, Scott was made a Sergeant, and that did not suit the rest of the corporals so they all "resigned," Anderson, Commington, Friend, Brenam[4], and so there was made corporals in their places Rutherford[5], Rosevelt, Conner, Chamberlain and Ainsworth they all make it go first rate, our Captains name is John B. Davis, 1st Lieutenant D. B. Loomis 2n J. S. Livingston, we are now in Buell's Division, the third Regment has had a

---

[4] James Brennan, one of Brainard's tent-mates, Co. F, 2nd Minnesota Regiment of Volunteers.

[5] George Rutherford, a Fillmore County friend, Co. F, 2nd Minnesota.

fight in Mumfresboro Tenn[6], and they had to fall back towards Nashville it does seem as though the government was loose somewhere, for they will let the rebels get back behind us and come in on the few that are left behind and either take them prisoners or drive them back again. I do not see but what we have got to stay and fight it out for the next two years, but I hope not for the sake of the country and for the sake of our loved ones at home, and I do not know as there is any one who has got any wife and children, that would give any more to see them than would your humble servant, and if I should have to stay two years longer I do not know what I should do, you will have to go right on and make your calculations as to living just the same as though I never was a coming home again, and then if I should not get home this fall, you will be all right. I wish that Father would write a few lines to me letting me know how things stand, on the farm, and what he thinks it is best for you to do this winter, and you must tell me how you get along and how you you think of doing this winter. God knows that I wish that I could be there, but I have enrolled my name for the cause of the Union, and if there is any prospect of its prospering I want to among the ones that help maintain the Government, but if not let us come to some terms, that is not to humiliating, but never give up the principles of the union. I know that you see more of the war news than what I do, but still we get more of an assortment of papers, than what you do. It does seem as though your letters could come through to me quicker than they do, the last one that I got was dated the 15, and Jim got one dated the 27th, so you see that you either do not write or else your letters are delayed on the road, but perhaps I shall get one to night, for our post master has gone after the mail now, so I will not write any more untill he comes back. I am on guard to day and night.

---

[6] 1st Murfreesboro, July 15, 1862, involving the combined cavalry forces of CSA Col. Nathan Bedford Forrest, and the Union forces under Gen. Thomas L. Crittenden, in which more than 1,000 Union troops surrendered (including parts of the 3rd Minnesota), and more than $1,000,000 worth of military supplies were destroyed.

Monday morning, 21st.

I am well this morning but sleepy[.] I have not got any news to write this morning, and as the mail is agoing out this morning I will send this out with it. I will send you another five dollar bill, which makes twenty dollars. I shall not send you any more this time, there was two months due me the first of this month. I expect that you have received a checque from St Paul before this time, there is not much danger but what you will use it to an advantage. I must close for the post master is a waiting for me, so good bye once more, good bye one and all, this from your husband and father in Ala

D. B. Griffin.

Chasing Gen. Bragg From Florence, Alabama to Louisville, Kentucky

Letters 47–53 (July 27–September 28, 1862)

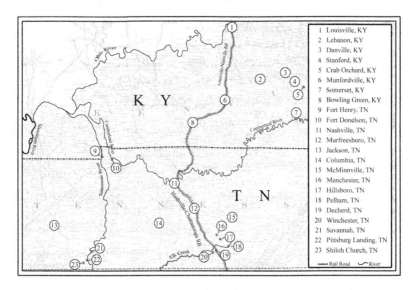

1	Louisville, KY
2	Lebanon, KY
3	Danville, KY
4	Stanford, KY
5	Crab Orchard, KY
6	Munfordville, KY
7	Somerset, KY
8	Bowling Green, KY
9	Fort Henry, TN
10	Fort Donelson, TN
11	Nashville, TN
12	Murfreesboro, TN
13	Jackson, TN
14	Columbia, TN
15	McMinnville, TN
16	Manchester, TN
17	Hillsboro, TN
18	Pelham, TN
19	Decherd, TN
20	Winchester, TN
21	Savannah, TN
22	Pittsburg Landing, TN
23	Shiloh Church, TN

Rail Road ⌒ River

Their correspondence continues, with Minerva's news from home of the farm, the children, and their extended family, as well as Brainard's financial and emotional support from the field. During the division's hundred-mile march to Winchester, Tennessee, Brainard's brigade commander is killed by Southern guerrillas, resulting in a two-day retaliation inflicted upon the area's civilians. Other stories sent home include information about the 3rd Minnesota being captured at Murfreesboro, the gathering of additional escaped slaves, and Brainard's thoughts about the federal draft. Returning north, his division spends more than a week atop the Cumberland Mountains in a defensive line to prevent a Confederate movement to Nashville before marching the eighty-five miles there themselves. During this period, initial news of the Sioux Uprising in Minnesota is received. After a week's stay, they again take off after Gen. Bragg in a race to Louisville, where Gen. Buell is regathering his army, though Buell's division commanders express doubts about his leadership. There, Brainard has his "likeness" taken to send home after a full year's service.

Major General Halleck,
Commander of Western Department.

Letter Number 47

Florence Ala July 27th 1862

My Dear Wife and little ones,

I will once more set down and talk with you. I am well this morning, and I hope that you are all of you in good health. We were relieved from bridge guarding on last Friday, and started for Tuscumbia we got there and had a good time with the boys. Charles Russell was there and I was very glad to see him, he is to work for the Sutler of the 2nd[.] I received a letter from you while there and was glad to hear from you once more, and was glad to hear that you were all well it was dated June 29. And was glad to have Edgar pen a few <u>lines</u> to me, but as they were written in some unknown toungue I could not read it, but I can immagine that I saw him and I know that he was <u>happy</u>. I hope that "<u>pa pa</u>" will come back from the war before many months, and see his little boy, it hardly seems as though I had a little boy that could call ~~my name~~ me "pa pa," but still I suppose that it is so, but I expect that I should not know him any more than he would know me. I wonder if Alice and Ida would know me, now. I recon that Nerva would not look the second time in order to know who I was if I should ever get home alive and sound, I do not think that I shall ever forget those faces which are engraved upon my <u>heart</u>. I have not a letter from Vt as yet nor any from any one else but you. I expect that James Nichols has been taken prisoner with the rest of his regiment, as I expect that you have read all of the particulars before this time, there is not much of any news around here, there is now and then a slight skirmish amongst our picquets and the bushwhackers or guarillies. I cannot tell where we are a going to from here but I expect that we will go to Huntsville Ala. The village of Tuscumbia is quite a place as well as all other places in the South, the country around here is good, there is some large fields of corn, but not any cotton to speak of, some fields of corn is getting to hard to boil, but we have all that we can eat, we came here to Florence yesterday, we are camped upon a beautiful grass hill which overlooks the Tennessee river the rebels burnt a very nice bridge here, on the Nashville rail road[.] I have not been into the village yet so I cannot tell you how it looks[.] I have sent you four letters this month with five dollars in eachone of them, let me know whether you get them all or not. I think that you have got all the money that I have sent to you before. We have very hot weather during the day, but quite cool during the night, so we can sleep well. I expect that you are a harvesting before this time, you must write as often as you can and let me know how things get along with you and the rest of the folks. I cannot think of much to write to day, but I hope that I can find more to write about next time, the boys from there are all well, Elicut is here in the tent, he is well, but I will bid you all a good bye once more, so good bye Nerva and all

D. B. Griffin. 2nd Reg.
Minn. Vol. Via Cairo Ill.

To P. M. Griffin
 Alba P. O.
  Minn

Letter Number 48

Camp near Winchester Tenn. Aug. 8th 9th 1862

My Dear Beloved wife and children,

I will once more write a few lines to you all. I am well this morning and have stood the march first rate as well as the rest of the boys, we have marched 100 miles since I last wrote to you at Florence, over a country thinly settled, but a good deal of it is good land and there is a good many handsom residences on the road, and a plenty of good water, we passed through a few small villages but not of much account except one called Athens, which is a very large, neat and beautifull place, the rest of the places look as though they had been built at least one hundred years ago. Florence is a nice place. We had not anything to mar our journey, or enjoyment untill last Tuesday, the 5th...on that day a band of Guerrillas attacted our Gen. and staff, (R. L. McCook) which was in advance of the Brigade some two or three miles, and they succeeded in taking a few prisoners and mortally wounded Gen. McCook, he lived about 24 hours, in loosing him we have lost a good man, one who was beloved by the whole Brigade and by the whole army, he was a true soldier and a man, we cannot get another commander that we can place as much confidence in. Our whole Brigade was perfectly frantic with rage, they destroyed and burned evry thing on the road that day, and the next morning I started out with my gun, and with a great many others with us, mostly from the ninth Ohio, we went around the country some eight miles, and burned evry house that belonged to a Secesh, taking evry thing that was of any benefit to us, such as horses, mules, beef &c, we compelled them to take their clothing and beds out of their houses before the torch was lit. It looked hard to me, to see women and children turned out doors, and to hear them begging of them to spare their houses, but all of their entreating was of no avail whatever, the mothers had to take their little ones in their arms and go out of the reach of the flames, it was hard to hear their screams and cries. I hope that I never shall witness the scenes again, there was three or four men killed and it is estimated that there was over a million dollars worth of property burnt. It is the first instance of the kind that we have had in our Brigade[.] I hope that it will have the effect to stop them some, they were very much frightened in Winchester for fear we would burn the place, they went to Gen Thomas, our Division Gen. and asked a guard of him, he told them that they could have a guard but if anything should happen to one of our men in passing through there, he had not men enough in his Division, to stop this Brigade from burning the town if we set ourselves about it, but there was not any thing happened to us, so we passed through without any trouble, we have camped about two miles from the Village and about one mile from the railroad that runs from Nashville to Chattanoga. We some expect to have a battle somewhere in this vicinity, the rebels are said to be getting in force at Chattanoga, it is thought that a part of the Richmond army is there, if so we may have to lay here some time, to get reinforcements, unless we are driven back, but I see that the President is determined to put this rebellion down in a short time, if men will do it. I hope that the people will turn out en mass, at once and help put it down for who or what nation could stand such a war, carried on as this war has been, for instead of taking anything from the rebels, there is a strong gaurd put over his or their property, as soon as we get into camp but that is about played out, and I am glad of it, we have got a good many contrabands in our camp, and a happy set of fellows they are to, they have their dances and songs after sundown, and you better believe we see the original nigger acted out, it beats any nigger-imitation that ever was got up, we have got four in our company, they are smart lively fellows, they are right out of the hands of the slave owners. I wish that the children could see some niggers and hear them talk and sing. I can talk nigger like fun. I received two letters from you yesterday, dated the

6th and 13 and was glad to hear from you all, and ~~th~~ to hear that you were all well, and in good spirits, and that Jery had been to see you. I expect that he could tell you all of the news especially the worst side of our treatment in the army, but you know that there is a great many folks that would not be suited if they had the fare of a King, but as to myself, I have had enough to eat, if it did not consist of pies sweetcakes and preserves, and have been treated well enough, because I have tried to obey the orders, and have done so, so far, as near as can be expected of anyone, and so I have not anything to complain of, and if I had I should not worry myself enough to make me grow poor, as long as I am well and know that my family is also well. I wish that you would tell me what Jery thought of the war. I think that he is dreadful feared that his wife would be hurt to see him come home, when she was expecting him too, when I go home I <u>shant</u> <u>let</u> <u>you</u> know it if I can help it, would you. I was glad to have Father write a few lines to me too, I think that Mother works herself to hard this summer, making cheese. I should like to have a tast of some of it this morning, and eat it with you too, and have some of your green peas too. I have not eaten any this year. I eat a dinner in a house the other day which is the second meal that I have eaten in a house since I left home, there was a number of <u>pretty</u> <u>girls</u> there and we had some nigger wenches to wait upon us and to keep the flies off, our dinner consisted of corn doggers and butter fried meat and eggs, the old woman was very clever and we had a long chat with the <u>girls</u>, you must not get <u>jealous</u>, for I ~~do~~ shall not forget you nor yours, [*] as long as we both live. I believe that I am not as bashfull as I was before I left home, and you know that I was very <u>bashfull</u> especially amongst the <u>girls</u>. It appears by your account that I have sent you ninety dollars, seventy of it you had got when you last wrote. I had received ninety two dollars from government, and if I have sent you ninety of it, it is pretty close, but I thought that I had sent five or ten dollars more, but was not certain.

---

* Unreadable

There is now due me from Government, or will be at the end of this month, fifty two dollars, there is so many of my letters that you had not received yet, (or when you wrote) that I cannot hardly tell what to write, concerning the course to have you take this winter, so I will say nothing about it this time. Father wanted to know if I could remember any thing about some wheat that he borrowed of Mr Bennet. I have nearly forgotton about it, but I am pretty certain that Mr Bennett got the wheat of me, when I thrashed, the first time, the oats that I borrowed of Father, Mr. Bennett had them fork in and he got them, but it is so long since, that I do not recollect any circumstances connected with it. I would like to ~~have~~ know how his reaper works, I think that you had not better try to winter any young stock this winter. I got a letter yesterday from brother Samuel[1], and right glad was I to hear from them too they were all well when he wrote July ~~18th~~ 21th, he is at work in Burlington for a Mr. Drew Henry and his wife live in B. somewhere. Mother had received a letter from you so they found out where to write to me. Mary, Sary and Sylvia[2] work out near Essex Center, so I guess that Mother lives alone. Uncle Elezar folks are all well and are all at home Uncle Harrison's folks were all well and Uncle Chancey[3] folks. Cousin Maria was married and had got a babe about 6 months old. Sidney enlisted in the first Vt Cavelry. Sister Marias[4] folks were well, they had bought a place among the hills and moved into it last Spring, he did not say where it was, Uncle Charles W. lives in Conn. and aunt Dolly Potters[5] oldest boy lives with them, uncle John's folks were well, Grandmother Griffin[6] is as well as usual, she is staying with Ellen Seaver and her man, they

---

[1] Samuel Ebenezer Griffin, Brainard's youngest brother, living in Vermont.
[2] Mary Louisa Griffin and Sarah Andelusa (Griffin) Bliss, Brainard's sisters, also living in Vermont.
[3] Chancey Woolcott, and the Maria, Sidney, and Charles Wollcotts who follow, are related in an as yet unidentified way to the Griffins.
[4] Ann Mariah Griffin (married name unknown) is another of Brainard's sisters, and will be a frequent correspondent through the rest of the letters.
[5] Dolly (Thompson) Potter is the sister of Brainard's mother.
[6] Sylvia (Bradley) Griffin is Brainard's paternal grandmother.

live in the White house at Butlers corner, and he works for Charles Day. Flavel Day and folks are well he works upon the railroad and Albert works with him, Grandmother T. and Fanny were well, but Grandfather[7] is no more, he died July the ~~eleventh~~ 18th, he had been quite unwell all ~~of~~ the spring, but had got quite smart, although he was not able to walk a step, on the day of his death he appeared to be quite smart, ate a hearty dinner, sat up all day...about half past four o'clock, he wished to lay down, Mary was there and she and Fanny helped him onto the sofa, when he fell back into Fanny's arms, and breathed his last at ten minutes past five o'clock, his funeral sermon was preached by the Rev. Mr. Parmaly, so another one of our ancesters has passed away, he is out of his sufferings and trials, may his soul rest in peace. I shall have to stop writing for this time, we have had some very hot weather here, but we all of us stand it well, when I am on the march, my clothes would not have a dry thread in them, I could wring the water out of my shirts, I weal woolen shirts, but I must stop and clean up my gun, kiss all of the babies for me, and except one from me (-) this from your husband and Father,

D. B. Griffin

Letter Number 49

Camp near Winchester Tenn Aug 13th 1862

My Dear Wife and Children,

I will once more write a few lines to you[.] I am well this morning, and so is the whole company, there has not been anything of much importance happened since I last wrorte to you, a squad of our boys went out last Sunday night and captured one of the worst bushwhackers there was in this part of the country, he had been watched for a long time, but had always managed to ~~elude~~ get away, but he came home last Saturday night, and Sunday morning a negro came into camp

---

[7] These are the Ebenezer Thompsons mentioned in letter 27.

and told us of it, so there was a squad of men detailed to go out and arrest him, taking the negro along with them for a guide they had not gone far before they saw three men a coming towards them upon horses they secreted themselves in the bushes, and when they came up, ordered them to halt, but they turned to run and three of our men fired upon them, bringing one of them to the ground which proved to be the man that they wanted, they brought him into camp, and he died the next morning his wife was in camp soon after he died, she took on rather hard, but she did not get much simpathy from any of the boys, he was the Captain of a band, of guerrillas, there was a train of waggons attacted by the rebels near Huntsville captured about 120 of the sick men that was a coming on to their regiments, but the boys from our regiment got away without being taken or hurt, they only captured one wagon, and 6 mules[.]

We have moved our camp about one mile on to a hill with a plenty of good cold spring water, there was a boy here last night from Co C of the third reg. that company was not taken. James Nichols is well and with his company. Rundell and Ed. Rexford was with the reg. when they was taken prisoner, and so they are prisoners, there is a good deal of censure towards the officers for surrendering without any struggle, they are set down as cowards by Gen. Buel, in his order. I hope that the 2nd will never be branded in the same manner, but if we do, it will not be the fault of the privates, there is a number of men from our regiment a going to start for Minn. in a day or two, for the purpose of recruiting for this reg. Mr Cutting of Co A. is agoing and I thought that I would write a few lines to you, and send you some money, I can get twenty dollars to send, and the man ~~felt~~ will wait untill payday for it, I think that it will be the safest way for me to do, and if you get it you had better keep it to pay the interest on our land, for it may be some time before I can send you any more. I am very anxious to hear whether you have received all the money that I sent last month (twenty dollars), in four letters[.] I have not received any letters from you since I last wrote. James Thornton got one yesterday dated the 20th[.] We are a looking for Jerry now, evry day. I hope that we shall all be able to go home for good before many months, and I do not see why it cannot be done if the 600,000 men are brought into the field immediately, and I think that that is the only way to decide the present contest between the North and South[.]

I expect that there will be some drafting done in Minn, and I would like to know who haves to go from about there, there is a good many around there that could go better than I could, and I would just like to see some of them down here amongst the rebels. We expect to stay here for some time, probably through this month if we are not drivin away by the rebels, we have a good number of contrabands in the reg. three in our Company and a happy set of fellows they are, we have a plenty of singing and dancing evry night, it is amusing to hear them tell over their adventures with their masters and others, in their innocent African talk. It is not quite as hot now as it has been some of the time. I have written a letter to Samuel[.] I suppose you have got a letter from them before this time. I cannot think of much to write to day. I expect to send this away in the morning. I see that they are a offering a bounty of 25 dollars extra to the volunteers, in Minn. I do not think that it is a fair show for I think if any one is entitled to anything extra, it is them that went forward and offered themselves to the Government when they was first called upon, them that are drafted will not get but 11 dollars a month, and no bounty. I hope that you will get all of the money that I have sent to you. Minerva when you write to me, write about the children, what they are a doing, and what they say. It seems like a great while since I ~~heard~~ see and heard them talk. Oh I hope that it will not be many months before I shall hear their voices and see their joyful faces again, and My darling boy, will he ever see his father to know him. God grant that he may soon ~~see~~ see him and know him, kiss him and the others for me, has Mr. Peters ever written to me but once. I have never received but one. I wish that you would send me 50 cents or a dollars worth of Postage stamps, for there is none to be got here. I have sent a number to you without paying the postage let me know whether they came through safe or not, tell All. that he must go to meeting as many times as I do. I have not been to a meeting since I came away from home, we hardly know when Sunday comes around, I have a good many talks with some of the boys on the bible, there is some strong endless misery ones, or was when they enlisted, but some which were church members (methodist) when they enlisted are the most profane ones there is in the company now, such is the influence of the army, but still they believe that he that does not <u>repent</u> of his sins, will be eternally damned, it makes no odds how bad they are now they are agoing to repent and get read of the punishment. I cannot say that I am living any nearer my Maker now, than I was when I enlisted, but I hope that I am not so far gone as to have no regard for my actions and doings while here, as some do, for I have some respect for myself and companions, I intend to do all that is requirred of me to do and that is all that we can do here, I do not look for any earthly reward, for what I do. If I should live to get home safe and be permitted to live in peace with my little family the remainder of my days is all that I can ask but I must draw this letter to a close for I have not got much more room to write in, and I have written more that I expected to when I commenced, you must all read my letters just the same as though I had directed them to you all Father Mother and all, good bye Nerva and the babies

D. B. Griffin

Letter Number 50

Camp, near Winchester Tenn Aug. 17th 1862

Dear Wife and Children, Friends and neighbors,

I will once more try to write a few lines to you. I am well to day, and have been so all of the time as yet. I had a long letter written allready to send to you by Mr. Cutting, but he has not gone yet, nor he does not know when he will go, so I will write a few more lines and put ~~with~~ along with that and send it along by mail, but I will not send any money in it, but will wait untill he does go. We expect to go away from here in two or three days at least towards a place called Battle Creek, which is about thirty miles from here, towards Chattanoga. We do not get any war news of any import since I last wrote, there appears to be a general calm through~~t~~ out the whole line[.] It may be that it will soon break out into a severe storm.

There has been ~~throughee~~ or four of the boys from Co C. of the third Reg. down here to see us. Tom. Douglass[8] was here and stayed over night he is well and tough again, he says that James Nichols is well[.] Ed. R. and Rundell were taken prisoners, they feel very hard towards their officers for surrendering up their reg. there was not but two men killed out of the reg. they say there is a good many of the boys going home from St Louis, perhaps you will see some of them up there. Co. C. is on guard at Murforsboro, they are anxious to get into some reg. so that they can have a chance to prove themselves, if they should ever get into another fight. I received two letters from you last night, dated Aug 3d with Mary and Sylvia's letter in one of them, I was glad (as I always am) to hear from you, and also from them, but was also sorry to learn that my mother has to work out for her living, when <u>one</u> who has had her property and used it, is a living near her, but I expect that his wife is so <u>high</u> up in the world that she could not look so low as to concent to have a mother <u>in law</u> live with them, and perhaps he is quite <u>large</u> too. I wonder if he ever borrows any ones <u>shirt collar's</u> to wear to church[.] I hope that I shall not live to see my mother suffer for the want of the comforts of a home, but I do not feel as though it was our duty to offer her a home with us untill we get one ourselves, which I hope will not be many years, and I think if we have good luck, ~~that~~ and I come home from this war safe and sound, and have my health, and my family have's it's health too, we will have a home in a year or two, and Nerva if I <u>do</u> come home I believe that there will be at least, <u>one</u> happy

---

[8] Tom Douglass, a Fillmore County friend, Co. C, 3rd Minnesota Regiment of Volunteers, mustered out in September 1865.

family in Minnesota, dont you think so <u>Nerva</u>. Samuel says that if I get home he is a going to go out and see us[.] I hope that they will all go out there and get them a home once more, it seems as though Mary still remains in a state of single blessedness it is a pity that some poor fellow could not share his <u>bed</u> and board, with her, but tell her that leap year comes again in one and ahalf years, so that there will be a chance for her to pop the question to some bashfull young man, once more before she gets to be a <u>confirmed</u> old maid. What I have written about Jery's being well, is just what the boys told me that saw him after he went to the hospital so if his wife blames anyone she must not blame me. I do not intend to write anything that is not so if I know it. It is a new Idea that a person can stay there as long as he is a mind to, by reporting to his Captain evry thirty days, it is not in the regulations[.] I hope that he will return to his Co. before he is reported as a deserter. I have just been and asked the Captain if he has had any letter from Jery he says he got one from him a day or two ago, and also one from a physician stating that he was not able to join the reg. the Cap. wanted that I should tell him if he wanted his discharge, to go to some army physician, and get a certificate filled out, certifying to his ~~in~~disability, and send it to him, and he will get a discharge made out for him, it is optional with the Captain whether ~~to~~ he can remain away by notifying him once in 30 days, if he does not report him, it is all well enough, if you see him tell him what the Captain says, or send him word if you can, Jim Thornton, Elicut and the rest of the boys are well at present[.] It is quite cool here nights, but hot through the day time, we have not had any rain for some time, and the roads are very dusty.

I guess that I have got nearly all of your letters now. I am glad that you got the 15 dollars all safe, I cannot tell you what to do towards getting wood this winter, because I do not know who has got any unless it is Mr Vincent, perhaps you can make a trade with him for some wood. I should like to know how they got along in raising men in Minn. I hope that they will turn out freely and fill up the ranks of the new regiments, and also to fill up the old ones, you need not send me any letter stamps, for if my letters go through without paying for them, you can pay the postage on them there, how does the folks over in the Abbott neighborhood get along this fall, how is Alfred and family getting along and all of the rest of the folks have you heard from Norm, yet. I have not heard from Watson for a long time. I should like to hear from them all, give my best respects to all the folks around there, particular the girls, how much does it cost you to get your hay put up. I do not know as I can ever repay Fathers folks for the acts of kindness they do for us, but if I am not permitted to do as much for them on this earth, may our heavenly Father reward them all in heaven, for remembering us. I know that it must be quite a task to see to their own affairs and to mine too, but if I had supposed that this war would have lasted one year, from the time I left home, I think that I should done differently, but here I am, and I cannot do any better now for, if I was at home, ~~now~~ I should probably enlist.

James Nichols has just come in to see me again he is well and looks well, he says that he has not heard from home for three or four weeks. Wm. Rundell and others came down with him, they are agoing back to morrow, there is a meting to night our Chaplain is agoing to preach, and I guess that I will go out and hear him, for it is sometime since I have heard any one preach. I have heard the sermon, and it was a very sound sermon, the boys have been in the tent all the evening, and we have had a good time in talking over old scenes and old times. I cannot think of any thing more to write this time, so I will bid you all good bye again, one and all, good bye Nerva, from your Husband

D. B. Griffin
you need not change the directions
of my letters for ~~the~~ it is the best way
for them to come to the Reg.

167

Letter Number 51

Camp on Elk Creek Tenn. Aug 23d 1862

Dear Wife and Children,

I will write a few lines to you this morning, so as to let you know how I am a getting along. I am as well as usual this morning, and I hope that these few lines will find you all enjoying the same good health. I have not got any news to write this morning of any account. We are camped in the woods about fourteen miles from Winchester, on the McMinville road. I do not know where we are agoing to go to from here. I went out into the country yesterday for the purpose of forageing, we got a good supply of pork, chicken honey, peaches apples &c, there is in most evry house a widow but we ask the niggers where there masters are, they say that they are in the Secesh army, so we proceed to confisicate what provision we can find for our own benefit, there is not many wealthy farmers about here, it is pretty rough land clost to the mountain, it is said that there is some bushwhackers in the mountain, but we have not seen any since we have been here, we came here three days ago, it is not so warm weather as it has been, it is quite comfortable now. I have not ~~see~~ received any letters for some time, in fact there has not been any mail for a number of days. I have not anything to write about, so I cannot write any more this time, the boys are all as well as usual to day. I will write as often as I can get anything to write about, you must write as often as you can, how does Jery get along and all of the rest of them, except these few lines from your husband in Tenn,

D. B. Griffin
P. M. Griffin and babies, kiss them all for me <u>good bye</u>

Letter Number 52

Camp in the mountains, near the middle gap, Aug 29/62

My dear Wife and friends, as I have got a sheet of paper and a pen and ink, I will commence a letter to you, but I do not know when I can send it away for we are up in the Cumberland mountains, near a little town called Pelham, about seventeen miles from Winchester. Our waggons have gone to the depot at Dechard, so we have been without tents for about a week, but it has been very dry so we have got along very well so far, we are here for the purpose of preventing the rebel army from coming through the pass, we have a strong position here, we are camped upon a side hill in the woods, among the rocks, there is a large flat in front of us, and beyond that is ~~our~~ the pass, it is rumored that the rebels are making for Nashville, but if they undertake to come through here, we are ready to meet them, and if they go on to McMinville, there is an army there ready to give them a warm reception, we have to go some ways for our water and it is not very good when we get it, we have been on half rations for the last week, but we get more to eat now, that we did before, for we have foraging parties evry day, and they bring in beef cattle, pork bacon, chickens geese and anything else that we can eat, and find with the secesh families and there is a plenty of it with them. It is all very quiet at present, but evry thing looks dark, we some expect to have to fall back as far as Nashville but if we do, woe unto the country when we come back over it again, for we shall be pretty apt to do it when all of the new volunteers get into the field and they are a pouring into Kentucky ata tremenduous rate, we do not get any news from Richmond or Virginia, for the mail has been stoped for some time but they say that ~~it is~~ the road is opened again, from Nashville to Louisville, so I hope that we shall get some mail before long. I have not had any letters since I last wrote to you. I thought them that the next time I wrote, that I should have something to write about, but I have not. I have been well all of the time, and all the rest of the boys, how does Jery get along, did you show him the last letter, has he moved up on to his place, yet. We expect to stay down here through the winter, and perhaps for the rest of the three years. We have heard that the Indian's are murdering the inhabitants around Fort Ridgley, but we think that the reports are greatly exagerated, if they are true, it is an awful butchery, it seems as though we were surrounded by enemies, both at home and abroad. I hope that the war with the South ~~with~~ will speedily be put down, without counting the cost, and we think that it will be ended before another spring, but so we thought one year ago. I hope that you will get along this winter without any trouble, you must have Hill plough ten acres of the land, take the last years breaking first and the rest where it needs it the most, and if you can get the rest of it ploughed, do so for it will be the best way. I do not know when we shall get our pay again, perhaps not for some time.

In Camp, Nashville Tenn. Sept 9th 1862

My Dear Beloved Wife and family,

I think that you will be glad to hear from me by this time, but I have not had any chance to finish this letter since I commenced it. I am well, and have been since we have been on the march, we have marched 85 miles since I commenced this letter, and it has been warm and very dusty, we stopped one or two days on the road and foraged some, we have been upon half rations for the last three weeks, but we have never had any better living for we could go out amongst the farmers and take anything that we wanted to eat, the last day that we marched, we came from Murfresboro, which is thirty miles from here, I got very tired I will assure you, but I went through with them, there was not but one man in Co. A. that was there when we stacked arms, the rest had fallen out to rest on the road, we passed through several small villages on the road, viz. Hillsboro, Manchester, Murfresboro &c the last place is quite a large place. Co C of the third reg. left there the same day that we did I did not see many of them, we came here last Sunday and I was on guard untill yesterday, and after I came off guard I got a chance to leave camp and go around ~~camp~~ the town, so the day worked off and I did not get a chance to write to you.

Sept 10th

Well, here I am again, I had to stop last night and pack up, so I did not finish my letter, we moved about $\frac{1}{2}$ mile on to a hill which overlooks the whole city of Nashville, it is a nice location[.] Co. C of the third moved right up by the side of our Company last night, so we had a grand visit with them last evening. James Nichols is well, and all the rest of the boys. Abe. Lamb[9] is in the Hospital he is so as to be around I have not seen him yet. I have not had a letter from you yet, we had a mail when we got here, but no letters for me, I hope that I shall get one to day[.] Jim Thornton got a letter from Dan, they say that Jery is at work making hay all of the time, and he says that he will not come back unless he was a mind to, other folks write the same thing, now that does not agree with the letter which he wrote to the Capt, he wrote to him that he was anxious to join his Co, but was not able to, he is reported on the muster roll as absent without leave, so I think that it will bother him some to get his back pay unless he comes back soon. Dan's wife says that you miss me, but that you do not make as much fuss about it as Jery's wife. I am glad of it, for I should not like to hear that you worry about me all of the time, be patient for a short time, and I hope that you will soon be rewarded for your patience before long. We are expecting to stay here untill we are driven away by the rebels, and I cannot tell whether we will get drove back or drive them back, it is reported that they are within a few miles of us with a heavy force, but I cannot tell any thing about it, nor can I tell anything about what is agoing on any where for we do not get any mail that amounts to any thing. I hope that we soon will have things straightened out in the country for I think this war has been carried on about long enough to accomplish something or other. I cannot think of much more to write this time. I will write a few more words about Jery the Capt. says that he cannot get any of his back pay unless he can bring certificates to show that he has been gone by the order of Gen Buel, and if he is gone a great while longer he will be reported as a deserter and that will be rather a serious thing for him, and it is not only him, but there is a good many others that are gone the same way, so he can have his choice. I expect that they will be mad

---

[9] Abe Lamb is another Beaver Township neighbor of the Griffins, Co. C, 3rd Minnesota Regiment of Volunteers.

at me for writing to you so plain, but I never have written anything but the truth that I know of, now I will end this letter and try to get it sent away, so I will bid you all good bye once more[.]

Good bye Nerva and the babies

D. B. Griffin

Letter Number 53

Louisville Ky. Sept 28th 1862

My Dear "Nerva" and Children,

I have once more an opertunity to write a few lines to you. I am well to day as usual, and I feel quite well pleased for I received two letters from you last night dated Aug 25, and Sept. 22nd there is one between them behind and one from Samuel. I was glad to learn that you were all well, and that you was agoing to live with Mary this winter, for I did not know how you would get along there alone through the cold winter. I think that you will get along first rate. I thought a good deal about you of late, and have wished a good many times, that I could be at home for a couple of weeks and get things fixed up for you, but I do not see but what you will get along first rate. We have had a pretty hard march since we left Pelham Tenn. I wrote a letter to you when I was at Nashville, but it is rather uncertain whether you got it or not, for the communication bettween Louisville and Nashville was cut off by the rebel Bragg[10], we started from Nashville two weeks ago to morrow morning, we marched to Mumferdsville 85 miles in four days. Gen. Bragg was there, and we were very anxious to pitch into him, but were kept back by Gen Buell, untill Sunday afternoon, when he started out with his advance guard, he came upon the rebel pickets about seven miles on the other side of Mumferdsville, they chased them into and through the place, killing and wounding some, and a

---

[10] CSA Gen. Braxton Bragg, commanding the Army of Tennessee, attempting to draw Kentucky into the Confederacy.

taking a good many prisoners on the road towards Louisville, where they were intending to march right into, but they changed their mind before they got quite here, and they took a road that lead off towards Lebanon and so we kept straight on marching from twenty to 28 miles a day striking the Ohio river some thirty miles below here, and we were pretty well tired out you may be assured, and hungry to, for we had been upon half rations, and that rather short to for about four weeks, we have not slept in our tents but a few nights either, since we left Dechard, but it has not rained but one night, and then it rained quite hard, but I laid down and slept sound, with the rain pouring down on my blanket for a "lullaby" when I woke in the morning I was wet through and through, but I did not catch cold, and have stood the march as well as any of the rest of them. We took the boats at the river and road up to within four miles of this place, the river is very low it does not look much like the Ohio of last spring, we are camped about one mile south of Louisville, we came here night before last, and it rained yesterday so that I could not write, there is about 100,000 thousand troops here, and it is very probable that we shall move towards the enemy in a few days, there is a good deal of dissatisfaction with Gen. Buell, and a great many reports about him but I cannot tell how true they are, but one thing I do know, that we have been on short rations but a good deal of the time we have been where we could forage a good deal, we have picked corn and grated it up, and made cakes, and mush and it was good too" the country between Nashville and this place, is naturaly a beautiful country, but it is quite destitute of fences especialy where the soldiers have camped, it will be a great many years before it will regain it's original prosperity, there is a good deal of murmuring among the troops concerning the movements of Gen. Buell, it is thought that he works for the South more than he does for us. I understand that Gen Thomas and McCook had quite an altercation to day with Gen. Buell, concerning the marching and usages of the soldiers, and still it does not amount to anything in the end, we all think that we could have cleaned Gen. Bragg's Army out entirely if we had not been kept back by Gen. Buell. We camped one night in sight of the rebel pickets and Gen Thomas, our Division Gen, was anxious to go ahead but he was prevented from doing so by Gen. Buell, so we laid still two days and give Bragg a chance to get away from us entirely, so now we are right where we were one year ago, but I do not think that it will take us one year more to clean them out, for most all of the important points are in the hands of the union, and if we are set to work before the roads get bad, we can travel as fast as they can, and not give them a chance to fortify themselves in any place, we can drive them out of the country in three months. Samuel writes that they are all well at present, he had been home about four weeks but had got back to Henry's then Sept 1st. Henry has enlisted for nine months and he is agoing to take his place in the meat market. Edgar and F. Albert Day and Marai Wolcott husband have enlisted, Samuel wanted to go but Mother did not want we should all go, he says that she feels dreadfully about me and Henry. Essex has made out her quota so they will not have to draft, any. Mother is at Simeon Bliss'es Mary is at Josiah Tuttles Mrs. Tuttle died sometime in August, he did not say what Mrs Tuttle it was, but I supposed that it was the Widow Tuttle, Sarah is at Foster Taylors, and Sylvia is up to Nelson Kelloggs, and Brainerd is in Louisville Ky, so you see that a family that was all at home but a few years ago, is all broke up and scattered from one side of the union to the other. Melvin Freeman had his thumb taken off with a mowing machine, Fanny F. is a teaching school in Essex, Nellia is at home, there was three men arested in Jericho as Secesh to Wit, Dr. ~~Seymour~~ Lyman, Dea Field's, and a son of Mathew Barney, they are in jail, awaiting orders from Washington, Charles Russell is the boy that Grandfather Thompson brought up. When we were at Nashville he started to go home but he had not got but seven miles from Nashville when he was taken by a band of guerrillas, but they did not harm him any, and they let him go, he came back to us again, but we left all of the teams with our knapsacks at Bowling green, I understand that they are a coming along, we have drawn new pants, shirts, shoes, and socks and we are a going to have hats, haversacks and canteens, I have got a plenty of clothes for winter, or can get them cheaper than I can have them sent back to me, we have not been paid yet, but we expect to be paid to night, if we do I will send you some money in this letter[.] James Nichols was left in Nashville sick I have not heard from him since we came away, the rest of the boys are well. ~~Wehn~~ When I read where you told what the children said when the mail was a coming, I could not keep back the tears, what would they say if pa was coming. I think I see their joyfull faces coming to meet me. I hope it will soon be a reality. Alice you must excuse pa for not writing to you. I can hardly get time to write to ma, you must read ma's letters I am glad that you write some to me, for I like to see something that my little girls do and say[.] I cannot write any more to night, but will try to write some more in the morning[.]

Monday Evening Sept ~~22~~ 29.

It has been quite a busy day with me to day. We got our pay this morning ($52.00), and I have been up in the town this afternoon, and got my likeness taken, and took a good look of some of the city, it looks some different from what it did last winter evry thing is green and pretty. I thought that I would get my likeness taken, and send to you, so that you could see me once a year it was a year yesterday since I enlisted, and you can see if I look any different than what I did then. Mr. Cutting is a Sergeant in his company he is a going to start for Minn. to morrow if there does not anything happen and I will put forty dollars ($40.00) in this letter and let him or some one else take it along with them untill they get somewhere near Minn. Co. C. of the third is ordered home, or to St Paul, they will all try to go home first if they can. I received a letter from you dated Sept the 8th since I commenced writing this evening, so I guess that that is all that you have wrote. I guess that you will think that the guerillas or something else has got me by the time you get this for it is a good while since I have wrote to you, but you will see by the letter what the reason is.

Gen Nelson[11], was shot and killed this morning, by Gen J. C. Davis[12], of Missourie, there was some words passed between them, and Gen Nelson slapped him in the face, and he turned around and borrowed a pistol and shot him through the breast, he did not live but a short time, it is reported that Gen. Buell has been superceded but I have not learned by whom. I hope that it is some one who will not work for the South quite as much as Buell did, the prisoners that we took all spoke well of Gen. Buell, they say that he is a gentleman, and a good officer, now if he had worked against them they would not liked him quite as well. We do not know when we are to move from here. We hear pretty hard stories about the barbarity of the Indians, it is awful to think of. I hope that they will not get down as far as there. I think that this regiment had ought to go home and fight them, but I cannot tell it is thought by our Col. that we will go, so I was told just now and it come pretty straight, too, if we do I may get a chance to go home for a day or two, but I will not build any "castles in the air" yet. I should have gone to the theater to night with the boys if I did not want to finish this letter. I went one night in Nashville, if I stay here long I shall go up some night.

I received the letters of yours and Mary's all safe some time ago, there is not many of your letters but what I have got now. I did mean any harm in saying that I thought I had sent home more than 90 dollars, only I had not kept it an account of it, and I did not know but what I had sent more. I knew that I had sent that much, and I did not know but more, that is the reason I wanted that you should let me know, I am well satisfied that it is all. I hope that you will get this $40.00 too, that will make $130.00 and there is one month due me now, on the year. I cannot write any more to night it is past nine o'clock, and the wind flares the candle, for my house is not very tight, when I

---

[11] Union Gen. William Nelson, in charge of defending Louisville, Kentucky.

[12] Union Gen. Jefferson Columbus Davis, upset by a rebuke from his commander, Gen. Nelson. Because of political pressure, Gen. Davis was allowed to return to active service without any punishment.

get up in the morning my blanket is wet through with the dew, well I must bid you all a good bye and go to bed again hoping that it will not be long before we shall see each other again, good bye Nerva, good bye one and all.

D. B. Griffin.

I have put in a few quince seeds

I think that Jery's 25 a month from U.S. will come out rather scant

This is the "likeness" Brainard had taken in Louisville on September 29, 1862, after a year's service in the 2nd Minnesota Regiment of Volunteers.

Chasing Gen. Bragg Out of Kentucky— Louisville to Bowling Green

Letters 54–57 (October 13–November 4, 1862)

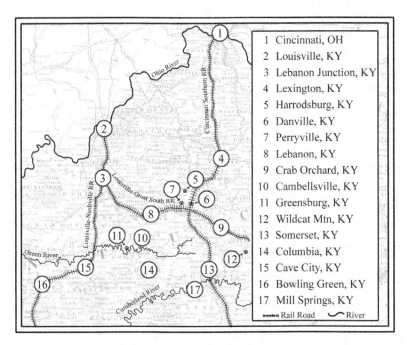

1	Cincinnati, OH
2	Louisville, KY
3	Lebanon Junction, KY
4	Lexington, KY
5	Harrodsburg, KY
6	Danville, KY
7	Perryville, KY
8	Lebanon, KY
9	Crab Orchard, KY
10	Cambellsville, KY
11	Greensburg, KY
12	Wildcat Mtn, KY
13	Somerset, KY
14	Columbia, KY
15	Cave City, KY
16	Bowling Green, KY
17	Mill Springs, KY
⊶⊷ Rail Road	⌣ River

Brainard records his regiment's rapid movement, without tents or backpacks, as Bragg's army retreats out of Kentucky. He provides fearful descriptions of the scenes during and after the Battle of Perryville and continues to detail his physical pains from marching, the condition of his regiment, and the general dissatisfaction with Gen. Buell. After a week's pause at Crab Orchard, they work their way southwest to Bowling Green. These letters include many expressions of his thoughts of home and Minerva's move to her sister's home in Spring Valley as well as the human cost of war. At Bowling Green, Buell is replaced by Gen. Rosecrans.

Letter Number 54

In Camp near Haroudsburg Ky Oct 13/62

My Dear Wife and Children,

I will try to write a few lines to you this evening. I feel quite well this evening, but I have been quite unwell for a few days, but not so but what I have been upon the march all of the time. I have not written to any body since we left Louisville for the reason that we have not been still long enough for me to write, we have been a chasing the rebels for about one week, and we have not had but one hard battle and that was last Wednesday at Perryville. We lost about two thousand in killed and wounded, but the rebels had a heavy loss, they left between 500 and 1000 on the field dead, besides any amount of wounded, our Brigade did not fire at all, but we were drawn up to support the Batteries, and the rebels fired shell and grape over, behind and in front of us within a few feet of us, they charged upon the Battery twice, but they pored such a deadly fire into them that ~~thest~~ they had to fall back, our Brigade has got the praise of winning the day, which is a good deal ~~f~~ in such a large army. I tell you when I heard their big shells coming towards us it was rather deathly music, some of them sounded like ~~an~~ a thrashing machine cylinder, when they went through the air and the grape shot sounded like hail in the trees and leaves, a grape shot is about as large as a walnut, but the Lord willed that we should all come out safe one man in the Battery got both of his hands shot off and five or six of our men were wounded. I went out to the edge of the battle ground the next day, and I saw enough, to satisfy me. I went into one secesh hospital, and it was a sight to behold, they were amputating legs and arms on all sides, some were dying, others crying and calling upon absent friends, and praying to die, it was a sight that I hope I may never see again. We have kept close to the rebels ever since, marching evry day and not going more than ten miles, we have [*] positions [*] It is known to night that Gen. [*] has taken one Division of rebels commanded by Gen. Polk to day, but we do not know for certain, but one thing is certain, that they are in a pretty close place, we have heard that they have had a fight at Corrinth, our men whipped the rebels bad. I have not heard from Virginia for some time. I suppose that you get more news than I do. I got a letter from Jery, he was in Chatfield waiting for a physician. I have not had any from you since I left Louisville. I sent you $40.000 by Thomas Douglass when he started for Minn, he said that if he did not go home he would put it in some post office. I hope that you will get it all safe. I will send you ten ($10.000) dollars in this letter. I think that I can get along and spare that much, perhaps I will send you more in the next letter, if I get any chance to write, we may have another battle in a few days, we cannot tell what a day may bring forth. We have had very good weather so far, there has been one frost (on the sixth) we have not had any tents yet, we make a shelter with rails and straw when we can get any, or roll ourselves up in our blankets and lay down by the fire, we are soldiering in good earnest, but the boys all stand it well, but we are all getting worn down, we need a good rest, but I hope that we can end this war before the first of January, for we are all tired of war, both the northern and southern soldiers, if I live to get home again I do not think that I shall learne war any more. I do not know as you can ever read this, but it is the best that I can do under the present

---

* Unreadable

circumstances, I am up by the side of the fence with my blanket hung up to keep the wind off from the candle, it looks like a city to look around and see the fires on the side hills, we have a good deal of trouble to get water enough to use, for it is very dry, where there was large rivers last spring, there is not a drop of running water, there is some standing water in holes, which we get to use. I cannot think of anything to write to night so I will stop for this time. I am bothered a good deal with the piles this fall, they are pretty bad to night. I shall send this off the first chance I get, which I hope will be in a day or two, so I will bid you all good bye, once more. Good bye Alice, good bye Ida, good bye Edgar and good bye "Nerva" with a kiss for you all   [kiss]

D. B. Griffin
To P. M. Griffin
  Alba P. O.
    Fillmore Co.
      Minn

Tuesday 14th 62

I am well as usual this morning, we have got to move this morning. I will put in some postage currency for you and the children, divide them up to suit yourself, there is fifty cents worth.

D. B. Griffin.

Letter Number 55

Crab Orchard Ky Oct 19th 1862

My Dear Wife and Children, and friends,

I will once more write a few lines to you   I am quite well to day, but I have had quite a time with the piles, they have been so that I could not march, but we have lain still ever since Tuesday night so they are better we get along very well considering, for we have no tents, and it is quite cool nights, there was a frost night beforelast, there is a heavy dew evry night, we have not got but one blanket apiece, so we double up and put our blankets over us, and sleep quite warm, we some expect to go back to Lebanon, and stay there untill we get our tents and teams, and knapsacks too, we have not got a change with us, nor have not had any since we left Bowling Green, and we have not had a chance to wash our clothes, since we left Louisville untill since we got here, so we got prety dirty, and some of us lousy too, but we have got cleaned up some, and got some more clothes, so we look better and feel better too.

As to the rebels I guess that they have scattered in all directions from this place, so we do not expect to have any more fighting in Ky. at least, they can beat us out in running, if not in fighting. I have not heard a word from Virginia for a long time. I do wish that we could get more of the news, from there for I want to know what they are a doing to end the war. I am afraid that there is not much progress towards the ending of it, but it does not seem as though it could last a great while longer. We are near the same town that we ~~pro~~ passed through last Feb. but we have came upon a different road most all the way, so we have had a chance to see a good deal of the country, it is a very nice country amost all of the way, but water is very scarce all through, there is not any place that the water runs but a short piece, it is a lime stone country, and a good many caves, so all of the water sinks into the ground. We have just received orders to be ready to go out on picket at three o'clock this afternoon, and it is now one o'clock, so I shall have to delay writing untill some other time, you must not worry about me if you do not get a letter from me evry week, for I cannot carry paper with me nor anything else but hard bread and coffee, sometimes three days rations at once, besides our blankets, gun and forty rounds of cartriges. I think it is ~~our~~ my loade that makes me have the piles, if they should get so bad again, I shall try to get along without marching so much, it looks very much as though we were a going to have some rain before long. I dread to have it rain, ~~f~~ untill we get our tents, for it is bad enough now and it will be worse if it should rain, there is not a great deal of sickness in the regment just now, but it is reduced down one half since we left Minn. one year ago, what will it be one year from now if the war lasts that long, but I hope that it will not last that long, for the sake of the country, if not for the people for whereever the army goes it nearly ruins it, and there is a larger army in the field now than ever before. I must close for a while and eat some dinner, before I go out on picket, so I will stop for this time.

Thursday, Oct. 23d

I will try to write a few more lines this afternoon I feel quite well this afternoon, but am pretty well wore out, for we have had a hard three days march, we went on picket that night, and it was a very cold frosty night, and we were not allowed to have any fire untill day light, my feet got quite cold, as well as all the other boys, we received orders to march about sundownrise, so we swallowed our hardbread and coffee and started, the regiment soon left me behind but I cought up with them again, and marched 20 miles to Danville, where we camped in a green woods, it was not so cold that night, we started the next morning and marched to Perryville[.] I got a letter from you in the morning, and you better believe I was pleased to hear from you once more, and to hear that you was well and all the rest of you at home. I had to ride part of the day, and I did not rest very well that night. I got into a waggon yesterday and we started about noon, and traveled very slow untill one o'clock this morning when we halted without catching up with the reg, we built up some fires, and got some coffee, and eat some crackers, add lay down at two o'clock to sleep, but it was a regular frosty night, and I kept up a fire all night, we had to start early this morning so as to get to the reg. for they were out of rations, we are camped about six miles in a southerly direction from Lebanon, upon the rolling fork river, or what was a large river last fall, but there is not any running water, we get water out of the deep places, it is better than some that we have had to use, we are expecting to lay here some time. I hope that we will stay here untill peace is declared, for we commenced our marches from Lebanon, and I hope that we will end them here

As near as I can learn the whole army is dissatisfied with the movements of Gen. Buell, we think that he could have given Bragg a cleaning out, if he had been a mind too, but he has let him get away with nearly the whole of his army, but I think that they have gone out of Ky. or nearly so, we hear a great many reports about the movements of the army, some say that hostilities have ceased for thirty days or so and that they are a going to meet, both the North and South, and try to settle this war, but I do not know. I have not seen any thing yet I hope that it may be so, for God knows that I am a getting sick and tired of the movements of our leaders. It does seem as though ~~that~~ we ~~had~~ have got traitors some where <u>pretty near</u> the head of the army, but I hope that time will develop all these thing in such a shape, that we shall be able to tell where all the blame lies.

Your letter was commenced Sept 25th one year from the time I left home. I wish that we could read each others thoughts. As I lay down to sleep that night, with the stars shinning in my face, as clear as ever they did in a cold winter night, my thoughts turned homeward, to my wife and children, of the many happy hours that we have spent together, I wondered whether we should ever spend any more happy days and hours together. I knew well that you were a thinking of me that night, we shall probably long remember that night, if we are permitted to live in the enjoyment of each others presence, and comforts on this earth again, and I believe that we shall, some time, but how soon we cannot tell. I hope and pray that "the time will fly swift around" and bring that welcome day," but in the mean time let us look up and trust for the best. As you wrote, it is a horrible thing, (war,) whether with the rebels in the South, or the Indians in the North. I cannot bear to think of it, you wanted to know what I thought about the people sending clothing to the soldiers. I will tell you I think that if any one thinks that they ought to do any thing for the soldiers, let them help the <u>families</u> of those that are in the army, for I think that they need it if any one, for they have sacraficed evry thing as it were in giving up the presence, and comforts of a son, husband, and father, perhaps to shed his blood on some distant battle field or to wear his life away in the tedious marches and cold nights, how many a family has already lost all that was near and dear to them in this "wicked rebelion" and how many more will be sacraficed before it ends, we are here atrying to do our duty to our country and it is not our fault if we do not do it, to the letter, and if there is any one that wants to aid in any way, I think that they could not do it in any better way than to help the Widows and orphans, and those that are deprived of the enjoyment of being in the presence of a Husband and Father, you may think that I say this for self interest but it is not so, for the government furnishes all the clothing to the soldiers that they can wear or carry with them, if they should send any to them, ten chances to one they could not get them, or would not be permited to wear them. I have clothes enough, and I can manage to send you nearly all of my wages. I sent forty dollars by Tom. Douglass and have sent ten dollars in a letter since, and there is two months due me at the end of this month, but I do not know when we shall get payed again. I have got a little left, and I will keep a little by me for fear I may want some before I get payed again. It is not so about Gen. Thomas'es sending back the negro for he is in the regiment and has been ever since, he has got his free papers, instead of being whiped out at Corrinth, we whipped the rebels badly too as you must have seen before this time, there has not been any battle at Chattanoga. I do not feel bad because Em. has got into office, it is well enough to have office while in camp, but I do not envy any one of their place, when ever my officers think that I am deserving of one, and there is a chance for me they will give it to me, I do not ask them for any office. I shall be glad if I live through the war, and get home safe as a private soldier. Where has Em gone to, we hear that the Indians want to settle the thing now, and that they have brought back the women that they took. I hope that they will make them pay pretty dear for their bloody work.

We are expecting to have our tents and knapsacks evry day now for we need them very much, we have not had any rain yet, it has been very dry here, has Hill gone away from there yet, I am glad that you have a chance to go to meeting, and that you have good meetings, I hope that I shall be there to go to meeting with you before another year rolls around. I suppose that you have payed Mr. Boynton the Interest. If you have any money to spare I wish that you would pay him for the small note, I forget just how much it is. I think if <u>you</u>, and I have good luck, we shall get all of our little debts paid up, in the course of <u>three years</u>, has Mr. Partch taken the cow, if so how much did he give for her, did Norm get the check, safe did you have corn enough to fat your pigs, how large were they &c &c. Perhaps you will want that I should direct your letters to Spring Valley, you must direct yours to Louisville the same as usual. I would like to write to you all of the time if I could find any thing to write about, tell Alice that I am very glad that she writes a few words to pa, I think of her and all of the babyes a good many times a day, I should like to have seen Edgar climbing up on top of the house, I guess I should have pulled him down by the heels or some other way, tell Alice that pa does not get so much time to write as I did one year ago, perhaps I shall have some more time after this, to write   Well it is getting some chilly and I cannot think of any more to write this time, so I will close by giving you all a good bye, hoping that I shall soon find out whether this war is agoing to last another year or whether there is any prospect of having a quick return to our families and friends. Goobye Nerva, good bye Alice, good bye Ida, good bye Edgar, good bye one and all, this from your Husband and Father,

D. B. Griffin.

the capt received a certificate of disability from Jery in the last mail

Letter Number 56

In Camp near Lebanon Ky Oct 28th 1862

My Dear Wife and Children,

As I have received two letters from you within the last few days, and we are expecting to move from here in a day or two, I will try to write a few lines to you to day. I am well to day, as well as the rest of the boys. We have received our knapsack's, and mine was all safe and sound, so I have got two blankets and a rubber coat, and I can sleep better and warmer than I did before. I will tell you how we have got along. As it looked a good deal like a storm last Saturday, we all went to work and fixed us up some shanties, and I wish that you could look down upon our camp, you have seen the picture of the camp at Valley Forge, but a picture of our camp would throw that in the dark. There is some built of rails, poles, brush, straw, cornstalks, blankets and any thing that would answer for a cover, and a windbreaker, well about noon it commenced to rain some, and it grew cold towards night, and the rain turned into snow about dark, and it snowed quite hard untill after midnight, the snow was about four inches deep. I woke up a number of times, and kicked the snow off from my blanket. We got up in the morning, and it was quite cold, and the way the rails walked into camp, (notwithstanding the order to the contrary) was a caution to the farmers in the vicinity, it was cold all day so that it did not thaw much untill just before night. I received a letter from you that day dated Oct. 12th in which was one from Eliza and Alice Ida and Edgar, and right glad was I to hear that you were all well, and that you had received the $40.00 that I sent by Tom. Douglass, and I got one last night dated the 19th in which you said that you had received my likeness. I was detailed Sunday night after dark to go to Lebanon, to load up rations we went and got there about eight o'clock, but the train had not got in we had to lay over untill yesterday, it was quite cold and froze quite hard that night. I laid down upon the floor in the bar room and slept about three hours, we got back last night, and I was tired and hungry, so I did not write to you, it was quite frosty last night, but it has come off very pleasant this morning. I doubt some whether you have had any colder weather in Minn. than what we have had here, there was not as much snow fell all last winter as we had the other night, but it has all gone off and the ground is dry again, we are expecting to go towards Bowling Green, as soon as we get our tents, we had orders to start yesterday morning, but our Gen. said that we should not go untill we got tents. I see by the letters that I get and the other boys too, that Jery has worked the card first rate, if he has contrived to get his discharge, and has been able to work all summer, but it is not any more than what others do, in the regiment, one person pretended that his lungs were affected so bad that he could not speak loud for a long time, but just as soon as he got his discharge papers, he could talk just as loud as any one, and told them that they might all go to h--l, for he had made out all that he wanted to. I do not say that it is the case with Jery, but still we all have our thoughts. I should like to be with you as well as ~~one~~ any one would like to be with his family, but when I go home, I do not want that any one should think that I have ever shrunk from doing my duty, while in the service of my country, but still we are all somewhat discouraged ~~by~~ in traveling over the country so much, and accomplishing so little towards the completion of the war. I suppose that you see in the papers how Gen Buell is talked about, we think that he is a traitor, and we blame "Old Abe," for keeping him in the command but we hear that he has had the command taken from him, and that McClallan was to take his place, if it is so I hope that he will do better.

I am glad that Father had good luck with his sorghum. I wish that you had had good luck with yours, so that you could had some to. I wish that I could be there and help you eat some custard pie. I cannot tell you whether I shall be there to plant any next spring or not, but I hope so sure. I have not heard from J. Nichols since we left Nashville. I have not had any letters from Vt. nor from Watson Freeman[.] If Norm. comes out there tell him to write to me, about all the folks in Ill. I hope that it will be so, that we can fix up our fence next spring[.] I should like to have you send your likenesses to me if you can for it would be some consolation to me to look at your likenesses once in a while, I am glad that you received mine all safe and sound, you do not say much about going a visiting. I do not believe that you go much, you think that it is pretty quick buisness to load a gun and fire it off three times a minute, but it is not any more to do than it would be to cap a gun twice and fire once[.] How much wheat did Father raise this year, I hope that he will get a good price for all of it, what teams has father got this fall, I hope that Grandpa will get well again for I should like to see him again as well as the rest of you, as to my looking sober, that is the way I generaly <u>look</u>, and "<u>keep</u>" but sometimes I get to raising <u>ned</u>, rather hard, but still I have managed to do my company duty and have kept out of the guard house so far. I do not think that you see my face in your dreams, oftener than I do your's in ~~miney~~ dreams[.] I am glad that the children all tried to write a few lines to their father and uncle. I hope that I shall soon be with them and enjoy their innocent plays, with them as I used to do heretofore, and <u>you</u> know that I never was <u>better suited</u> than when I was a rolling upon the <u>floor</u> with my (our) babies. I hope that I, and they, will be spared to roll on the floor a good many times more before we get old enough to to enjoy youthfull plays. I do not feel any older now than I did one year ago, but my head or hair says that I am, for it is quite gray now, but still sometimes I feel quite stiff in my joints after marching all day. Elicutt got a letter from Mrs Bonested last night, they were all well, he is well, Charles Phillips is in Louisville he was well a few days ago, Jim Thornton is well, he got a letter from Dan. last night they sayd that Jery was agoing to St Paul for his discharge and his pay. I hope that he will get it, and then I hope that they will not blame me for his enlisting, for if he gets all of his back pay up to the time he gets his discharge, and be at home all of the time, it is a good deal better than what I have done. Mrs. Paul says that Mrs Bender has got <u>your</u> <u>man</u> away from you, but she thinks that you are not sorry any for the loss, what is Hill agoing to do, take Mrs. Benders place, if so I hope he will do well, what is Chipman a doing this fall, the Case boys are well at present, in what Co. of the seventh regiment has Emery enlisted, where are they stationed this winter, how does he like soldiering. I think that I shall direct my next letter to Spring Valley, for I hope that you will go there before it gets to be cold weather, how does Mary make it go takeing care of two babies, I expect that they are almost as <u>large</u> as she or Em is. I hope that she will excuse me for not writing to her, but still if she has read your letters, it is all the same. I hope that she will write a few lines to me in your letters. I should like to see all of you, very much, I will assure you, Wife and children, Father and Mother, Brothers and sisters, Grandparents, Neighbors and all. I cannot think of much more, if any, to write this time, here is a little trinket for Ida, which I got with my paper, tell her not to <u>cut her fingers</u> with it. I must close for this time and bid you all good bye, once more, from your husband and Father and friend, good bye.

D. B. Griffin   (kiss.)

Letter Number 57

In Camp near Bowling Green, Ky. Nov 4th 1862

My Dear Wife and Children,

As this is the first day that we have lain over, since we started from Lebanon, I will take the opertunity and write a few lines to you. I feel pretty well to day, we started from Lebanon on the morning of the 29th and have marched evry day early and late untill to day making about 80 miles, a part of the way over a rough hilly country, first to Camelsville, then to Greensburgh, and through to Cave City where we struck the pike road from Nashville to Louisville, and came on to Bowling Green, which is 72 miles from Nashville, some of the time it has been very dusty and windy which makes it very disagreeable marching, it has been quite warm evry day and cool evry night so that it freezes, but we have got new tents, and we get along very well, we do not expect to stay here but a day or two, but go on towards Nashville, we are camped about three miles from the village near where we camped when we went through before, near a plenty of water, so we have been a washing up to day. I have washed up my shirts, and myself, got and eat my dinner, laid down and took a good nap, the first that I have had in a long time.

We do not know much about the movements of the enemy, but we see by the papers that they have left Ky. pretty much, now and then a squad of guerrilla's, the rail road from here to Nashville is not in running order, but as we advance it will be fixed up again. I see by the papers that Gen. Buell, has been superceded by Gen. Rosencranz[*], he has proved himself to be a fighting Gen. and I hope that if we get a chance to fight the rebels again, that he will pitch in and clean them out, but we may not have a chance at them again. I hope that something will turn up before the first of January, that will tend towards ending the war one way or another, and let the soldiers go home to their families and friends[.]

I cannot think of much to write to day. I wish that I could, for I know that you like a good long letter, but somehow or other it is hard work to think of anything to write. I should like to be there with you, and I could talk more in one hour than I can write in one week. I shall direct this to Spring Valley, where I expect you will be by the time this gets there. I hope that you will have a good time along with Mary, but it seems as though you would be as thick as three in a bed, but you will have to be so much the more pleasent. I hope that Em. and myself will both be there before spring, do you hear from him has he been in any fight with the Indians yet. I heard that the seventh had been in one or two small fights, did they have to draft any one in Minn, who has gone from around Spring Valley in the New Reg'ts   I cannot write any more to night as I see, but I will try to write to you as often as I can if only a few lines at a time. I have not had a chance to be weighed in a long time, but

---

[*] Union Gen. William Starke Rosecrans, who will reorganize his forces into the Army of the Cumberland and remain in command through the disastrous Battle of Chickamauga.

I do not weigh near as much as I did last spring and summer, but still I am not very poor, nor do I feel quite as well as I did then, but am not sick so but what I do the marching, and my company duty too. I hope that I never shall be any the less able to do my duty, and I intend to do it as long as I can, when I get so (if I ever should,) that I can not do any service to my Country, then I want that they should give me my discharge and let me go home, nor do I want to go home before I get my discharge give my best wishes to all of my friends at home and abroad, the rest of the boys are well as far as I know. I have not received any letters since I last wrote, you must except these few lines, and hope for more the next time, from your husband and father, in Ky to Mrs. "Nerva" Griffin and the babies.

D. B. Griffin

Guarding South Tunnel and Cunningham's Ford, Gallatin, Tennessee

Letters 58–61 (November 16–December 14, 1862)

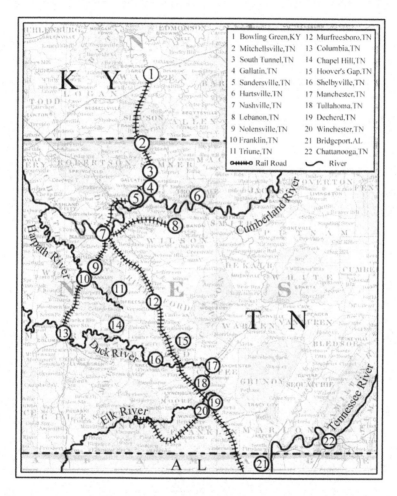

1	Bowling Green,KY	12	Murfreesboro,TN
2	Mitchellsville,TN	13	Columbia,TN
3	South Tunnel,TN	14	Chapel Hill,TN
4	Gallatin,TN	15	Hoover's Gap,TN
5	Sandersville,TN	16	Shelbyville,TN
6	Hartsville,TN	17	Manchester,TN
7	Nashville,TN	18	Tullahoma,TN
8	Lebanon,TN	19	Decherd,TN
9	Nolensville,TN	20	Winchester,TN
10	Franklin,TN	21	Bridgeport,AL
11	Triune,TN	22	Chattanooga,TN
⊶⊶⊶o Rail Road		⌣ River	

Because rebels have blocked South Tunnel on the Nashville Line, a week is spent unloading railroad cars for overland transport, then another week at the tunnel itself to clear the fallen rock. Continuing on through Gallatin, Tennessee, Brainard's division finally sets up camp at Cunningham's Ford of the Cumberland River, just above Nashville, where he relates a remarkable experience of being shot at by Confederates. These letters are filled with light banter about family matters, eating and sleeping, farm concerns, their friends and neighbors, and their second Thanksgiving Day apart. He and others also respond to President Lincoln's Emancipation Proclamation. An attack by Gen. Morgan's Raiders in nearby Gallatin does not directly threaten the forces at the Ford. Pictures arrive, one of Minerva with their son and one of their two daughters, to Brainard's great joy. He also announces his appointment as corporal, with its new duties. Initial good news about Fredericksburg is corrected when notice arrives of the heavy losses suffered there. To all this, Brainard adds an accounting of his first year of service's clothing bill.

Letter Number 58

Camp at the South Tunnell, Tenn. Nov. 16th th 1862

My Dear Wife and Companion, Children and Friends, one and all, I bid you all a good morning. I am well this morning, with the exception of a lame knee. I had the misfortune to hit it a rap on a car that we were at work on yesterday. I wrote you a short letter when we were at Bowling green, and it has so happened that I have not had a chance to write since. I have been quite well ever since, we marched from there to Mitchellsville some twenty five miles, in two days we went into camp in the woods near the depot, and no water less than from one to two miles, that was fit to use, we stayed there some four or five days, standing guard and unloading cars, as all the rations for Nashville had to be unloaded here, the trains do not run beyond there at present, the road will soon be opened through to Nashville, we are camped on a hill under which the tunnell goes through, the rebels destroyed the tunnell by running cars loaded with wood into ~~the t~~ it and set them on fire, the heat of them causing the rocks to crack and crumble off so as to fill up the track with stones and rocks, it will take two or three more days to clean it out, our regment, or a detail from it worked upon it yesterday, and while I was there I went to jump upon one of the cars, and I struck my knee against it, hurting it a considerable, but it feels better this morning, it is nothing serious, we are about five miles from Gallatan   I received a letter from you yesterday dated Nov. 2, and was glad to hear from you, for I had not had any letter from you since I left Lebanon. I am glad that you have good health, as well as the children. I hope that we shall remain an unbroken family, untill permitted to join each other <u>at home</u> which I hope will soon be. I see that Edgar had to <u>set his foot in it</u>, that is in the letter, I wish that I could see him, or his likeness in it You must try and keep his shoes on, so that he will not get any more thornes in his <u>feet</u>, you wrote that you had sore lips. I have got a sore <u>lip</u> to, I think that the same <u>medicine</u> that would cure <u>yours</u>, would cure <u>mine</u> also, I should like to try it any how. I am glad that you have got a good lot of potatoes. I wish that I could set down to a good meal of potatoes, and hot buiscuit and butter, pies and wheat bread, &c a regular family dinner such as <u>you</u> used to get, I think that it would do my <u>stomach</u> good, we do not get any ~~shuch~~ such things this fall, we get hard bread, rice, beans, beacon, beef and coffee, sugar, and salt pork, and each one cooks his own dish. I have stoped drinking coffee, for I think that it hurt me to drink it, so perhaps I can sell my rations for something else. I have not heard a word from James Nichols since we left him. I expect you must have heard from him before this time, if he is alive, there has not been any mail from Nashville untill within a few days, since we left there, probably that is the reason that his folks have not heard from him. We have had very pleasent weather so far, it rained a little the day we came here, just enough to lay the dust, there was not any frost last night, there has been a frost almost evry night since it commenced to be cold. I sleep with a young man by the name of James Brennam[.] I have got two blankets, and so has he, and we get straw and husks to put under us, so we sleep first rate, but still I had rather go to bed in a good <u>warm</u> <u>bed</u>, and have a good <u>bed fellow</u> than to lay down here, it is almost fourteen months since I left home, and I have not slept with my pants off but twice since, I dare not take them off for fear of taking cold, and a good many times I do not take off my shoes or coat, but still I do not complain for if I live to get home, I shall know how to prise such things.

One of the boys got a letter from Jerry last night, stating that his boy was dead, it is hard to loose those we hold dear to us. Minerva I think that we know how to sympathise with them in their loss, he writes that he got his discharge, and his pay up to the time of his discharge, without any trouble, he regrets very much that he could not be with us to fight for his country. I think that if I could get my discharge and be at home, I would let them fight their own battles, for all of me, and not regret it very much either. I should like to know whether he got any more than 13 dollars a month or not. I see by the papers that the Indian war is at an end for the present, and that the sixth and seventh Reg. are ordered South, you must write to me where ~~and~~ Emry is and what they are a doing, as often as you can hear from him, if he should come down this way I shall try to find him if I can, you sayd that Hill did not get all of the work done, how much did he do for you, he should have ploughed ten acres for you, I hope that he will have a long life and a happy life with Mrs. Bender may they have plenty of <u>children</u> to comfort them in their old age, but I do not hardly think that Mrs. Bender wanted to get married bad enough to have an "Old Maid," for a husband. If you see Alfred S. tell him that I wish him much joy with his little son. I see that the Govenor[*] has appointed Thursday the 27th as a day of Thanksgiving and praise. Oh! how I wish that I could spend that day with you, would it not be a day of Thanksgiving with us if it could so be, little did I think one year ago now, that another year would find us still in the South, and apparently no nearer ~~home~~ the time to go home than we were then, it is not the war that we thought it was, it is a war of parties and the southern party has to many simpathisers in the northern army. I hope that they will all be ferreted out, and be dissmised from the service, and those put in that will work for thee Union, and the good of the nation, instead of working for themselves and a few politicians of the day, we the soldiers were cheated out of our votes this fall, but I hope that Minn. ~~has~~ has been true to her interest and not gone the "Secession" tickit but I will let that pass. Our Company has gone out on picket to night, and I was lucky enough to get off, for it set in to rain just before they started out, and it rains hard now, it looks as though it was agoing to be a rainy time, my knee is a good deal better to night. I cannot think of any more to write this time, you must not worry if you should not get a letter from me evry week, do you take a paper this winter, and what ones do you take, the boys have some papers occasionly from all parts, of the

---

[*] Minnesota State (and before that Territorial) Governor, Alexander Ramsey. Gov. Ramsey had come to visit the 2nd Minnesota Regiment of Volunteers in Corinth following the Siege of Shiloh, a fact Brainard did not mention.

country, the rebels are said to be concentrating at Murfreesboro, where they may have a fight, but I hardly think that they will be any before they get back to Chattanoga, our forces are steadily driving them back, both here and on the Potomac. I hope that they will not give them any rest untill they will be ready and willing to cry "enough, let us stop," but we may meet with many drawbacks, but I hope the Federal army will never give up the ship, there is some few gurrillas about here, but they are pretty quiet, two boys from this regiment have been missing for the last three days, we expect that they are taken prisoners two Companies have gone out to day to hunt for them, and to fetch in a family of children, their father was killed by the guerrillas last July, and the woman wants to get North where her friends are, the country is nearly striped of evry thing fences and all, it looks like an old deserted place. I will close by giving you all a good bye, good bye one and all this from your husband and father with a (kiss).

D. B. Griffin.

Letter Number 59

Camp at the big island ford, Cumberland river Tenn. Nov 27th 1862

My dear Wife and Children,

as it has been some time since I have written to you, or received a letter from you, I will write a few lines to you to day, and let you know how how I am, and what we have been about. I feel pretty well to day, as I have ever since I wrote before (the 16th), except a touch of the diareah, and getting very tired, it rained, and kept lowry for three or four days, but it cleared off and froze quite hard, but would thaw out in a little while in the morning. Last Saturday our company went out a foraging for beef we went out into the country about five miles, we got about 50 head of beef, the country is a rough, rocky and hilly, and the soil is not the best, there is now and then a good farm, while we were gone the reg. received orders to stand ready to march, at a minutes notice, but they did not go that day, the guerrillas attacked a reg. of men on the Cumberland about nine miles from the Tunnell, but our men held their ground without any loss. Sunday passed off about as usual, untill about Sundown, when we received orders to pack up and march, and we started about seven o'clock, and marched untill midnight, about nine miles, to the Gallatin ford on the Cumberland we went through Gallatin, and I should think that it was a very pretty place, it is quite a large village, it is a place where the rebels are very strong, and they have given the North a good deal of trouble about there, we laid down and slept about three hours, when we were ordered to go to another ford about six miles from there, it was quite cold and we did not march very fast we had to go acrost the fields through lanes and cornfields, over a very rough country, we went through one little village called Cairo the buildings all look as though they were built in the year one, [the windows all out and everything around looked as though they had been forsaken. There was hardly a road there or away from there. But we got along very well for the teams were not with us, they came up to us that night, but it was late and we laid down without our tents and I have not slept as well in a good while. We got up the next morning and came here, about three miles. We are camped in the bend of the river. It is not over one half a mile across, and the citizens say that it is about ten miles around by the river. We are right in the timber, and heavy timbers too—maple, hickory, elm, white wood, black walnut, etc. We have all the walnuts and hickory nuts that we can eat. I wish that you could get a few of them to crack. Now I will tell you what transpired yesterday, or something that I shall be apt to remember as long as I live. Now do not be scared for I am not hurt any yet, but the Rebels have got to shoot at me the second time before they hit me, for they shot at _me_ for the first time (as far as I know anything of) yesterday, but they shot about a foot to one side of my legs. Now I will tell you the circumstances as near as I can. About ten o'clock I took two canteens and started down to the river after some water, which is about eighty rods from camp. As I came up to the banks of the river, I saw a man sitting upon a horse on the other bank. When I came, he asked me if there was any chance to cross over to this side. I told him that I was not acquainted with the river and did not know. He then said that he wished that I would take that canoe, pointing to one on this side, and come over after him as he would like to get over and he did not want to take his horse over. I told him that I could not row a canoe. He said that it was not anything to row one, and he would give me a dollar if I would come over after him. I told him that I could not go after him and asked him what he wanted to get on this side for. I began to think that he was a Rebel. He said that he did not want to get acrost as much as he wanted to get the boat over there, and he would see me back all safe. I told him that he could not catch me as easy as that, and upon that I heard him speak to someone else and ride off into a cornfield. I could then see another man laying by the side of a tree. I then stepped back to make sure that I saw someone. I stood out about four feet from the tree in plain sight and was standing still when crack went a rifle and whiz went a little bullet, about halfway up to my knee and about a foot from my leg. I then saw another man step from behind a tree some four rods from where the one lay which was the one that fired at me. I then stepped behind the tree and took a good look up and down the river, but saw no other men but the three. I came back to camp and reported to the Col. He sent down seven men with me and told us if we see anyone that looked suspicious to drop him if we could. But we did not get a sight at them again. We destroyed the boat and came back to camp, so we all had something to talk about the rest of the day, but they have got to shoot better than that, or they will not hit me. Today there is not much stir in camp. We are looking for orders to march any minute. There has been heavy cannonading all the morning in the direction of Lebanon, Tenn., but we have not heard what it is about. We may look for a forward movement now any day for the tunnel is opened and the cars run through to Nashville. Now I will send you a piece out of a paper written about a week ago which will tell you more than I could in a good while on paper. I have not received any letters from you since I wrote before nor from anyone else. I see by the papers that the Sixth and Seventh[*]] reg. are not agoing south yet, I hope that they will not beeneeded here at all, for it does seem as though we had men enough in the field now if they would all be put into the right place in the right time, but here we are, another "Thanksgiving" day has come, and we are not at home yet. I did think, one year ago, when I was writing to you about Thanksgiving and about your suppers, that I should certainly be with you before this time so that I could set down to supper with <u>you all</u> <u>to night</u>, but no here I am away down in Tenn. a watching and guarding against the enemies of the Union, and they a sneaking around trying to shoot down any of us that they can catch away from the reg, when will such a curse end. I am afraid not untill the <u>whole</u> south is entirely ruined and laid dessolate by the sword and bayonet, but I try to look on the bright side of things, and hope that before another year we shall all be at home by the firesides ~~af~~ of our wives and families, to eat our next Thanksgiving supper with our own friends, may God grant it to be so, but time flies swiftly around, and it will not be but <u>nineteen</u> months more before the three years that the reg. was sworne in for will be up. I suppose that you have got moved before this time, you must tell me how you get along, and where you keep all of your things, in such a <u>little</u> <u>house</u> for you could not hardly find room for all of your things in our <u>big</u> <u>shantee</u>, you must write as often as you can to me, and let me know what is agoing on and how you all get along in Spring Valley have they got a good school there, I hope that they the children will be able to go to school all winter, kiss them for me won't you "Nerva." Mary must write some to me too. I must bid you all good bye, again, so Good bye, all, from

D. B. Griffin.

---

[*] The enclosed material constitutes the only uncopied original material and is recorded here from an earlier transcription made by a relative around 1940.

Letter Number 60

Cunningham's ford Tenn. Dec. 7th 1862

Dear "Nerva," and "babies,"

I will write a few lines to you to day, although I hardly know what to write for I have not got any news to write to you, and I have written three letters to you since I have received any from you. I do not see the reason why I cannot get letters as well as others, Jim. Thornton has received three or four from D. Paul since ~~you~~ I received the last one from you, which was written Nov. 3d. I know well enough that you write to me as often as you can, but I suppose that they are delayed somewhere. I think that they will be very welcome when they do come. I am quite well to day, but I have been quite low for the last week, my stomache was quite out of order, but I took an Emetic, and phisic, and it helped me right up again, so I feel as well as ever to day, we have not removed camp since I last wrote and we do not know when we will go from here, nor do we care whether we go from here before peace is declared, or not, for we do not have much duty to do now, we have to drill about two hours in a day, go on picket once in ten days and on guard, once in two weeks so we do not have to hurt ourselves, there has not been any rebels seen about here for some time. We were called out two nights ago, but it was a false alarm so we went to bed again and slept untill morning. Capt, or rather Maj. Davis, Lieutenent Wait, Sergeant Cutting and others arrived in camp last Tuesday, and we were all glad to hear from our friend and relatives at home[.] At least I know that I was for one, Cutting says that you looked well and felt first rate, I was glad to hear it.

I hope that I can see for myself in the course of a year or two at most, but I will wait untill <u>my</u> time comes to go home to Minnesota and then I hope that you will all be alive and well, as well as myself.

The boys tell some pretty hard storye's about the barbarities of the Indians, it is awful to think of. I hope that evry one of them that is guilty of any of the acts of barbarity, will be speedily punished, and not be kept there on at the expence of the government. I have seen the Presidents Message[*]. I think that he means to stick to what he says concerning the Emancipation, it is not but a short time now before the first of January, and we all are in hopes that they will either make peace...or else go to fighting and fight it out at once, and let us know how we are to be governed, if by the South, let us stop at once, but if by the Constitution, let us conquer at once or be conquerd for we are getting rather tired of "doing nothing" all of the time.

We have had some pretty cold weather the last three days, last Friday we had quite a snow storm, it fell about 2 inches deep, and all the boys had a fine time of it, a snowballing each other. I stood by and saw them but I did not feel like throwing any snow balls, yesterday was a cold day so the snow did not go off. I was on guard the night after the snow, and came off last night. I was on post while the Eclipse of the moon was on it was a total eclipse for about one hour and a half, it was worth seeing, last night was a very cold night, the coldest one that we have had this winter, but I slept as warm as I ever want to and a good deal better than I have for a good while before, it does not thaw any to day I tell you. I commenced to write in the tent but my "fingers" were to cold so I am setting on a log by the fire, but it is rather disagreeable, for it smokes and the ashes fly, and my back gets cold while my face burns, we keep a large fire all the time for we have got a plenty of wood and it is handy by, so we have not been uncomfortable cold yet, dinner is ready so I will stop untill after dinner[.]

I have been to dinner, would you like to know what we had well I will tell you, we had some beef soup and hard bread, not the kind that you used to make, with potatoes, onions, turnips and seasoning, but simply some beef boiled and the soup thickened

---

[*] The Emancipation Proclamation, issued September 22, 1862, following the Union victory at Antietam. As a war measure, it was to free all slaves in areas still in rebellion, and it was to take effect January 1, 1863.

with a little flour, it makes a very good change. I wish that I could eat some that you make, perhaps I shall another fall, you wrote that you had received the money all right, but you did not say any thing about the united states currency bills of 50, 10, and 5 cts or of that kind did you get the letter with them in the ten dollar bill, that is all that I have sent, since we was at Louisville ($50.000). We some expect to get ~~paiyed~~ payed again before the first of Jan. Charles Russell has been to Minn. and took his wife and boy down to Mass. and has come back again, he is in Gallatin. I have not seen him yet. I have not heard a word about James Nichols yet, there was some of our boys in Nashville all of the time but they were not in the same hospital that he was, so they did not know any thing about him, or whether he was there or not if you hear from him let me know, the third did not get a very good name through Minn they pillaged and plundered just the same as though they were in an enemy's country, we get some fresh pork or a chicken once in a while, but I can say with truth that I have never taken but four chickens, and a few potatoes, without paying all that the things were worth, but I suppose that it is just as bad to help "eat stolen fruit," as it is to steal it, but one thing is certain, we generaly know whether they are <u>secesh</u> or union "chickens," probably once in a while a "<u>union</u>" chicken or pig or turkey, duck, goose, sheep, or whatever we find that "<u>runs right at us</u>" finds its way into camp but as a general thing they belong to secesh persons, there is very few others here.

There is a great many opinions as regards the Presidents Message, some think that the plan he lays down in regard to Emancipation can never be carried through, that the South will never consent to any such measures, it would be a good thing for the country if they would agree to that or some other propasition that will put an end to the war, for it seems as though this war had lasted about long enough. The report has just camp into camp that Gen Morgan[*] the ~~Gen~~ rebel Gen, made a dash on our men somewhere east of Gallatin, and captured

---

[*] CSA Gen. John Hunt Morgan, Cavalry Brigade Commander.

four regments of our men but I do not credit it yet, it is getting cold and most night, so I will stop for to night.

Monday Eve,

The above report is true, they were taken about ten miles from here, after we got our supper we got orders to go on picket, we went about eight o'clock, it was a very cold night, the coldest yet, we have just come of from picket, there has been heavy firing heard all day up the river but we do not with what results it is getting dark, and I have not got any letter from you so I will wait untill morning.

Tuesday morning Dec. 9th

As the mail has gone of this morning and I did not get this done I will write a little more. I am as well as usual this morning, and it has come of quite pleasent, so I guess that what little snow there is will go off to day, the birds are a singing like spring. We were called out at three o'clock this morning, and ordered to stand by our arms, as it was expected that "Morgan" was agoing to attact us this morning, but he did not come, so evry thing passed off as usual, it is said that there is was about twelve thousand rebels under Morgan, Van Dorn, and Forrest, attacked about three thousand of our men, and succeeded in capturing them after fighting two hours. I have not learned how many was killed on either side nor have I learned what regments were taken except the 106 Illinois infantry, an Indiany and a Kentucky regiment, the 2nd Indiana Cl Cavelry, and two pieces of Artillery, amounting in all to about three thousand, they were obliged to ford the river about waist deep after they were taken. The rebels were driven back acrosst the river by Gen Col Harlan, who succeeded in taking most of the arms back again. If they should make an attack upon us I expect that we should fight pretty hard before we are taken, but there is not but about two thousand men here, and we could not do much against a large force, unless we should receive reinforcements, but I do not apprehend any danger here, for there is not a very good fording place here.

We do not hear of our men a doing any thing any where, and it makes the boys uneasy, they think that we have got men enough, both here and on the Potamac, to go ahead with the war, if they are agoing to do any thing this winter but perhaps there will be something done in Congress before the first of Jan. that will do something towards settling the war, we look anxiously for it, and will except almost any terms that will bring peace and prosperity to the land again, may the tine soon come. The mail just came in but no letters for me, it is strange that I do not get any letter from Nerva, it is over four weeks since I have heard from you the last letter being dated Nov 3d. I suppose that you have got moved before this time. I should like to look in and see how you and Mary look this morning. I suppose that the children are in school this morning as they have a good school, and who is their teacher, what books do they study, tell Alice she must write a few words to me once in a while so I can se how fast she learns to write, she must not feel bad because I do not write a letter to her for it is hard work for me to write at all, for we have not got any conveniences for writing. I have got an old cheese box on my knees to write upon, and it is cold writing. I have not written to you since the 27th of Nov. I can not send this off before morning, so perhaps there will be a letter for me to night, I hope so sure. I cannot think of much more to write this morning so I will wait untill after the mail comes to night[.] We have got to go out now and drill an hour, ~~now~~ from eleven till twelve.

Evening.

Well it is the same old story, "no letter for me." I shall begin to think that evry one has forgotten me, but you and I know that you will not forget me while we both live, if we are seperated from each other for a few days or months, I know that you seem nearer to me now than you used to before I came away, may our seperation be a blessing to us while we live. There is not any more news to night, of any account, it is quite warm to what it has been for the last few days, I think we are agoing to have some fine weather again, you must excuse me for not writing before, but it has been so cold, and I did not hear any thing from you so I thought that I would wait a few days, but I could not wait any longer, kiss the babies for me, and tell Mary to kiss <u>hers</u> for me too, I would like to see her little girl as well as herself, and all of the rest of you too, don't <u>you</u> <u>believe</u> <u>it</u>? well I will close this time by giving you all a "good bye" with a (kiss), from your husband, and father, in the 2nd Minn. Vol. Cunningham Ford <u>Tenn.</u>

to, Mrs. P. M. and Alice J, Ida May, Edgar L. Griffin, and all the rest of the <u>folks</u>
D. B. Griffin

Letter Number 61

Camp Cunningham Tenn. Dec. 14th, 1862.

My Dear Wife, Children and Friends,

As I have a few moments to spare, and feel first rate, I thought that I would begin a letter to you. I am well and hearty again, and I hope that I shall remain so during the war. I received a letter from you on the 12th, dated the 2nd, and you may be assured that I was well pleased to hear from you once more, and to hear that you were all well, and that you had got moved up to "Aunt Mary's," as Alice says. It is the first letter that I have received from you since Nov. 3d[.] You sayed in ~~that~~ the letter that I had probably received your likenesses before I had got that, but I had not, so I felt rather bad that I could not get my mail as regular as others do. But when the mail came in last night it brought along your pictures, and I took a <u>good</u> <u>long</u> <u>look</u> at them now I tell you. It did me good to see that familiar look of yours, and to see you looking so well. I could almost imagine that you was agoing to speak to me, but I was contented to have you look at me, through a "<u>glass</u>." Alice and Ida look as natural as the "pigs," evry one that looks at them thinks that they are pretty girls, they all remark something about Ida's "black eyes," they will bet that she is a "scheemer," a "witch" "that's my girl," &c, but <u>I</u> <u>think</u> that they are "<u>my</u>

girls." I guess that they will everage with the rest of the little girls in Minn, if they will always be as good as they look, I shall be content. I think that they have grown a good deal since I last saw them. I guess that Ida is about as large as Alice is by this time, is it not so? But there is one little fat chubby boy sitting in his Mothers lap, that "takes my eye," he looks up as though there was something a going on, that he did not see into, exactly. I cannot see any familiar look in his little fat face, he looks well and as pert as a mouse. I hope that I shall be permitted to see all of you as you are, before many months. I shall have to stop for to day, for we have got to go out upon picket in a short time, we expect to move to Gallatin to morrow.

These are the "likenesses" Brainard received on December 14, 1862, of Minerva and the children. Left to right, Edgar Lincoln, Minerva, Alice and Ida May Griffin.

Tuesday Dec 16th

We are still at the ford, not going to Gallatin as we expected, the reason I do not know. It is rumored that Morgan is a crossing the river at Hartsville some ten miles from here up the river, the place where he had a fight one week ago, if so, we may see some work done before long. We got some good news from "the army of the Potomac" we learn by the papers that Burnside had a fight at Fredericksburgh, and succeeded in crossing the river at that place, and that several movements are on foot, which looks as though the army was about to do something at last, and also that Grant has got ten miles below Grenada, in Miss., and the fleet has started or about to start down the river, so we may expect to hear of some battle before long if the rebels do not run to fast for them, and if there is no Traitors amongst the Officers. I think that the Federal army will be the victors, and if they are, and follow up their victoryes with success, this war will not last six months longer.

We look anxiously for the news evry day, both in Congress, and in the army. I see that the Indians that were found guilty are to be hung, or be have been hung before this time in Minn. they had all aught to be hung or driven out of the country entirely, so that we shall not again be troubled with the treacherous race, especialy in Minnesota.

We went out upon picket as I wrote and we did not have a very bad time of it, for it was warm and pleasent untill about two hours before we were relieved, when the wind whirled around into the north, and it commenced raining very hard, but I had my rubber coat with me, so I did not get wet any, some of the boys got pretty wet, we came in and made for our tents, and did not come out of them again untill this morning. I eat some crackers and drank some water, and went to bed, and slept well, it stopted raining sometime in the night, and come off cleare but the wind blows hard from the south, and it is quite chilly, we have been out a drilling this forenoon in the manual of arms, and in marching, it was some cold for the fingers. I have not yet told you the news. We had an order read to us on the tenth, notifying us of the promotions in Co. F., G. Wallace was made first Sergeant, J. T. Riggs, fifth Sergeant, and David B. Griffin, C. Crane and Wm. Chapman, appointed Corporals, so you may tell Emry that he is not much ahead of me yet, as far as office is concerned. I am the sixth Corporal. I did not know anything about it untill the order was read. It did not make me feel very big. I have just been out upon Batallion drill, and I have got to go upon guard to night, so I do not know when I shall finish this letter, perhaps I shall write some more to night. It is quite chilly and my fingers get numb so I will stop for this time.

Thursday, Dec. 18th,

I will try to finish this letter this afternoon. I had to go on guard Tuesday night, and came of last night. I was Corporal of the guard for the first time, it is the duty of the Corporal to relieve the guards evry two hours, and stay at the guard tents, ready to go on any duty that he may be called upon to do about the camp, so I did not get a chance to write any yesterday, and I have been out two hours this forenoon a drilling, in the bayonet exercise, and the Batallion drill, it was pretty cold for our fingers in the morning, but it is warmer now.

The news received from Burnside last evening was not quite as good as we would wish it to be, he has retreated back acrosst the river with a heavy loss, but we have not the means of knowing the cause of such a movement, it may be done in order to let Banks'es and the other expeditions get into position in the rear of Richmond, or for some other purpose, we wait anxiously for the results, there is no news of interest from Nashvill, it is said that Jef. Davis is in Murfresborough, inspecting the troops around there. We were expecting to be relieved yesterday morning, but the order was countermanded, as it was expected that Morgan would attact us early yesterday morning, or this morning, so we were up and under arms at four o'clock both days, but he did not see fit to come on, so we remain here yet, we will most likely go to Nashville from here, if we are not whiped out before we get there, by Morgan's men, but if he makes the attack, we will give them the best that we have got, if the officers stand up to the fire, and we have a good deal of confidence in them at the present time.

I see by Jim. Thorntons letter that James Nichols has got back to his regment again and has been home, it is the first that I have heard from him, if you had written anything about him, I have not got the letters. I expect that there is some letters remaining behind. I have not heard anything from Vt.

you may send the first likeness of mine to Mother if you see fit to do so, and tell them how I get along and ask them to write to me as often as they can, you can see by this letter that I do not have a great deal of time to write, when it is so cold, we do not have any fires in our tents, so if it is quite cold, we set or stand around the fires made from logs and rails, the rails disappear very fast these frosty morning's. We are having a different winter this winter from what we had last, it is dry most of the time and clear, the regment stands is well, there is not many sick, and we are getting pretty well rested, ready for another campaign, but I hope that it will be a short and decisive one.

I am as well to day as usual. Pete, is well and all the rest of the boys from around there, you must let father see my letters and tell them to write to me as often as they can. I do not see what Hill took away any thing that did not belong to him for, such as stakes and the like, I hope that there will be no trouble to have him do the rest of the ploughing, there was about nine or ten acres ploughed[.] I know because we talked about it, and there is about eleven acres in that new piece, and I had it all done but about one days ploughing besides what was ploughed around the barley field, but there was a little piece acrost the end that C. ploughed if Hill does not plough as much, Chipman will owe you for it, unless there is some agreement between you and C. about it with Hill, but if I am alive and well I had rather send the money and pay for the ploughing than to have you have any trouble about it. What is Jerry about this winter, he will not get any bounty nor any one else that gets a discharge inside of two years, unless the war ends. I do not think of any more to write just now, so I will wait untill after the mail comes in, the call is made for us to go out upon drill, so I must stop now[.]

Evening, there was no letter for me, no news of any importance in the papers, we had a very good Batallion drill. I have to look at your likenesses often, they look so much like home, "When shall we all meet again," "meet ne'er to sever," Lord hasten the time. The account of my clothing bill is put down on this paper[.] I thought you would like to see it, and I could not get quite all that I wanted to say upon one sheet, so I took this, you must excuse me for not writing any oftener, I will write all that I can think of[.]

when I do write, I cannot say where I shall be when I write again, you must give my respects to all of my friends, but take my love to yourself and babies, love and cherish them for me, I remain your affectionate husband for life, kiss _all_ of the children for me, and accept _one_ for yourself [kiss]

"Corp." D. B. Griffin.

Attachment to Letter Number 61

Oct 1	1 O. Coat	7.20	1 pr. Shoes	1.94
	1 D. Coat	6.71	1 " of socks	.24
	1 pr. Shoes	1.94	1 Shirt	.88
	2 " Socks	.52		3.06
	2 " Drawrs	1.00		
	1 Hat	1.55		
	1 shirt	.88		
	1 Blouse	2.63		
	1 Blanket	2.95		
Nov 5	1 Shirt	.88		
8	1 Cap	.63		
	1 pr. Pants	3.03		
March 10	1 " "	3.03		
May 3	1 Blouse	2.63		
July 22	1 shoes	1.94		
Aug 18	1 drawers	.50		
Sept 29	1 hat	1.55		
	1 pants	3.03		
	1 shirt	.88		

	43.48
	3.06
	46.54
I am allowed the first year	45.97
and I have taken up the first year	38.
	02
which leaves	7.95

my due on the first year and I shall not take up near as much the second year. We are allowed about 35.00 the second year.

In and Around Gallatin, Tennessee

Letters 62–68 (December 23, 1862–February 18, 1863)

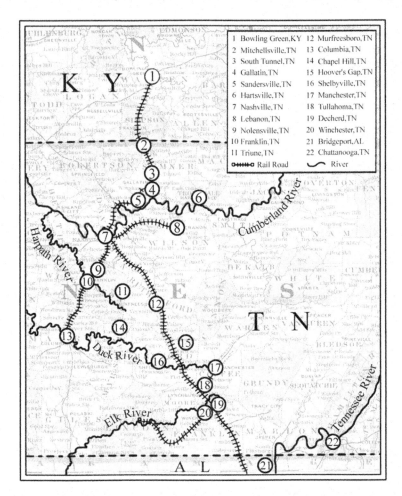

1	Bowling Green, KY	12	Murfreesboro, TN
2	Mitchellsville, TN	13	Columbia, TN
3	South Tunnel, TN	14	Chapel Hill, TN
4	Gallatin, TN	15	Hoover's Gap, TN
5	Sandersville, TN	16	Shelbyville, TN
6	Hartsville, TN	17	Manchester, TN
7	Nashville, TN	18	Tullahoma, TN
8	Lebanon, TN	19	Decherd, TN
9	Nolensville, TN	20	Winchester, TN
10	Franklin, TN	21	Bridgeport, AL
11	Triune, TN	22	Chattanooga, TN
	Rail Road		River

After four weeks guarding the Ford, the division makes several scouting passes beyond Gallatin, with the brigade Brainard belongs to eventually encamping near Gallatin to respond to rumors of impending rebel attacks. Christmas, New Year's, and his birthday and wedding anniversary are marked with wistful dreams of home and questions regarding his term of service. News of the Battle of Stones River arrives, and half of his brigade moves down to Nashville as a hard winter sets in. Brainard relates a delightful story about his "initiation into the cavalry," and an interesting tale of digging up ninety barrels of lard rendered and buried by the Confederates. A reunited brigade then rejoins their division near Concord Church, south of Nashville. Their stay there is, ironically, on the farm of Col. Battle, commander of the Confederate forces, which the 2nd Minnesota had faced across the fence at Mill Creek! The last two letters are filled with domestic images (farm and camp) and politics, along with small bits of war news and the exciting story of the bravery of the 2nd Minnesota's Company H.

Flag of the seas! On ocean wave
Thy stars shall glitter o'er the brave.

Letter Number 62

Pilot Knob, Tenn. Dec. 23d, 1862

My Dear Wife and Children, Friends & Neighbors,

I will again try, to write a few lines to you to day. I am well to day, and in ~~the~~ fine spirits. We had a regimental review last Sunday and the day passed of fine, we were expecting an attack in the morning from Morgan, but he did not see fit to pitch into us, we went to work the day before and fell large trees, so as to have them touch together, around in front of our camp, they made a good breastwork for us, but we did not have to use them, and in the evening the order came for us to move in the morning. We have had a long rest, of four weeks the longest rest that we have had at any one time since we started on the march, the first day of Jan. 62, and the boys are all in good spirits and feel well. Yesterday morning we struck tents and started about ten o'clock for Gallatin, we had to march about five miles before we struck the pike road, over a very rough road, and a poor country, but after we came on to the pike the country was better, and as we neared Gallatin, there was some handsome plantations. Gallattin has been a handsome place, but the ravages of war, have striped it of all it's beauty, so that it looks like a dessolated country, there is not much business done, except with the army, and the fields are striped of the fences, wherever any of the regments camp. Last night we camped along by the side of the ninth Ohio, and the eighty seventh Ind. reg. so the whole of our Brigade is together again, except three or four companies, as soon as we get together, we will start for Nashville or somewhere in Dixie. We are camped on a meadow near a place called Pilot Knob, on the Nashville road about six miles from Gallatin.

It is quite pleasant weather at present, it has not froze ~~one~~ any for the last three or four nights, the sun shines out as warm as spring. I have seen a number of flocks of wild pigeons, and the robins and blue birds sing as they do any time in Minn, but I see that you are having a good winter so far in Minn. I received a letter from you last night, that you wrote the 25th

Nov, it was not put into the office untill Dec 13th[.] I expect that it was mislaid somehow or other, but I was glad to get it as it was. I see that you have payed the interest on the land, and ten dollars on the reaper, by selling the reaper for five dollars, I am glad that you got rid of it, I suppose that there is about ten dollars more due on it, if you have payed Partch in cattle, you can nearly pay all of our small debts by spring, the first of next month there will be fifty two dollars due me from "Uncle Sam," I do not know when we will get our pay, but when we do I will try to spare 45 or 50 dollars of it, you wrote that you had just received my letter, which was written while we were in the mountains near Pelham, so it seems that some of my letters do not go straight through, any more than some of yours. I have not heard of any movements in the army for the last week, it seems to be all quiet again, but how long it will remain so we cannot tell, it seems as though the rebels were strongly fortified at Fredericksburgh, they may have to wait for new events to turn up before moving again at that point, we may have a big fight near Murfresboro before long, but there is no knowing, anything about it, but we will wait for the events of war. I cannot think of much to write this time, perhaps I shall get a letter from you to night, if I do I will write some more in this before I send it away, the mail came in but no letter for me so I will bid you all a good bye again, this from your husband and father with a kiss for all, (kiss)

D. B. Griffin.

Letter Number 63

Gallatin Tenn. Dec. 28th 1862

My Dear Wife and Children,

I will try to get a few lines written to you to night, but I do not know when I can send it away, for there has not been any mail sent off for the last two or three days, on account of the track being torn up between here and Green river, but I believe that it is fixed up again, and the men that tore it up caught, so we will get some mail again before long.

I am well today, and have been all the time since I last wrote to you, the 23d. On the morning of the 24th we were called out at two o'clock and got our breakfast and was ready to start at three, but we did not go untill five, we marched to Gallatin by day light, and halted[.] It was rumored that Morgan was agoing to make an attack on Gallatin, but he did not come on, so we marched back to camp again, arriving there at twelve o'clock. Our Co. went out on picket at three. I was up all night, my post was up close to a house, and as it was Christmas Eve, the Negroes had a dance in their quarters, they appeared to be very happy. I saw them dance some, and talked with them some, but one thing I will tell you I am a <u>republican</u>, but not an <u>abolitionist</u>. We were on picket all day so we kept <u>sober</u> all day, but there was quite a jolly time in camp, but all went off very quiet, and we went to bed thinking that we would have a good night's sleep, but we were disapointed, for we were ordered up at one o'clock, and ordered to have evry thing ready to move in an hour and a half, we were ready in time, but did not start untill five o'clock, when we started for Gallatin where we arrived just at day light, and went into camp, about one mile south of Gallatin, in a very pleasent piece of timber and a dry place, we had barely got our tents up, and cleaned up the camp when it commenced raining, it rained all the afternoon and through the night, and was showery all day yesterday, but the sun set clear and red, and it cleared of cold, but not so as to freeze any, but this morning we had a white frost and foggy but it cleared away and we had a pleasent day to day. I have washed and cleaned up some, but I could not clean up as much as I wanted to for I had not got a change, but we have sent for more clothes, and are expecting them evry day. Yesterday we could hear heavy canonading in the direction of Nashville, during the afternoon, and we have heard to night that there was a skirmish on the Nolinsville pike, and our men succeeded in Capturing two pieces of artillery, and a number of prisoners but no news of certainty as yet. Our Brigade is left here, and the rest, or a portion of the Division has gone back towards Lexington Ky, to drive Humphrey Marshal[*] if they can do so, it is reported that he is advancing on that place, but as we do not receive any mail from that way, we do not know what is agoing on in the North or East, I hope the mail will soon come in again. As I have no news to write to night I will stop now and finish up this letter as soon as I can send it off, so good night one and all.

Tuesday the 30th   I am well to day but am pretty tired as you must know, by what we have been doing. We had a batallion drill of two hours and a noncommissioned officers drill of one hour in the afternoon yesterday, and evrything passed of quiet untill after we had all got to bed, when the news came that some of the rebels were crossing the river about three miles from here, the 2nd Minn. and the 9th Ohio and two pieces of artillery were ordered to go out and watch for them to come along, we started about ten o'clock, and went through fields and pastures around a by way, about three miles, we got there about twelve o'clock, when we were ordered to lay down behind a fence and keep perfectly still, but it was hard work for them to keep still for it rained some and it was quite cool, but we lay there untill daylight this morning, when we came back to camp, again we had but just broke ranks when we were ordered to "fall" in" again, we fell in, and stacked arms, and swallowed a few mothfuls of breakfast, and started again, we marched and countermarched around all the forenoon, but we did not get a sight of a rebel, there was a few rounds of artillery fired off at the river, but they did not attempt to cross over to this side, if they had we should have given them a warm reception I will assure you, for we have been a fooling around after them a good while without seeing any of them, we came back into camp about noon, got our dinner, and lay down and took a nap, it rained some this afternoon and the wind whirled around into the North west, and blew very hard and chilly, so it is quite cool this evening, we have not had any news, nor any mail yet, we expect a mail through to morrow. I hope that we shall have a

---

[*] CSA Gen. Humphrey Marshall, serving under Gen. Braxton Bragg.

good night's sleep to night, for we will have to go on picket in a day or two again. The year 1862 is almost gone and we are still at war with the south. I did not think one year ago, that we should not see one another before 1863, but so it seems, I wonder if another year will pass in the same way, I dare not hope any differently, for fear our hopes will not be realized, I hope that you will spend a happy New year, which I wish you all. I will not write any more to night for it is cold and I am sleepy, and I cannot send it away if I get it finished. So good night Nerva, and the babies, & Mary & babies.

Jan 1st, 1863

Dear Wife and family, I wish you all a "happy New Year." I am having one, and I hope that you are all well and happy this afternoon. It is warm and pleasent today here and we are having a fine time of it in the regiment, there is a good many of the boys that feel their <u>whiskey</u> pretty well, the Major, he who was our Captain, gave a treat to our Co, and there is a good deal of it brought in to the Co. besides, but I have not got any money so I can go without which I prefer by far. Whiskey is sold at two dollars a quart, and it goes just as quick as it would at sixty cents a gallon, with them that has got the money and drink whiskey, they are all very quiet so far, there has not been but one or two fights, and they were in another company. We had a regimental review and inspection in the forenoon yesterday, and muster in the afternoon, it was quite cool all day but pleasent, and to day it is quite pleasent and warm, it froze some last night. We have got to go out on picket to night, and I hope that it will be warmer for we are not allowed to have any fire while on "post," we have not got any mail from the North yet, and it is not certain when we will get any, for the rebels have broke up the rail road at Elizabethtown, and taken possession of the place, it is about forty-five miles this side of Louisville, but if the river raises so that boats can run up to Nashville, it will not do as much damage, it is reported that they were having a fight near Murfresboro[*] yesterday, our men driving them slowly, but not without a loss on our side, but we have not seen the report yet. I have not any more news to write to day so I will end this letter and put it in the office, so that if the mail should go out before I come of picket it will go with it so I will end by wishing you all a good bye hopeing that we shall see another before another New Year, good bye all, from

D. B. Griffin.

Letter Number 64

Gallatin, Tenn. Jan. 9th 1863

My Dear Affectionate Wife and Children,

I will try and get a few lines written to you this morning, so as to let you know how I am, and where we are at this time. I am well this morning and in good spirits. We are still in camp near Gallatin where we have been for the last two weeks, but I do not suppose you have received my last two letters, as the mail has been stopped ever since Christmas, but it has commenced going again, we received a mail on Wednesday, and I got a letter from you dated the 15th Dec. in which I learned that you were all well, and enjoying yourself as well as you can. I suppose that Em. was there with you Christmas and New Years, but you will see by my letters where I was on both days, but you may believe that I thought of you all a good many times, through the day, as I do evry day of my life, and see you in my dreams at night, as well as Mother brothers and sisters. I was a dreaming the other night about Vermont, and my folks, when I called "Mariah" so loud that it woke up some of the boys in the tent, and myself to, but you was there to. It is so far from here to Minn. that it would not pay me to go home on a furlough, but I hope that it will not be many months before I

---

[*] Battle of Stones River, December 31 – January 2, 1863, pitting part of Union Gen. Rosecrans's Army of the Cumberland against CSA Gen. Braxton Bragg's Army of Tennessee.

can go home for good, <u>if I live</u> through the war[.] I do not think that it will be a great many months before you will see me there. There has been a hard battle of five days duration at Murfreesboro and according to all accounts it is the hardest fought battle of the war, but Gen. Rosecrans has succeeded in routing them out of their strong hold, but not without a heavy loss on our side, but he is still following them up some ten or fifteen miles beyond Murfreesboro. We have not seen any official account of the fight yet. I am thankful that we were lucky enough to ~~escape~~ escape, being the fight, for it has brought death and destruction to the homes of thousands of the soldiers who sacrificed their homes and friends and all that was dear to them on earth, and enlisted under the stars and stripes in order to save the Union as it was from the hands of the Southern Traitors. I hope that it will never be my lot to be in any such a battle, as they have had at Murfreesboro[.] I see by the papers that Vicksburg is in our possession, but we cannot credit any reports untill they are given Officially, if it should prove to be true, the Miss. river is open again, I hope they are true. It seems that they are ~~not~~ doing little or nothing in the east, I expect that the western army will have to go there and help them fight before they will do anything towards taking Richmond, but there is no us of fretting for we are here, and have got to await the movements of the Government. You wanted that I should tell you whether the Government could keep us for a longer term than three years if the war lasted longer than that[.] They <u>cannot</u> keep us any longer than three years, for that is the extent of the time of the Presidents call for Volunteers, but they can keep us three years if the war does not end, but if the war should end to morrow, or next week they could not keep us any longer than the war lasts if it ends within the three years, but <u>three years</u> is the longest time that they can keep us if the war does not end before that time, so you may look for me <u>home</u> in "<u>eighteen</u> <u>months</u>" if I live till then, if folks tell you to the contrary notwithstanding.

We have had a day or two of cold weather, but it has come of very pleasant to day, but I see that you have had a fine winter in Minn thus far[.] I hope that you will not have as cold weather after this time of the year as you did last year, but if you do, I do not think you will suffer as much with the cold as you did last winter. I am in hopes that I shall be at home by another winter at fartherest, if I am permitted to live and come home at any time. I think that there will be a "Thanksgiving day" for us all[.]"

We have had pretty heavy Guard and Picket duty to do for the last two weeks, for a part of our Division has been gone on detatched duty, our Co. went on Picket New years day, then on the fifth day, and we have got to go out to night and then they come on guard evry fourth day, in camp, but it does not come quite so hard on me, for I do not come on guard quite as often as the privates do, but when we are out on picket I have to be up all night as a general thing, but the Division is a getting together again, and we will be apt to move from here in a few days, towards the front, probably towards Chatanoga. The river is up now so that boats have commenced running to Nashville, so that the breaking up of the rail road by Morgan's men, will not put us back much. Morgan has been run back acrosst the river again, we get our mail by the way of Nashville now, but the rail road will soon be fixed up again, and we will get it by rail again, soon. I hope that the mail will not be cut off again while we are here.

I wish that Em. would write a letter to me and let me know where he is and what they have been a doing and what they are expecting to do. I see that the thirty Eight Indians were hung at Mankato last month[.] I hope that the indians will not bother the setlers of Minn. again very soon if ever. You must let me know how fathers folks get along this winter, it is such a bother for me to write this winter that I do not write to any one only you, but as it gets warmer I may get time to write to others if they will write to me. I have not had a letter from any one else this winter. Have you paid the taxes, or have you got enough money by you to pay them. We have not got our pay yet, there is four months pay due us, when I do get it, I will send all that I can spare of it, to you, so if you should get short a few dollars, you need not be afraid to borrow some if you can get it. You just tell <u>Mary</u> that I guess if I was there, I would find some place to sleep, besides down cellar, if we had to sleep as thick as "<u>three</u>" in a bed," but if it gets warm weather before I get home, I can take a blanket, and sleep out of dorss.

There is five Negroes in the guard house, for burning up two houses and trying to rape a young woman, they are in irons[.] I do not know what will be done with them, but probably some of them will be shot, there is a white man implicated with them, that belongs to the 35 Ohio, the blacks do not belong to this regiment, and I am glad of it. I cannot think of much more to write and as I have got to go out, at 3 o'clock, on picket, I will have to close for this time. I hope that Alice and Ida will have a good school and that they will learn fast for it will be as good a chance for them to go to school as they will have for some time to come. I see your "<u>faces</u>" almost evry day, and they look just the same as they did when I came away, except little 'Edgars[.]' I can see nothing in his little fat face that looks natural, but then he has ~~grown~~ grown so much that he has <u>run</u> out of my sight. I would give almost anything to see you all again, but I must wait patiently untill my time comes. If you get any news from Vermont let me know. How does "Hill" and Mrs "Limber" get along <u>together</u> this winter, do you suppose that they are <u>near</u> and dear to each other, are they married, what is Chipman adoing this winter and all of the rest of the folks around there. I will send you a list of the prices in Georgia[.] I should think that Spring Valley was hard up if they could not furnish one pair of shoes. Are you not afraid that the mice will get at your things in the shanty, while you are gone from them, but you have fixed them up as well as you could I know. All of the boys are well as far as I know, give my respects to all of my friends in Minn. and take a large share of my <u>love</u> <u>yourself</u>, tell Alice that she must write to me as often as she can and let me know how she gets along in school this winter, and what books she is a studying and who is in the class with her and Ida too. I must stop for want of time, so you must excuse all mistakes and except these few lines from your husband and father in Tenn, hoping that I shall soon be with you all again, so Good bye one and all for this time,

Corp. D. B. Griffin.
To "Nerva" Griffin)
   Alice Griffin)
                    Spring Valley Fillmore Co. Minnesota
   Ida   Griffin)
& Edgar Griffin)

Letter Number 65

Gallatin Tennessee Jan. 18th 1863

My Dear "Nerva" and <u>babies</u>,

I will try to write a few lines to you this afternoon. I am well this afternoon as I have been all the time since my last, (the 9th)[.] I went out on picket that night and it rained hard most all night, but it came off clear the next day, and warm. On the eleventh I received a letter from you and Samuel, I was glad to receive one if there was not but a few lines. I like to hear from home and from Vt. to. I should have thought that Samuel could have told where Henry was as well as the rest of the boys from Essex. I have written a long letter to him since I received one from him but probably he did not receive it, or he has written to me and I have not received his but I am glad that he did not enlist, for there is more of us in the army now than I wish there was, not because it is wrong, but because the war is carried on through a few political leaders, if a Democrat is at the head of an army, the republicans are not satisfied with their movements, and 'vice versa,' and so it goes on, superceeding one here and one there, and giving none of them a chance to do as they would, and the soldiers have to be content with all their movements. It seems by what news we can get, that the union army has met with a repulse at Vixburgh instead of a victory, and we have not gained a great deal at Murfreesboro, although evry thing is kept out of the papers that would give us any satisfaction, and we have not had any papers since the 14th, for the water took off a small bridge between here and Nashville, and the road is not open to Louisville as yet. I went upon guard the twelfth and was intending to set down the next day, my 32nd birth and our eleventh wedding day, and have a good long talk with you and yours but things so turned out that I did not write any and the weather has been such that I have not written since. We received orders at 12 o'clock to march, taking evry thing with us, at three o'clock in the morning of the 13th. I did not sleep a wink, the regiment were up at a short notice and soon the camp fires were burning lustily through the camp, and all had their breakfast eat, and knapsacks packed, tents struck and ready to march by time, we got under motion about four o'clock, and headed towards Nashville, the 2nd Minn. in the rear. I was on guard and we had to guard the prisoners four, two soldiers, and two negroes, the negroes were chained, with a chain and ball, the ball weighed 24 lbs, three of the negroes that were in the guard house, made their escape the night before I went on guard, we marched about fifteen miles on a good pike road, and through a very good country, we passed through one small place, about the size of Spring Valley, called "Sandersville," we got into camp about one o'clock, and got pretty well rested, the wind blowing hard from the east or south east. I went to bed, and slept sound, we were called up in the morning at "reville," and ordered to go back to Gallatin, the 2nd Minn, and the 87th Ind, the new reg. that joined us at Louisville, we were ready and started in about one hour, the other two reg, the 9th and 35th Ohio going on to Nashville. We had not marched but a little while before it commenced to rain, and it rained hard all day, but we all managed to keep quite dry by having rubber blankets and coats. We went into camp about three o'clock, one mile east of Gallatin we struck our tents, and got straw for our beds, which was quite handy, and got up a pile of rails for fire wood, and got into our tents, and stayed there the rest of the night, for it rained hard all night, but in the morning of the 15th the wind changed into the North, and it began to snow and rain and it kept it up all day, untill it froze into snow and snow fell about six inches deep, it did not stop storming untill the next morning, the 16th and the wind blew cold all day long, it is the worst storm that we have had since we have been in the South it raised the Cumberland river about eleven feet in two days, but yesterday was some warmer but still it did not thaw any, to day it has thawed a considerable, but still it is quite winter weather to night, but it will not last long I think, for the wind is in the south east now, but we are better off than thousands who are on the march, and without their tents, we have good fires and a plenty to eat such as it is, these two regiments are kept pretty busy standing picket and guard, around Gallatin, some of the boys coming on evry third day. I cannot tell how long we shall be here, but perhaps not long, we have not had any mail for a few days, nor has there any gone out, I do not know when this will go out, as it is quite chilly in the tent now I will stop writing for to night.

Jan. 20th

Well, as the mail is agoing to go out to night I will try to write a few more lines to you to day. I am as well as usual this morning. It is a wet slopy morning for it rained amost all night, and the snow is allmost all gone off, but it is not very cold so we get along first rate, it is foggy and some misty, a regular spring morning, but I expect that you are having pretty hard weather about this time in Minn, but I hope that you do not suffer any for the cold weather this winter, for I think you have enough to contend with without suffering with the cold. Yesterday was the aniversary of the battle of ~~the~~ Mill Springs ~~fight~~ and we were intending to have had a supper in grand style. Major Davis went to Louisville for stuff for the supper, but he did not get back, we shall probably have one when he does get back. We were called out yesterday morning under arms, with the expectation of being attacked by a band of Morgan's men, but they did not show themselves, so the day passed off like all of the rest of the time, we all getting our meals and answering to our names at roll call, and so the time passes along from day to day, & from month to month, untill a year soon passes off, little did I expect at my last birth day, that I should be in the army this birth day, but so it is, and I do not see anything to give us any reason to think we shall not be in the same shape another year if we are alive and well, but I hope that something will turn up between this and the first of July, that will let us know what is agoing to be done[.] I wish that I could be at home by that time, don't you, "Nerva?" you say "yes, I do, you know I do, without asking me." May God answer our prayers, and let our wishes be granted, and may we all be again permitted to live together on this earth an unbroken family, if not permitted to, I know that we shall all meet in heaven. I would like to be there and attend some of the meetings with you, for I know that I should be greatly interested in the sermons. I hope that you can go, and that the folks will be able to keep up the meetings[.] I am willing that you should take any paper that you want to take and as many, I do not know when we will get our pay, but I hope before long for I am afraid that you will want some money. I have sent to Louisville by Charles Russell, to get me a watch, that will cost from $15. to $20.00 if he gets one, I cannot send quite as much to you, but I will send you some as soon as I get any myself. It is raining some to day. I hear that the cars are a going to run through to Louisville to day, if so we may get our mail regularly once more. I hope that you get all off my letters I know that I do not receive all of yours, but I do not blame you for it. I wish that you would tell me where Emery's Co. is stationed this winter. I ask you a good many questions which you have answered and the letters do not get to me untill after I ask you again so you must not blame me for it, will you. I must stop for want of room

D. B. Griffin

Letter Number 66

In Camp near Nolinsville Tenn Feb 5/63

My Dear Wife and Children,

As it has been sometime since I last wrote to you, (some three weeks,) I will try to write a few lines to you all to day. I am well to day, and have been so ever since I last wrote. We have had a good deal of wet, cold and bad weather and it is not over with yet. Since I last wrote to you, we have been around the country a considerable. In the first place while we were at Gallatin, I went out on picket in the place of one of the privates, about three miles from Gallatin, on an out post. In the evening a negro came in with a report that there was about twenty guerrillas met together (without arms) some ten or twelve miles from there. So the Cavelry officer asked us if four of us would go along with them, out there, so I volunteered to go with the rest. We got ready to start out about nine o'clock, when we mounted our horses and put off, we went about four miles on the turnpike, then we left that and went through the country, letting down the fences, and opening gates &c for about six miles, stopping at a few houses on the route and searching for arms, we found a couple of rifles and a pistol or two, but when we had got within about two miles of the place where the gurrillas were, we learned that there was about eighty of them there, and that they were all armed, so we concluded that our force was not strong enough to attack them, there being only seven of us, that we would not go any farther, so we stoped in a negro's hut and warmed us a while, then started on our way back, we all got along first rate, until we got back onto the turnpike, when we thought we would try the speed of our horses, after running a short distance, the horse that I was upon, stumbled and fell, throwing me "end over appetite" and the horse was going so fast, that he ended over "end for end" and fell upon my leg, and when he got up, my foot was twisted and cought in the stirrup, and my head was on the ground, but as he stood still, I got up all right, and as fate would have it I was not hurt much, my wrist was quite lame for a day or two and also my thigh, but nothing more. We had a fine ~~lagh~~ laugh about my horse turning a samerset, and my being initiated in the Cavelry[.]

In two or three days after that our Co. and three others and three ~~Co.p~~ Com's in the 87th Indiana, were ordered to be ready to march at three o'clock in the morning. We were up and ready in time, and started for the Lebanon ford, we got there just at the break of day, about four miles, we got acrosst the river in canoe's and on flat boats, we went about three miles on that side of the river, away back into a cornfield and were ordered to dig in such a ravine, we did so, and what do you suppose we found. We found ninety barrels of <u>lard</u>, that was burried there by the rebels over a year ago. We dug them out and pressed in teams and hauled it to the river, and it was nearly all sent to Nashville. Just as we got ready to start back it set in to raining, and it rained about as hard as they generaly let it, we got back to camp about eight o'clock, wet and cold, but we had our ration of whiskey and got into bed and soon got warm, and slept sound, untill morning. On the morning of the 29th I went out on picket about 2 ½ miles from camp, we had not been out there an hour, when the order came for us to go back to camp for we were ordered to Nashville, we went back, got our dinner and packed up as soon as we could, and marched down to the depot, got on the cars, and soon the old Iron horse started we were about two hours in going, to Nashville 26 miles, we went out about one mile from the City, and camped, as the teams did not get through untill about ten o'clock, we slept without our tents, the next day we started about two o'clock to go out on the Nolinsville pike. We marched through the City by the ~~step~~ music of the martial and bugle band. We marched about ten miles, pitched our tents amongst the rocks on the old Murfersboro pike, the next morning we crossed over the country on to the Nolinsville pike, we got there just at dark, and were ordered to get ready to march immediately with two days rations in our haversacks, we got evry thing ready, and it commenced raining, and we expected to have a hard night, but the order was countermanded, and we pitched our tents and lay down in our blankets listening to the rain falling upon the tent, and thankful that we did not march. In the morning we woke up at revelle, and found that the water was running through the tent and right under where I lay, but as we had our oil cloths under us, we were dry, we got our breakfast and started in the rain for a two days tramp without our tents, we went as far as Nolinsville, 5 miles, then took a road towards Franklin, we went as far as the Willson pike, that night, and camped near a fine house which belongs to secesh, we had traveled through the rain and mud, and it had turned around cold. We had orders not to burn any more rails <u>than we wanted</u>, so we soon had a plenty of fire, got our coffee eat our crackers, and as there was a big pile of lumber there, we went to work and built us a shanty, and lay down to sleeppp we kept a fire all night, and kept warm, we started for the Franklen pike, we came on to it about eight miles from Nashville, it was froze quite hard, we went on that pike a few miles towards Nashville, then struck acrosst the country and came back to our camp about noon, when we were ordered to move camp as soon as we could get dinner[.] We came into this camp in the afternoon and have been here ever since, three days now. We are camped about twelve miles from Nashville and about four from Nolinsville, on a creek called "Mill Creek," on a farm owned by a Col. Battle[*], he was in the Battle of Mill Spring in the rebel army. I think that he is a Gen. now. We do not spare the fences at all yesterday the teams went out and got some potatoes, so I had a mess for breakfast the first that I have had for a long time, they went first rate but they are not such potatoes as we raise in Minn. I expect that the next move we make will be to join the other Brigades in this Division and go to the front, but I cannot tell how soon it will be. We were expecting this morning to go on a scouting expedition to day, but as it rained and snowed we did not go out, the snow is not all gone off yet, and it is so cold, that I have to stop every little while and warm me. I should have written to you before if it had been warmer when we were in camp, for I know that you look anxiously for a letter from me when the mail comes in, and I have tried to write often so you must overlook my neglect this time, and if it is warm enough to write, I will write oftener, although I have not received a letter from you since the one you sent Christmas day Samuel's and yours together, and you better believe that when the mail come's in I am on hand to see if there is one for me, but I get the answer "<u>none</u>," and I feel like droping a secret tear, for it

---

[*] CSA Col. Joel A. Battle, serving under Gen. Zollicoffer.

seems strange that my letters do not come through as well as others. You know well enough that I do not blame you for <u>not</u> writing for I know that you <u>do</u> write as often as you can. I have thought of you a great deal of late, and some nights I dream all night about <u>you</u> and the children and the rest of the folks in Minn. and away back in Vermont[.] I am afraid that you are not well, all of you, or that something does not go well with you all, but I shall try to wait patiently untill I hear. The regiment is about as healthy now as it ever was, there being a very few in the Hospital at present. "Pete" and the other boys that you know are well[.] I see by all accounts from Minn that the Indians are intending to make another raid in the spring, but I hope that the Government will take steps to stop them before they go to far, for I think that the country has got about as much to tend to now, as it wants. We have not got our pay yet, but we expect to get it in a few days, I hope so for I expect that you want some to pay your taxes with, let me know how much the taxes are[.] It is so cold and it is getting long into the afternoon, so I will have to bid you all good bye once more hoping that I shall soon hear from you all, so Good bye "Nerva" and the babies, and all the rest,

D. B. Griffin

Letter Number 67

In Camp near Concord church Tenn. Feb. 13/63

My dear Wife and Children,

I will again write a few lines to you, as it is a very pleasent day and I feel first rate too. I am as well to day as I have been for a good while, but still I have not been sick any. I was just weighed and I weighed 162 lbs so you can see that I am not very poor in flesh. I received a letter from you three days ago, but I could not get a chance to write untill this afternoon. It was dated Jan 28th, just one month from the time the last one that I got from you, and you can assure yourself that I was glad to hear from you, and to hear that you were all well, for I was afraid that some of you were sick, for I had heard that it was quite sickly there, with the fever and measles, but it seems as though you had escaped them, but I shall expect to hear that some of you get the measles before spring[.] I have forgotten whether Alice ever had them or not, but, I thought that Henry was old enough to have them before this time. I did not know that Eliza, lived at Fathers this winter. It seems by your letter that you had written to me, since Emery came home, but I did not get any, you merely say that he had gone back to the Fort, and that he was at home most four weeks, but where he is, or what Co. or Reg. he belongs to, I cannot find out. I presume that you have told me in some of the letters that I have not received, but if he does not think enough of me to write a few lines to me, and let me know where he is, it will save my writing any to him, how does he like <u>to 'be a 'soldier</u>," and how does he stand it. There is some talk of this Reg. being called home, in the Spring, if the Indians should again make a raid into Minnesota, but I do not build any hopes upon such rumors. I hope the Indians will not make another attempt to drive out the whites, for the people of Minn. have already got enough to do to take care of themselves and friends, while this war with a traitorous south is in the country, but if they should raise I think that the Second could do <u>as well</u> as the third did, while they were there, that is if they could get as many <u>furloughs</u> as they did, but I hope that we should not get the name that they have got, for "plundering" amongst friends, it is bad enough to plunder from your enemies. We do not do as much <u>at that</u>, this winter as we did last, but we get some things in the eatable line, such as poultry, pork, flour, meal, &c. We have had something of the kind in our "mess," all of the time since we have been here[.] I have not been out but once since we came here, and then we went "<u>to mill</u>" to get a grist <u>ground</u> we "<u>drew</u>" the wheat while we were out after forage for the ~~the~~ teams, and the corn we "<u>drew</u>" in one story of the mill, and took it down into the next, and "<u>changed</u>" it for meal, so we came home with quite a grist, and it goes first rate I tell you. We make bread, pancakes, doughnuts, &c, with it. I set some 'risings' this morning, and I made two "<u>good</u>" loves of bread, you

233

need not lough for the boys say that it is "d--- good." I got a good bake on it then I went to work and made a "whole pan full," of sweet nutcakes, and they are good to, for I had some in my coffee for supper and some fresh pork that was "drawn" by one of the boys. I changed off some coffee for butter, so it makes my bread slip down easy[.] I have sold about three dollars worth of coffee, this winter, but I drink coffee again, now, and do not have so much to spare as I did. I do not think you have drank much tea, nor had things very sweet, if you have not had but one lb of tea, and one dollar's worth of sugar since I came away, but I expect that you have had some good sorghum molasses to sweeten "pies & thing." I wish that I had been there yesterday, so as to have gone to the Donation visit, but all that I could do was to think of you all day, for I was out on picket all day, so you must enjoy yourself as well as you can in your visits, and hope for better times to come. I know that you cannot help worrying some about me, but you must not believe the reports that you hear, untill you are certain that they are true. Do you know what Jery, is a doing this winter. I hear that Amelia Postle has got a boy, you know that they was not agoing to have any any babies, for a "good while" no sir, is there any more young soldiers about there this winter. I should like to be there some of these evenings, and "snap" some corn with the children, and play with them in it, on the floor too, does Mary's boy and your's have any "fights" with each other, I expect that your's will throw hers down, how is it Mary? I hope that Dan will manage to get out there in the spring, and get him a home of his own, if he is able to, if not he can do as well out there as he can in Vermont. I was glad to hear that Mother and her family were well. I hope that they will not any of them come out there before I get home if I live, to get home. Did your wheat keep good this winter, have you let out your farm yet if so how did you let it out, do you have any trouble in getting your wood and getting it cut. We expect to get our pay the first of next week, for the pay Master is here now, and I will send you a part of your "salary" in my next letter if we get our pay before I write, and I hope that you will get it all safe. I did not get me any watch this time, but I may get one before the next pay day. I hope that we shall not get payed off but once more and that before long too. I do not think that it is best for you to send any paper to me, for I do not get all of your letters, if there should be any short pieces in them that you want that I should read, cut them out and put them in your letters. I will stop writing for to night for the boys have all gone to bed and it is a getting a little chilly so good night all of you,

D. B. Griffin

Saturaday Feb 14th

I will try to write a few more lines to you this morning. It is not quite as pleasent to day as it was yesterday, it rains a little and it looks as though it was agoing to rain a good deal. You wanted to know if my views regarding slaves were any different now than it was before I came away. I told you that I was not an Abolitionist, that is I am not in favor of freeing the slaves, and let them run at large through the country, for they are deceitfull as a race, but I think that the President's proclamation is a good thing as regards the cripeling of the rebellion, but we have got to conquer the country, before we can take the slaves away, or set them free, and I think that we can do it, if our leaders are true to us. There is evidently something going to be done before long, both here, at Vicksburg and at the Rapahannock, and I hope that it will be a decisive blow. We are all very anxious to have the war ended, and go home, but not in disgrace, if the country needs us, we are willing to stand by it as long as life lasts, but we want it to make some effort towards ending this war, but perhaps we cannot see what is the best just now. I cannot think of much more to write now, so I will wait untill after the mail comes in, and if there is any letter for me, or any news I will write some more[.] 3 o'clock, no mail for me, nor any news s[o] I will finish this and send it of. It has been a raining quite hard. Write as often as you can, for I may get once in a while a letter from you if you do. I will try to write often. I do not know when we will move from here. I must stop for this time, so good bye one and all, hopeing that we shall soon meet one another, again, good bye

D. B. Griffin

Letter Number 68

In Camp near Concord meeting house Tenn. Feb 18/63

My Dear Wife and Children,

As it is quite a dull day, and we do not have to drill any to day, I thought that I would try and write a few lines to you. I am as well as usual to day. We have had a good deal of rain since I last wrote to you, so that the streams are up and it is very muddy at the present time, but I have not been out of camp, and we are camped on a dry place, so we get along first rate[.] We have a plenty to eat, drink and wear, but we do not get any money yet, nor I have not learned when we will get any, perhaps not for some time yet. I think that it is to bad that we cannot have some to send to our families, many of them are in want, and they are depending on the money that their husbands, fathers and friends send to them from the army. If we do not get our pay before the first of March, there will be six months pay due me, but I do not know whether we should get payed for six months or for only four.

We do not get much news for the last few days, but we get enough to show us that there is agoing to be something done somewhere, in a short time, probably at Charleston, Vicksburgh, or some, great point. I do not hardly think that there will be much fighting done here. It is rumored that the rebels are a leaving Tallahoma, and going to Vicksburgh, if true then we need not look for any battle on this side of the Tennessee river, perhaps at Chattanoga or Corinth but I hope that we will not be called upon to fight again, while in the service. There has been a great many troops landed in Nashville ~~for~~ within the last two weeks, but where their destination is we do not know, and perhaps it is not for us to know just yet.

We have had the monotony of the few last days broken, by a little exploit of Co. H. Last Sunday Co. H. was detailed with a Co. of the ninth O. reg. to go along with a foraging train, they were out beyond Nolinsville, some five miles from here, when a part of the teams stopped at a house in order to load up some corn, and fourteen of Co. H. were left with them as guard, the rest of the Co and the ninth O. Co went on to another place with the rest of the teams. In a short time a Negro came to the Sergeant and told him that there was some rebels acoming over a hill, so they were on the sharp look out, but they kept on a loading up the teams. In a short time two Co.'s of Wheelers (rebel) Cavelry came charging down the hill, with their hats a swinging, and they a shouting, "Surrender you G -- d --- Yankees." Some of the boys asked the Sergeant what they should do, he replied "fight them" boys "go in on your own hook," so they secured themselves in and around some old corncribs, and when they, (the rebels) got down into a lane close to them, they opened fire on them, emtying a number of saddles, the first fire, they kept up a brisk fire on both sides for about fifteen minutes, when the rebels withdrew, taking with them the most of their wounded, but leaving four or five on the field, together with several dead horses and loose horses. As soon as the way was clear, our men came out and got away with all the teams, except one mule that was shot, and not a man hurt to amount to anything, one or two being slightly scratched with a spent ball, they brought in three of the rebs, prisoners and two or three horses, the rest of the Co. did not get to them untill after the <u>fourteen</u> had driven them back there was, one hundred and twenty five of the rebels. We had an order read to us on dress parade last night, from the Col. Comanding the Brigade[*], commending them very highly, telling them that it was one of the most darring resistance and brilliant defeats that has happened during the war. I hope that the 2nd Minn will do as well if ever called into action as that little handfull of men did on that occasion, there was a squad

---

[*] Complimentary Orders of Col. Ferdinand Van Derveer, Appendix 14, *The Story of a Regiment*, Judson W. Bishop.

went out the next day and they found a number of wounded at a house near by which were paroled, they wounded some fifteen or eighteen, some mortally. So you can see that we have never learned to surrender as yet. Day before yesterday one of the boys kicked a "shell" into the fire that had been laying around camp ever since we came here, it had not lain there but a few moments, when it burst with a very loud report, throwing pieces in evry direction through the camp, but as fortune would have it no one was hurt, it is almost a mericle too for there was boys standing around the fire[.] I hapened to be a looking right towards it when it burst, so I know how one looks, it was a twelve lb shell. As to other things, in the reg., every day is alike when we are in camp. We get up at day light, get our breakfast, (we all cook for ourselves), then dinner and supper, when the weather permits, we have to drill two hours a day, and come out on dress prarade at sundown. We read what books and papers we can get hold off, and watch the mail when it comes in (if perchance there is one, and it comes nearly evry day now,) for a letter from our loved ones at home, and set around the fire or in our tents and talk over old times, and the topics of the day, and wishing that the war would end so we could go home once more, but we do not desire "Peace on any terms," as some of the Northern "Copperheads*" wish it. I hope that such men will be obliged to come into the army and fight for their country as we have done, and then see if they would be willing to give up the Honor of the country for the sake of "peace," such men do more towards encouraging the South, than they would if they were in arms against us, they are foul Traitors, and ought not to be allowed to utter their Treason at large. We all of us desire peace, but rather than have the Union broken up, and the Constitution trampled upon by the nation, we are willing to fight untill the last for the maintainence of the Union and Constitution, but I will not say more.

I received a letter from you yesterday, dated Jan 5th, 6th &c, so you see that they come through after a long time[.] I was

---

* Those known as "Copperheads" were antiwar "Peace Democrats," named after the venomous snake.

glad to get it to, for I see that you had written a little about your affairs with Hill, and I was glad that you got along with him as well as you did, for I do not believe that he is worthy of the name of "Man," most noble work of God." I am glad that Father took your part in settling with him. You said that he payed you for pounding "rosa," tell me all about it, wont you? I hope that his oxen got fat. How does your oxen get along, are they not getting old, if they are had you not better sell them in the spring, or summer and buy a younger pair, you can talk with Father about it, and do as he thinks best with them. I would not fret about that debt of Partch'es for it is not on interest I think, and if you have not got any cattle that he wants let him wait, you need not pay him any money, before I come home.

I do not think that it would be best for you to move back [to*] the claim in the spring, that is if you and Mary can agree [to*] live together, next summer, for it will cost you both less for wood and the like, by being together, and I think that father will see to the place, if you are not there, just as well as he would, if you were there, and he would have less to see too, besides if you can raise enough on the place for you to eat, I will try to save enough out of my wages, for you to use to get your other things with, and to keep our little debts down, &c, &c. I am glad that you got the letter with the rings, I have not got any shells now, but if I can get hold of some I will try and make you one, and also one for the girls, if that one is the right sise for them give it to them, together, and then if I can get another one you can fix them all up right. I am glad that all of the babies remember me enough to write a few lines to me. I see that Alice improves in her writing a good deal this winter, she will soon beat her father. I hope that she will be a good schollar and learn fast, does she get many head marks this winter what books does she study, and I guess that Ida is a trying to write some to, that is right Ida learn as fast as you can, and beat Alice if you can, Ma says that you are as large as Alice is. I don't know as I shall know my girls again if I should come home, but I guess that somebody would tell me who they are, and my boy to, I see that he wants to "ite" to pa, to. I cannot tell what it is that he wrote, but I guess that he knows, and someday he will tell me if we both live, he will be two years old by the time this letter gets there and what a two years it has been to us all, I can hardly realize it[.] I hope that we shall soon meet each other, and [then*] we can talk over our adventures, with each other, w[ith*] the interest that we could never realize before. I hope [and*] pray that the time will soon come, let us keep up good cheer and put our trust in a just God, and all will be well in the end. Write as often as you can, and you need not be afraid to tell me all of your trials, for I hope that you can trust me with your secret troubles, if not you can put your trust in God, he has promised to comforts us if we will obey and put our trust in him. I cannot think of much more to write to night, and in fact I have written more than I expected to when I sat down to write. I have not stopped before, but it is dress prarade call now and I must stop untill after dress prarade. I cannot think of any more this time so good bye all,

This from your husband and Father in Tenn.
D B. Griffin
(P. M. Griffin, [kiss] "Nerva")
(A. J. Griffin [kiss])
(Ida M. Griffin [kiss])
(E. L. Griffin [kiss])

---

*Missing words inserted from torn corner.

In and Around Camp Steadman, Triune, Tennessee

Letters 69–85 (March 2–June 20, 1863)

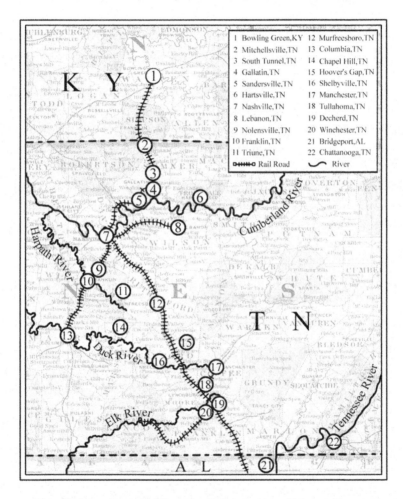

1	Bowling Green,KY	12	Murfreesboro,TN
2	Mitchellsville,TN	13	Columbia,TN
3	South Tunnel,TN	14	Chapel Hill,TN
4	Gallatin,TN	15	Hoover's Gap,TN
5	Sandersville,TN	16	Shelbyville,TN
6	Hartsville,TN	17	Manchester,TN
7	Nashville,TN	18	Tullahoma,TN
8	Lebanon,TN	19	Decherd,TN
9	Nolensville,TN	20	Winchester,TN
10	Franklin,TN	21	Bridgeport,AL
11	Triune,TN	22	Chattanooga,TN
o⊞⊞o Rail Road		⌒ River	

The division moves fifteen miles south to Triune, Tennessee, a heavily fortified headquarters position for their next three months. The 2nd Minnesota, with support, continues down to secure a ford of the Harpath River and is joined by the rest of the brigade on a sweep as far south as Chapel Hill, chasing retreating rebels all the way then circling back to Triune. Brainard mentions sending home some mussel shell rings he made and some cotton seed for them to plant as well as money and various magazines and newspapers. He also writes about camp life, missing his family, the politics of "peace" at home, and that death, desertion, and discharge have reduced his company to forty-three men. Here, the regiment is issued new two-piece shelter tents as well as Enfield rifles to replace their muskets. Occasional contact with Confederate troops keeps them on their guard as they forage and drill. Unable to keep the letters received from home, Brainard expresses his hope that his to Minerva are being saved for review when he returns. He also clarifies several miscommunications resulting from late or missing letters. On the war front, he passes on news of Hooker's defeat at Chancellorsville, Grant's movements against Vicksburg, and the first hints of what will become the Gettysburg Campaign. Brainard's new Division Commander, Gen. Gordon Granger, calls for a "grand review" of all twenty-three regiments, followed by a hard all-night march during a major thunderstorm to Franklin, only to arrive too late to engage the raiding cavalry of Gen. Bedford Forrest. During their final three weeks back at Triune, with more forces arriving for a push south, Brainard continues to write about camp activities and his great longing to be at home with his wife and growing children.

Letter Number 69

Camp near Concord Church Tenn. March 2/63

My Dear Wife and Children,

As we are expecting to move in a day or two from here, I thought that I would write a few lines to you this evening. I am well and hearty this evening, and I hope that you are the same. I received a letter from you to night dated Feb. 20th, in which you had enclosed Samuel's letter. I was glad to hear that you were all well, and that, the folks in Vt. was well when he wrote. I should think that he could tell where Henry is, so that I could write a letter to him. I guess that I shall have to write to him another letter, and ask him a few questions, but it does not do much good, for I cannot get any answer from the last one that I wrort to him. I see that they had a surprise party, I hope that it will be so that you can have a surprise party, before long, if it there should not be any one else there but your humble servant. I received a letter from Em. two days ago, stating that he was well, and enjoying himself first rate. I suppose that you hear from him often. I guess that I have received nearly all of your letters, or the most of them, I do not know as I had ought to say any thing about your letters untill I get them. If you get Samuel's likeness so that you can send it in a letter, send it to me, and I will send it back again to you. I am glad that the folks are kind to you, and I hope that they will receive their reward in doing so. I am glad in my heart that you have good meetings, and a good minister of the Gospel. I hope that you had a good visit, I have said something about it in my other letters. I do not think that Father is a getting very rich in selling town lots, where abouts has Chipman put up his house, does he think of marrying the "schoolmarm" yet. I think that Hill rather beat him, but still he can take the "Old Maid for his "daddy in law," by takeing "Careline[.]" You do not say anything about Allen, whether he is agoing to get a woman, or not, tell him if he will come down here, I will get him as many as he can carry home, but perhaps they are not of the coller complexion that he would wish, we have about a dozen wenches outside the camp, and about 25 "<u>buck</u> <u>niggers</u>" they can all find enough to do, as teamsters, cooks, waiters &c, they have came in under the proclamation, evry regiment has as many or more than we do, I hope that they will all be taken away from the secesh, for it will go a good ways towards cripling the rebellion[.] I see that the Richmond (Jef. Davis'es papers,) begin to look on the dark side of the rebellion. I hope that they will feel the dark part of it, they think that they are in the last stage of the war, that they have got to fight, or die, or give up in shame. I hope that they will soon give up, so that we can all go home, in a short time.

We went out a foraging yestergay, we went some seven miles and some of the roughest country I have seen for a long time, stony and hilly, the boys got some potatoes, hams, chickens, turkeys, eggs, tobacco &c, besides filling the waggons with corn and fodder. I got a few cotton seed, that I will send to you. I think that it will grow in Mary's garden, you must plant it about the same time that they do corn, so that the frost will not kill it all that you will have to do to it is to plant it in the ground. I have been to work on the bridge to day, we finished it all up to night.

In Camp near Tryune Tenn. March 9th 1863

You will see by the date of this letter that we have moved since I commenced to write. I had to drill in the forenoon of the 3d, and in the afternoon we got orders to be ready to march at four o'clock, with two days rations, so I did not get any chance to write that day.

We were all ready and we started with the first Tenn. Cavelry towards the rebels, we marched about fifteen miles that night and came up to the rebel pickets, when we lay down for the rest of the night, our men took a rebel Major, prisoner that night, the next morning we were up at light, and our Cavelry commenced a skirmishing with the enemy, all the while driving them back, they captured about seventy rebel cavelryman, wounding five or six, and taking a large number of horses and mules, about noon we were reinforced with the rest of our brigade, when we started on, we crossed little Harpeth river on trees that we fell across the stream, as the bridge had been burned, we went about six miles more, but did not get into any brush with the rebels, for they skedaddled to fast for us. I had to go on picket that night, it was quite cold, so that it froze hard, but nothing hapened through the night, the next morning, the 5th we started about ten o'clock, the advance soon coming up to the enemy's pickets but we did not meet with any opposition untill we got to Chapel Hill, about five miles, here our advance came up to their rear guard when sharp skirmishing commenced, as we were the rear regiment we were ordered up on a double quick, which we took for about three miles, when we formed in a battle line, and marched on, but the rebels did not make but one stand, and then they charged upon two companies of our Cavelry, but they came back in order to draw the rebels back to where we were formed, but they did not come a great ways before they wheeled, and we went after them, some three miles further, but they had crossed Duck river, we had to wade a stream which was about half knee deep. As we had obeyed orders and done with one brigade, what Gen. Rosecrans ordered two to do we started back, for we were some fifteen miles in the advance of the army, we marched about two miles back of where we camped the night before, our regiment did not fire a gun nor received a shot, the next day we started about four o'clock and marched some six or eight miles to this place, (Tryune) where we stayed that night, it rained hard all night, but we had some rubber blankets to stretch over us, we did not get very wet, and as I was very tired and sleepy, I fell asleep and slept so sound that I did not hear it rain, the next day we sent back for our tents and knapsacks, and moved about one mile, to where we are now, our tent came about ten o'clock, and they were very welcome, for we had barely got into them when we had as heavy a thunder shower as I ever saw, but we spread down our blankets and got a good rest, yesterday we had to poliece up, (that is clean up) the streets and fix up our tents and beds, we had not got that done when we heard heavy artillery in front, and we were soon ordered to "fall in," we marched out and got a position, but the firing soon ceased, they were a shelling a house in which were a lot of rebel cavelry, which made them scatter double quick, we stood in line untill four o'clock when we came back to camp, and we got our supper, and then we had a heavy shower and it was quite cold, so we were glad to go to bed, so I did not write any, this morning it has came off fair and it is some warmer, and we have got polieced up, and I have wrote so much, and now I must stop and get my dinner for it is after dinner time I am agoing to have some beans for my dinner.

I received a letter yesterday from you and Alice and Ida, and was glad to hear from you again and hear that was all well, it was dated Feb 25th and had the sermon, and a story in it, I like the sermon very much. I would like to hear him preach, and to go to meeting with you but I cannot tell whether I shall ever be permitted to or not, but if not, I <u>know</u> that we shall meet together in Heaven. I have not answered Em.'s letter yet, but intend to as soon as I can. I have got three rings partly finished <u>two for you</u> and one for the children and I will send them along, you can polish them up by rubbing them with cloth, if they are not large enough for you, you can get someone to file them out a little larger, if you do not want them both, give the colered one to Mary, and keep the white one, if I can get any shells, and we are in camp for any length of time I can make some nice ones, let me know if they are of the right sise, the cotton seed some of them I picked out, and a few I left them in the cotton just as they are picked of. I hope that they will grow so that you can see how it looks[.]

I do not think that the Indian's will ever get down as far as you are, for I think that the Conscription will place enough men there to protect you. We got a great deal from the rebels on this last trip, in the way of forage, pork, turkeys and chickens – so we had enough to eat all of the time, this is a rough, hilly country, but there is a good many good farms, but they do not look quite as well after we have camped upon them awhile, for we burn evry rail that we can get hold of, and evry negro man goes away from them and goes with the army, they make good teamsters, megro families are sent to Nashville.

We have not received any pay yet, nor I do not know when we will get any, but I hope before long[.] I do not get any more than a private, except a little extra clothing but not enough to make any difference. Wesley Baldwin has got his discharge, and if he gets home well, he will go and see you, if he does you must let him see my letters, and tell him to write to me, there is no foundation to the report that the Potomac army is demoralized, it was started by some of the northern Copperheads. I hope that they will all be punished as they deserve to be. We have not received any news that is reliable, since we have been out, it is all together likely that we will remain here untill the whole army advances, which I think by the movements will be before long, we are now in the front, on the Nashville and Huntsville road, between Franklin and Murfresboro, and about twenty five miles from Nashville, and about the same from the other two places, M. and Franklin[.]

I did not expect to write so much when I commenced, but I do not know when to stop. If I could talk with you for a <u>few days</u>, I could get catched up, the boys are all well, and are anxious if there is a fight, to be in. I do not think that you will find any of the "2nd" back out when the moment comes, there was one man buried on the seventh, in Co. B, our Co. has not got a man in the hospital[.] We muster 43 men, now, which is about the average of the other Co's, the rest of them have died, deserted , or been discharged from service. I am as well as can be expected. I weigh 167 lbs. I will direct as you wish me to, but I think that "<u>Nerva</u>" <u>is a good name for me</u>, kiss all of the babies for me, and tell them that pa likes to have them all write, and I hope that I shall soon see them all, <u>and you to</u>, give my respects to all, these few lines from a "soldier" to his wife and children, may God protect you in his mercy, <u>good bye</u> all,

D. B. Griffin
[kiss]

Letter Number 70

Camp near Tryune Tenn. March 17th 1863

Dear Wife and children,

As We have not got much to do this Afternoon, and I do not know what to do, but to write a few lines to you, although I have not any news to tell you. I am well and hearty all of the time, as well as the rest of the boys. I do not think there is a dozen men on the sick list in camp. We are a getting very hot weather for the last few days, and the trees and grass begins to put forth their green leaves and blades. I saw some peach trees yesterday, that had commenced blossoming, so you see that we shall soon have summer, again, but I hope that we shall not have to stay down here during another summer, but things look now as though we were agoing to remain here for some time, to come, for we are fortifying very strong, through the whole line, and if the rebels undertake to drive us away, I hope that they will be met with a warm reception. It is reported here that the rebels are evacuating Vicksburgh and concentrating at Chattanoga, but if we have nothing of any reliability just yet, if it is so they may undertake to drive us back from here. We do not get only now and then a paper, and when we do there is not anything in them worth reading. I have not received any letters since I last wrote to you. I have written to Emery, the reason why I have not written to you before, is because we were expecting our pay evry day, but we have not got it yet, and when we do get any we do not get but two month pay, but they tell us that it will not be but a few days before we get the rest of our pay for six months[.]

I hardly know what to write for I have not got any thing to write about, it is very warm and the boys are playing ball, pitching quaits, &c, and when we are not drilling or on guard, we pass away the time as best we can. I have partly learnd how to play chess, so I study at that some. We had a sermon last Sunday from the Chaplain of the 1st East Tenn. Cav, he preached very well, that reg. is composed of men who have been driven from their homes in Tenn. by the rebels, for their

Camp near Tryune Tenn, March 17th 1863

Dear Wife and children, As We have not got much to do this Afternoon, and I do not know what to do, but to write a few lines to you, although I have not any news to tell you, I am well and hearty all of the time, as well as the rest of the boys. I do not think there is a dozen men on the sick list in camp, We are a getting very hot weather for the last few days, and the trees and grass biging to put forth their green leaves and blades, I saw some peach trees yesterday, that had commenced blossoming, so you see that we shall soon have summer again, but I hope that we shall not have to stay down here during another summer, but things look now as though we were agoing to remain here for some time, to come, for we are fortifying very strong, through the whole line, and if the rebels undertake to drive us away. I hope that they will be met with a warm reception, It is reported here that the rebels are evacuating Vicksburgh and concentrating at Chattanoga, but we have nothing of any reliability just yet, if it is so they may undertake to drive us back from here; We do not get only now and then a paper, and when we do there is not anything in them worth reading, I have not received any letters since I last wrote to you, I have written to Emery, the reason why I have not written to you before, is because we were expecting our pay every day, but we have not got it yet, and when we do get any we do not yet, but two months pay, but they tell us that it will not be but a few ... before we set the rest of our pay for six months ...

Union sentiments, and they sware vengunce on those that have driven them away from their families and friends, they cannot even hear from their loved ones, at home as we do.

Wednesday morning 18th

I have nothing new to write this morning, but I am well and I hope that I shall hear from you soon and hear that you are all well, and getting along well. I expect that there will be quite a time amongst the old ~~batch~~ bachelors, for they will all try to get married, in order to avoid the conscription, on the first call.

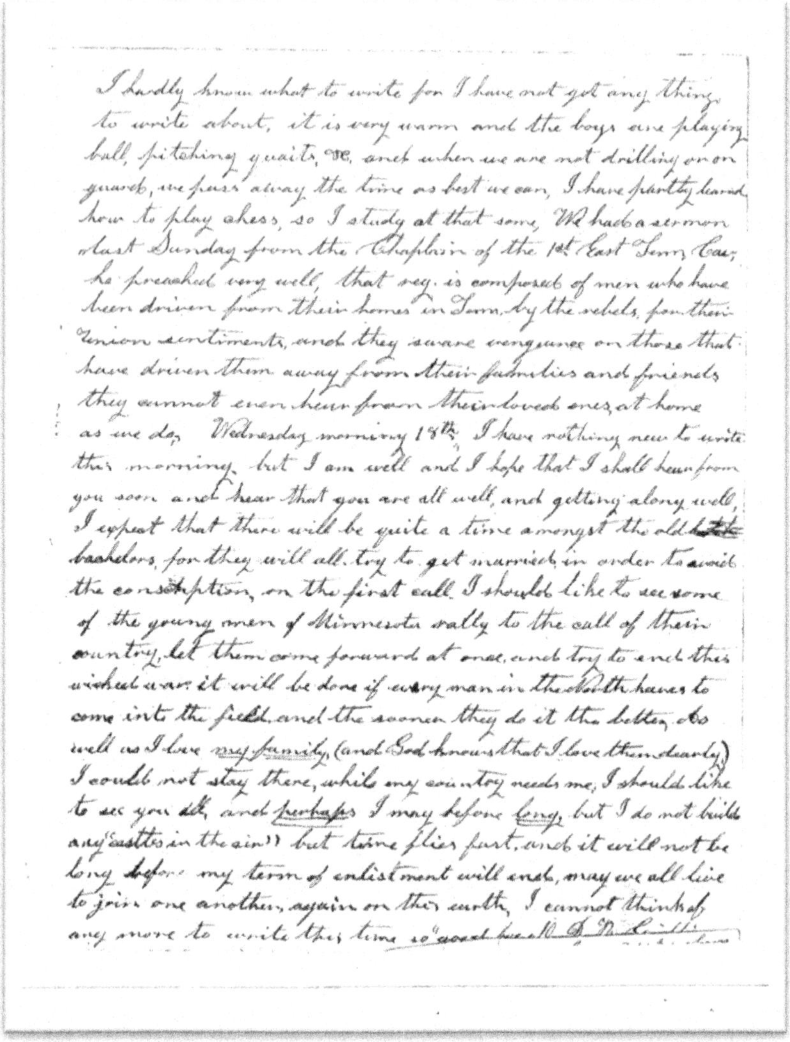
I hardly know what to write for I have not got any thing to write about, it is very warm and the boys are playing ball, pitching quaits, &c, and when we are not drilling or on guard, we pass away the time as best we can, I have partly learned how to play chess, so I study at that some, We had a sermon last Sunday from the Chaplain of the 1st East Tenn Cav; he preached very well, that reg. is composed of men who have been driven from their homes in Tenn, by the rebels, for their Union sentiments, and they swear vengeance on those that have driven them away from their families and friends they cannot even hear from their loved ones, at home as we do, Wednesday morning 18th I have nothing new to write this morning, but I am well and I hope that I shall hear from you soon and hear that you are all well, and getting along well, I expect that there will be quite a time amongst the old ~~bach~~ bachelors, for they will all try to get married in order to avoid the conscription, on the first call I should like to see some of the young men of Minnesota rally to the call of their country, let them come forward at once, and try to end this wicked war, it will be done if every man in the North haves to come into the field, and the sooner they do it the better, As well as I love my family, (and God knows that I love them dearly) I could not stay there, while my country needs me, I should like to see you all, and perhaps I may before long, but I do not build any "castles in the air" but time flies fast, and it will not be long before my term of enlistment will end, may we all live to join one another again on this earth, I cannot think of any more to write this time so good health

I should like to see some of the young men of Minnesota rally I should like to see some of the young men of Minnesota rally to the call of their country, let them come forward at once, and try to end this wicked war, it will be done if every man in the North haves to come into the field, and the sooner they do it the better. As well as I love <u>my</u> <u>family</u>, (and God knows that I love them dearly) I could not stay there, while my country needs me. I should like to see you all, and <u>perhaps</u> I may before long, but I do not build any "castles in the air" but time flies fast, and it will not be long before my term of enlistment will end, may we all live to join one another, again on this earth. I cannot think of any more to write this time so "good bye all,"

D. B. Griffin

Letter Number 71

In Camp near Tryune Tenn. March 22nd 1863

My Dear "Nerva" and babies, friends and neighbors, one and all,

I will try to write a few lines to you to day. I am well to and in good spirits. We have not had a great deal to do for the last week, but still it has been a prety busy time in camp, for the pay-master has been here and payed us off for two months, so we have had a little money to pay up our debts, and get a few things that we need, and a good many things that we do not actualy need, such as Whiskey at $2.00 a quart, and quick sales at that, cheese 50 cts a lb....&c, but as your humble servant thinks more of his little family, than he does of gratifying his own desires, I have not indulged in such "costly" luxury. I will send $20.00 to you in this letter, and I hope that it will not be long before I shall be able to send you more. I have got all the money that I want to keep, for I do not need any thing but paper, ink, envelops and stamps. I have got 25cts. worth (24 sheets) paper, and I have sent $1.00 for stamped envelops, I owed $2.00 which I have payed, and have got $2.50 left, so you see that my "spree" did not cost me much[.] But the Capt. told us this morning, that we had had a two days spree now, and discipline was laid aside, and no notice has been taken of what we had done for the last two or three days, but that he wished it all stopped now, for the enemy were right in our front and that we were expecting an attack from them at any th time and he wished that we would all be ready to fall in at a moments notice, and be ready to "fight" if called upon to do so, and we are all ready, and willing too, and if needs be to benefit our country and friends, to die in the service of our country, and if thei̶r̶re was a few of the Traitors of Fillmore Co. or Minn. in the lines of the enemy to stand up and fight in the ranks of the rebels against us, they would stand higher in our estimation to day, than what they now do. I have heard a good deal of talk amongst the boys of the Reg. in denouncing their <u>friends</u> <u>even</u>, or them who they supposed were their friends, but they have denounced the doing of the administration, and are a trying to discourage, those who have left all, home friends, and <u>evry</u> <u>thing</u>, in order to save the country from ruin and infamy, and in so doing they (the Copperheads) have got the ill will of all good <u>Union</u> loving men, and Officers in the army, and if they persist in uttering their traitors sentiments, in the North I, nor any one else will not be responsible, if their <u>folly</u> <u>falls</u> upon their own heads. The K. G. Cs[1]. are nothing else, but a den of lothing, hissing reptiles and if the soldiers ever go home "victorious," (and <u>I</u> <u>believe</u> they will,) they will <u>spurn</u> them as they would so many <u>serpents</u>, wreaking vengense on them where they can find them, amongst which are the editors of the Chatfield Democrat, and others in Fillmore Co, but I hope that they will repent and help save the union. I am anxious to see the conscript act enforced, but I hardly think that they will ever be brought into action, but we cannot tell, what may turn up before three months rolls around. We hear a good many rumors about Vicksburgh, we heard the same rumor that you did, but no one believed it, it is the general belief that they are evacuating Vicksburgh, they had a fight at Yazo Pass, our men taking a good many men and boats. I think from the present appearences that it will not be long before the Miss. river will be open for the navigation of the North, but we can not believe hardly anything that we hear in the army. I do not intend to write any thing to you that is not true. I received a letter from

---

[1] Knights of the Golden Circle. The secret society's original objective was to create a "circle" of at least 25 new slaveholding states out of territories annexed from Mexico, Cuba, and other parts of Central and South America and the Caribbean, in order to guarantee constitutional control by the South. It later favored succession. During the Civil War, Southern sympathizers, mainly in the Northern states of Ohio, Illinois, Indiana and Iowa, were branded with that earlier name.

you on the 20th, dated the 10th, so you see that it takes about ten days for a letter to go through by mail, and I will try to write one to you evry week, if I can get time. I should like to have been there and had a visit with you, when the Mrs. Wheelers and others were there. I hope you had a good visit. I hope that Leonora is not that bad put to for a beau, that she would concent to have an old gray headed "married" man go home with her, I do not think that "little Dan" steps up to her very prompt[.] It seems that the "Old Maid," (Hill) got his "Ebenezer" raised a little when he was a milking "Rosa," and he could not contain himself. You wrote that evry thing was very high there, and that you did not know how people were a going to get along, but if you could see some of the folks down here, and they not able to get anything at any price, you would not worry at all, about it, if we all live through it, and are able to gain ~~our~~ the day, times will be better again. I hope that the weather is warmer up there, by this time. It is quite warm and pleasent here, some of the trees look quite green, peach trees are blossoming and garden flowers are in bloom, so you see that it is a good deal earlyer here, than there, but still this is called a late spring, some years they plant their corn in March, but there is not much farming going on where the army stops, in fact they cannot do anything, no negroes, no horses, no fences, no cattle, nor anything left but houses and land and unless they are union men, that will not be of any use to them. It is amusing to see some of the old rich secesh, beg of when we are out after forage, but it is of no use, for where we can find any we take it, such is the way they are a getting their Southern rights.

I can see that Alice gains in her writing some. I receive her little letters with a good deal of pleasure. I hope that she will continue to write to me, can she read my letters? tell her that she must get her new dresses done, so that when I come home, (some off of these days,) she can show them to me, but I hope that she is a good girl, and helps her Mother and Sister and little brother. I thought that Edgar would weigh more than 33 lbs. by the looks of his picture, but he has got to grow some before he gets as "big" as his "daddy," and Ida, "my black eyed girl" she tries to write to me once in a while, if she keeps on a trying, she will soon get so that she will write as well as I can, you must write about all of them. I hardly think that they will escape both the meazels and hooping cough, but if they get either, be carefull and keep them warm, and they will get along, and Mary and her babies too. I think of you all, and often. Mary you must write a few lines to your brother, if you can, you and "Nerva" can simpathise with each other, in your husbands absence, do you ever hear anything from Em's brother in the army, if so where is he now if living. I have not heard from nor seen him since we left Corrinth. Now "Nerva" I cannot think of much more to write this time. I want that you should answer this as soon as can, for I shall want to know whether you receive the money or not, we will probably get payed off again in the course of a month or so, but if we do not, and you get this, it will last you some time yet, but I must stop for this time and I hope that this will find you all in good health, the health of the Reg. is good as yet. Now I will bid you all a good bye once, more, hopeing that it will not be but a short time before we shall be permitted to meet one and another, on this earth. I remain yours forever,

D. B. Griffin.

Here is a couple of rings, which I have made, one for you and one for myself. I do not know but it is to large for you, but I guess not, they are made from muscle shells got out of the Cumberland river. I have got another on my little finger, if I can get time and anything to make them with I will make the children some may our love be like these rings, having no end.

Letter Number 72

Triune Tenn. April 2nd 1863

My Dear Beloved Wife and Children,

I will try to write a few lines to you to day so as to let you know how I am, and what we are about. I am as well to day as usual, and I hope that I shall remain so during my term of enlistment or during the war, which I hope will be ended before another Winter, and for one I cannot see, for the life of me, what will hender the North from putting down evry armed traitor in the South, before that time, and I have faith to believe that it will be done. We are getting a strong army here again, and we are strongly fortified all along the line, both with siege pieces and field, and line after line of intrenchments, so if the rebel army sees fit to attact us, they will meet with a "warm" reception, but it is not generaly thought, that they will make an attact, but if they do not old "Rosy" will go out to see them before a great many weeks rolls around, and I do not think you will find many of the boys but what will march boldly up to the scratch, at the first sound of the bugle, for we are anxious to end this contest and return to our families and friends, but we do not wish to go home, before we can do so honorably, and have our country at peace, not untill evry traitor shall be silenced and put down never again to show themselves, as such, as long as we have as good a government as we live under now, although they may do acts under the present circumstances, that would, in times of peace, be deemed unconstitutional. I hope that no one in Minn. bi will go against the administration, nor any of its acts, untill the rebellion in the Southern states is put down, for ever.

You must not think, because a man is a Democrat, that he is opposed to the doings of the North, and in favor of the South, for there is just as strong supporters of the present administration in the democratic party as there is in any other party, in fact a man cannot be a democrat unless he is in a supporter of the union.

Afternoon,

Well we have been called out to meet the rebels, we went about two miles, and took a position behind a hill, and laid in readiness for them, but the 1st Tenn Cavelry drove them back acrost the river without any loss on either side, so after laying there about two hours we came back to camp and got our dinners. It is very warm to day, but the wind blows hard, the last week in March was a cold blustering week, there was a frost nearly evry night, and the two last days we had "snow squals," and rain, if it was as cold up there accordingly, you have had pretty cold weather[.]

I received a letter from you last night, dated March 23d, and was glad to hear from you all again, for it was almost two weeks since I had heard from you. I am glad that you all keep well, for I should not like to hear that any of you were sick, and I not able to get home. I am glad that your neighbors see a little to your wellfare, if nothing more than to shovel the snow off from your wood pile. I wish that you ~~will~~ would give Mr. DeGrooat my best wishes. I hope that he is not a "Copperhead" as they call the "K. G. Cs," and I do not think that he is, for I do not believe that any man, who wants to save the Union, can be one. I hope that all in Spring Valley will try to encourage those who have enlisted in the cause of their country, by urging them on, by kind words, and kind acts to their families, and friends in their abesence, and if we ever ~~we~~ are permitted to join our friends and families, that they will be amply rewarded, in having a peacefull and prosporous land to live in the remainder of their days, and if we cannot reward them with our hands, may God reward them in his mercy.

I wrote a letter to you a few days ago, in which I put $20.00, which was all that I could spare, and I hope that you will get it all safe if not write to me as soon as you get this we only got two months pay. We are expecting the other four months pay this week or next, and then I will send you forty or fifty dollars more, and you had better keep the most of it for your own use, for it may be a long time before we are payed off again. I have sent for the Weekly Nashville Union for six months, and it will be sent direct to you, you will find nearly all of the news from the army in that and a good deal better than I can write it to you, and also a good deal of other news, there has a good many of the boys signed for it in the same way, I think that it will do you more good than the dollar. I think that you have got the children some very good dresses, if they were dear, if you lived in the South you could not get them any, at any price, nor hardly any thing else, if all accounts are true, I do not see how they are agoing to live another year in the way they do now, almost entirely cut off from all communication from any other part of the globe, and their slaves leaving them, and where ever we go they do not raise anything, if they do, it will not do them any good, so unless they give up soon, they will be almost in a starving condition by another winter, but we look for some great change to be made within the next three months, and I think that it will be for the better for us. I sent three papers to you a few days ago, and I will send you a few more, if I can get hold of any good ones. I will stop untill after supper.

Evening

Well we have been to supper, and had dress praderade[.] I had some beef stake, and coffee and crackers for supper. We have got orders to be ready to march in the morning at seven o'clock with two days rations in our haversacks, with shelter tents and blankets, picks and spades, so I think that we are about to advance our lines some. We have just had shelter tents issued to us. I cannot tell how I shall like them, they are pieces of canvass about six feet long and five foot wide, they are so fixed that two of them go together and make a good shelter, they are to be all the tents we have. We have also changed our muskets for the Enfield rifles, which are better guns and they are not as heavy as the muskets were, so you see that we are fully armed and equiped for the summer campaign, we have also got clothes enough to last us untill July, so you see too that "Uncle Sam" feeds and clothes his boys better than any other army in the world. I hope that Dan will come out there this spring and get him a home as soon as he can. There was two or three regiments taken prisoners at Franklin, as you said that you had heard, but that is about twenty miles from here. We were out some ten miles yesterday after forage, we did not see any rebels, we got all of the waggons loaded up with corn and fodder, and got back to camp just at dark, the peach trees are all in full bloom, and I saw a few apple trees in blossom, the forrest trees are getting quite green, so I think that we will not have any more cold weather this spring. I have not got any shells to make rings with now, but if the streams get low again, perhaps I can get some. As it is a getting late and this sheet is nearly full I shall have to close, so you must excuse me for this time. I should like to talk to you all night if I could, but I must stop and bid you all a good bye, so good bye "Nerva" Alice, Ida and Edgar, with a kiss [here]

D. B. Griffin.

Letter Number 73

In Camp near Triune   April 11th 1863

My Dear Wife, Children and friends,

I once more have got down upon my knapsack, with my pen in my hand, to write a few lines to you all, it has been a number of days since I last wrote, and I have been a putting it of, in hopes that I should get a letter from you, but I will not wait any longer. I am as well to day as usual. It is quite warm and dry, we have not had any rain for some time, and the springs are a getting rather low around here. The trees are a putting on their new dress of green, and it begins to look like summer. There is not a great deal of farming done in this vicinity. I have seen them a planting corn in one place. We have been kept pretty busy since I last wrote, we have been out in front, a reconoitering and feeling of the enemy, but we did not see any here. There has been a number of skirmishes near Franklin[2], we could hear the fireing here, and we were called up in line, ready to reenforce them if called upon, but we were not called upon. We are called out evry morning, with arms and accoutrements, and then we are either on drill, inspection, muster, review, or on

---

[2] On April 10, 1863, CSA Gens. Earl Van Dorn and Bedford Forrest attacked Union Gen. David Stanley at Franklin, Tennessee, then withdrew back to Spring Hill.

working details, foraiging or upon guard or picket, so we find a plenty to do all of the time. I have not got any war news to tell you, if I had, you will get the news in the Nashville papers, which I have had directed to you. We hear that they have commenced bombarding Charleston, and we all are anxiously awaiting the result, and also we look for something from Vixburgh.

I have sent you $20.00, and this makes the second letter since, I will let you know of it in evry one I write untill I hear from it, or from you. I was asking Capt. Barnes to day if he knew Mr. Gaskill in Spring Valley, he sayed that he did, and that Sargeant Gaskill of Co. B. was a son of his, so I went to him and told him what you said about his brother being sick, he had not heard of it, he is anxious to hear from them, you must write about them, when you write, we are all anxious to hear from our friends, no matter from what source, so when you write you must write about all of the friends of the 2nd. Sargeant Gaskill is well. I have just heard that Luther Peasley and Willard Scott of Napierville were both Captain in the 105th Ill. regiment, now at Murfresboro, and that Thad. Scott, had got a divorce from his wife, she was Elonor Butler, there is a good many of the Ill boys that I knew there. I shall be glad to see them, and shall go and see them if I get a chance. We have just received orders to have three days rations ready for our haversacks, so there is something for us to do <u>I expect</u>. We were mustered yesterday, in order to know how many men it will take to fill up our regiment, there has not many of the Deserters returned as yet. I do not know how many men there is in the Reg. but there is between 5 and 6 hundred.

I sent three papers to Alice the other day, so she must excuse me from writing this time, we have not got payed yet but expect it in a few days. I do not think of much to write this time so you must wait untill I get something to write about, the boys are all well that we knew, write as often as you can and oblige your husband, and friend, so Good bye all, this from "Corp." Griffin, Co F. 2nd reg. Minn. Vol.

Letter Number 74

Camp Steadman, Triune Tenn. Apr. 16th 1863

Dear Wife and Children,

I will write a few lines to you this afternoon, in order that you may know how I am. I am as well as usual to day, but as I was on picket duty last night, I am some sleepy and tired. There has not anything turned up of any interest since I last wrote to you. We have been out a foraging once, and as the fortifications are nearly all completed, we do not have as much to do, as we did have for a while. The rebs. attackted our men at Franklin, but they "mistook their man," and come off "second best," but you will see an account of it in the Nashville paper, which I hope you have received all right. I have only sent it for six months, so you will know how to pay the postage on it. I see the daily evry day, and there is nearly all in the weekly that there is in the daily, so if you get them, all correct, you will get more news from the army than I possibly could write. I think that it advocates the views of the soldiers about as well as any paper that I have seen, you must try and let Father's folks read them, as well as others. I received a letter from you two days ago, which was dated the 4th in which you sent Samuel's likeness and his letter. I cannot see the <u>first</u> look of <u>Samuel</u> in the likeness, some say that he resembles me, but I failed to see it. I have not received any letter from him[.] I received a letter to day from Em dated the 4th, he was well, and was expecting to move from there, in a short time, to where he did not know, he says that ~~his~~ his folks, and Dan's folks, were expected to be there, (with you) this spring, and that if we were there, we could have a nice visit, but thinks that if we ever get home we can make up for lost times and "back rations." I hope that we will be permitted to join our littl family circle before another fall, and <u>I</u> think that I shall be at home by a year from this fall, if living, so keep up good, cheer, for the time flies fast around. I was glad to learn that you were all well, and that you had received the money all right. "Nerva" <u>I</u> enjoy myself <u>better</u>, when I know that you are not a suffering for the want of any thing, to make you comfortable, than I should to keep more money by me to spend for that, that I do not need, and if, you do not blame yourself, no one will blame you for getting what you need, and what the children need. I think that you sacraficed comfort enough when you let me go into the army, but I hope that we shall both live long enough to be amply rewarded for all of our trials, and that we shall again see our country at peace with all nations, and all traitors blotted out from the face of the earth.

I think that Mrs. Nichols is rather getting the start of you and some others. I should think that she was old enough to do better, but then I expect that the world will keep a rolling around untill the end of time, and that the people will multiply and replenish it. I would like to see Alf's boy, and them to, till them to write to me, perhaps I shall see some of the Minnesota boys down here before long, to fill up the regiment, as conscripts, and I hope that they will all come willingly. I see that you are having an early spring. I hope that you can raise enough on your place to eat, and some to spare. If you have any way of paying off our little debts, do it and in any way that you are a mind to, but I want that you should keep enough money by you for your own use. I guess that I can send you some more in the next letter, the boys are all well and hearty. I do not think of any more to write this time, so I will bid you all a good bye again and close, this from your husband and father,

D. B. Griffin

Letter Number 75

Friday morning Apr. 17th 1863

Good morning "Nerva,"

It is a very pleasent morning here, how is it there. The first Tenn. Cav. had a skirmish yesterday with the rebels, in front of us, they captured six or seven, including a Lieutenent, and wounded and killed a number, our loss was three wounded, one mortally. We were expecting an attact from them this morning, and we were up and ready for them, but they did not come on. We have had a considerable of rain for the last few days, but it has come off pleasant this morning, the trees are nearly as green as they are in the summer, but it is a late spring for this country. I will send you five ($5.00) dollars in this letter and will try to send you some in my next, we are to be payed in a day or two, for four months. I have sold enough of my rations to come to about four dollars, and when I am payed I am agoing to send Harpers Weekly to Alice & Ida, it will not make them <u>feel</u> <u>bad</u> will it? and perhaps some other papers. I had thought some of getting a furlough this spring if I could but I have given up the Idea, for it would be only a few days that I could be with you, and when I had to come back you would feel worse than you ~~to~~ would, not to see me at all, so I will stick to it, untill the end of my term, or to the close of the war, if I am well and lucky. I should like to see <u>you</u> <u>all</u> well enough but it will hardly pay. If Dan comes out there, (but I hardly think he will) tell him to write to me, and I should like to have others write to me to. You have never told me how much your taxes were last winter, I wish that you would, how much is a good cow worth up there? or the two year old? steer, what is wheat worth?

The Paymaster is here to day so we shall have some ~~mo~~ green backs, again. We have a good deal of reading matter in the camp just now. We take the Daily Nashville Union, and we get the Louisville and the Cincinati papers, and a plenty of other reading matter, so we manage to enjoy ourselves first rate. My bedfellow has been unwell for some time past, but he is on the gain again. I will close this letter again and bid you all a good bye, again.

Good bye   "Nerva,"}
Good bye   Alice,}   From your husband
Good   Ida,}   and Father   D. B. Griffin
Good bye   Edgar,}

Letter Number 76

Camp Steadman, Triune   Apr. 27th 1863

Dear Wife and children – I will write a few lines to you this morning. I am well, as usual, and hope that you are all as well. I have not any news to write to you, we have not had any fight here yet, the reg. was out after forage the other day, and there was a squad of rebel cavelry near there, but a man gave them some signs, that the Federals were a coming, and they skedaddled, but we took the <u>man</u> prisonor and told the woman if she had any thing in the house, that she wanted to save, to take them out, quick, she took out some of her bedding, and the match was lit, and soon the house was in ashes. I like to see the General's come down close upon the rebels, and their simpathisers. We are looking for something to be done before long, somewhere in the army, the news in the papers, go to show, that the move has commenced in the right way, the people are coming out for the Union every day.

I received a short letter from Samuel, which I will send to you. I wrote to him yesterday and I have asked him a good many questions, I tell you. I will ~~tell~~ send you ten dollars ($10.00) in this letter, which makes $25.00 this payment, you must keep count, so as to know whether you get it all or not. I am a looking for a letter from you, which will tell me all about the folks upon the Prairie, as I suppose that you are there now. I should like to be there with you but there is no use of <u>wishing</u>, do you get any of the papers yet, and how do you like them, does anyone read the Nashville Union.

We are having very nice weather now, but it looks a little like rain, this morning. I cannot think of any thing to write this morning, so I will not try, the boys are all well, in the Co. and in the reg. I hope that we will remain so, the Tenn Cavelry lose a man about evry day, and there is a good many sick, you will see a good many letters from them in the Nashville Union, they are true union men, if some of the Copperheads had to go through what they have been through, they would curse the South, <u>slaves</u> and all, as bad as they do, may they soon be permitted to see or hear from their friends and families in east Tenn, but I must stop for the want of something to say so good bye one and all, this from your beloved husband,

To "Nerva," and the babies
kiss them all for me and
take one for yourself.
Corp. D. B. Griffin.

Letter Number 77

Camp Steadman, Triune Tenn.   May 4th 1863

My Dear Wife and Children:

Again I will try to write a few lines to you all. I am as well as usual this evening. We have kept ourselves pretty busy since my last. In the first place we had to turn over our Sibley tents, and fix up our shelter (or "dog") tents as the boys call them, we button two or four together, and then fix them up from the ground, about four feet at the sides and 7 or 8 feet at the top, and then fix up our beds under them, and then we fixed up a shade over us and in front of us, so you see we can sit in the shade, or lay down and enjoy a good nap. I have just finished fixing mine this forenoon.

We had muster the last of Apr, so U. S. owes two months more pay, and I guess that we will not have to wait so long for our pay as we did before. I have sent you $25.00, $5.00 in the first and $10.00 each in the two last letters that I wrote to you, and I will not send you any more untill I hear from some of that. I hope that it will all get through safe, for you need it, or will sometime, but I have been quite lucky with what I have sent, some of the boys have lost some money through the mails. We have been a drilling a Briggade drill, that is the regiments in the Briggade all drill together (four reg.)[.]

We went out this afternoon to drill, but after drilling about one hour, in battallion drill, there came up a heavy shower, and the Gen. thought that it was a going to be most to heavy for us, so dismised us, and we came back to camp on a double quick, we had quite a shower, and it is quite cool and comfortable this evening. We have had some pretty warm days here already, but we were in camp.

It has been all quiet about here for sometime, our reg. has not been out for anything for a good while. We were some expecting an attact yesterday morning, but, as usual, the rebs, did not come. It is not impossible for them to try us some of these days, but we are ready for them, as I hope we always will be. We are strongly entrenched and fortified, and I think we can stand a strong pull, with them. The papers give good accounts of the army both at the Rapahanack and on the Mississippi. I hope that evry thing will be sure and to the purpose if they do have to move slow. I hope that the war will be ended before harvest, and I be able to go home safe and sound, don't you "Nerva?" I received a letter to day dated the 27th Apr. from you, and was glad to hear that you were enjoying yourself down upon the Prairie, amongst your folks and friends, and where we have passed many a hapy day together, and I hope that we will be spared to pass many more. I do not see but what you get along with the farming first rate. I hope that you will enjoy yourself better this summer, than you did last, and I think you will[.]

I have sent you three papers, which will keep your spare moments occupied some, if you get them all. I want that you should keep the pictorials, for us to look over together, if Providence permits me to return home, to my family. I was sorry to hear of the trouble that Thomas Douglass had got into but I think that he will come out all right, for I think he was a good soldier, and done as well as he could do, probably, it is not as bad as represnted, I hope not. I got the same news by James Thornton's letters from Dan. Paul. I wish that you had told me where the third reg. was, and where J. Nichols is and how he is, if you can find out by his folks. I shall look for a good long letter from you when you get back to the Valley again you must tell me how they all are, and how they all get along. You must send me a piece of Mary's "new dress," if you want one

265

like it, or else tell me what kind of a dress you want, and if it should hapen right, I might send one to you, if I could not bring you one. I hope that I can, sure "Nerva." You say that all of the folks send there best respects to me, why dont they write a few lines to me, which would be much more acceptable, but I am glad that they do not all forget me, and I hope that they will not forget my little family in my absence. I will have to stop for to night for the wind flares the candle, and it is long past bed time, in the evenings when it is pleasent, the boys have good times in dancing   I do not dance much myself but I enjoy the fun of the thing first rate. I think that we shall have some more rain before morning, but I must bid you all good night, and go to bed and dream about you which I do often. "Good night."

Tuesday morning, April 5th

I am well this morning. It rained quite hard in the night but it has ceased now, and the air is clear and nice, the boys are all busy now, some are getting their breakfast, others washing, &c, &c. I expect that you would laugh to see us cooking our meals, we all have the same things to cook, but we all cook in our own way, and in our own dishes. I have baked bread a number of times, and have good luck. I make water "risings" and they come up as nice as you please. We are getting bread from the Comissary now, which is very good, we have a plenty of hard tack[.]

How many bushels of Wheat have you got left after saving what you wanted? is there enough to last you untill next harvest? do you keep a cow at the Valley? or any hen's or pigs, how does Father take the place? or let it out? I do not think that you need to look for Dan, for I do not think that he will go there, but still he may. I hope that he will, and get him a home on the prairie, did you buy any of the white willow? how do they set it out, if it does well this year perhaps I will set some out for you next spring. I see by the papers that the K. G. C.'s are a little stiller than what they were, it is best for them to do so, for the Government, is taking hold of them in some places, and they are not received with any encouragement in the South, but as you are getting the Nashville paper, now I know that you will get nearly all of the news how is the paper liked there? does Mary take any papers? Why don't she write some to me. I sha'nt <u>kiss her</u> when I come home if she don't. I want that she should have "lots" of good things to eat, when I come to see her, but I cannot tell her when <u>that</u> will be, but I must stop for this time, you can see by my letters that when I get a letter from you, that I can find something to write about, but when I have to write two or three letters between your letter's I do not find much to write about. I had put of writing this time longer than I should if I had got one from you, perhaps you wrote one between the two last ones I got, the 12th & 27th. Write often. I will close now and go and get my breakfast[.] I must bid you all Good bye with a <u>kiss</u> and my <u>love</u> for <u>yours</u> from your Husband, and friend,

D. B. Griffin

Letter Number 78

Triune, Tennessee May 11th 1863

My Dear Wife, Children, and Sister Mary, one and all,

I will try to write a few lines to you this afternoon, although I have not much to write, for evry thing remains quiet here[.] No advancement being made from either side, and as the country is prety thouroughly cleaned of its forage, we do not have to go out a foraging. But the Gen. finds enough for us to do in the way of drilling. We had a Co. drill this forenoon and the boys are out on a Division drill, both Brigades drilling together. I ~~staid~~ stopped in camp so as to draw rations for the Co. I am well to day as usual. I received a letter from Samuel to day which I will send to you with this. We have been a watching the reports of the Telegraph from Hookers[3] army, but as yet we

---

[3] Union Gen. Joseph Hooker, facing CSA Gen. Robert E. Lee in The Wilderness at the May 1-3, 1863, Battle of Chancellorsville, a follow-up Union loss to Fredericksburg, though the Confederates suffered the loss of Gen. Thomas "Stonewall" Jackson.

get nothing reliable, but there was a good deal of rejoicing in camp to day when the news came in the mail, that the "stars and stripes" were a floating over the rebel capital, Richmond. I hope from the ends of my fingers, that the reports will prove true, but we will have to wait a few days longer to get the real truth of the matter, but they have had a hard fought battle, there is no doubt, but if our army is victorious, and the enemy is hemmed in between two armies, they will have to give in between this and next _____. I wont say when, would you? but God grant that it may be ended before long, and let the men go home to their families and "sweethearts," parents and friends, but we, or the most of us have no desire to go home before the country is at peace, "honorable peace" too," do you want that I should Nerva? I know you don't, but as you get the papers, (as I hope that you do) you will get all the news in them that I do, here. I have not got any letters from any one (except Samuel) since I last wrote, and I do not like to write <u>two</u> letters to you evry time I get one from you, for I cannot find any thing to talk about in the second one, but I cannot wait so long, so I write a <u>little</u> in order to let you know how I am, and where I am, and when we stay in a place a long time, and there is not anything a going on, it is the same thing right over and over. I like to write, and <u>talk</u> to <u>you</u> on <u>paper</u> even, and I know I should like to talk to you by "<u>mouth</u>," but as we cannot, we must talk to each other all we can on paper, so you must write all the news, and ask all the questions you can think of. I have to burn up all of your letters, because I have no way to keep them but I expect that you have got a <u>few</u> of mine laid up for future perusal. My prayer is that I may be spared to rejoin my little family, in health. We enjoy ourselves as best we can, there is a floor laid right in front of my tent, and four of the boys have dressed themselves up in <u>female</u> apparel and are having a hapy time a dancing, one of them has got on my flag for an apron, we have had it a flying in the camp ever since we have been here, as it is now long after "taps" I must close, we have got orders to fall in with our guns and accoutourments to morrow morning, but as we get that order so often we do not think anything about it, but we may have a skirmish with the enemy before many days. I will not write any more this time, so I will bid you all good night and go to my bed. Good night "Nerva," with a {kiss} for you and the babies[.]

This from your husband in Tenn.

D. B. Griffin.

Letter Number 79

In Camp Triune Tenn. May 18th 1863

My dear Wife and Children,

As I received a letter from you to day dated the 11th I will write a few lines to you this evening. I am as well as usual this evening, but am some tired as I have been to work upon the breastworks all day. The Gen has made some alterations, in the old ones, and made some new ones, and when they are all finished they will have some very strong works. We are expecting to have a fight at this point, if the rebels make the attact, if not I do not knot know whether we will have any fight or not, but I hope that we will not meet with the same success that the Eastern army has at Fredericksburgh, it is an awful loss to both armies, and nothing gained on either side. We think that Hooker is a good Gen. but there is something wrong, probably there is to much interference in other places, but as you get the papers now you can see what they are a doing both there and here, and elsewhere. I have not received any letters since my last, and I was glad to get one from you to day, but was very sory to hear that my boy was not well, but was glad to hear that he was some better when you wrote. I hope that he will get well, and that we may be permitted to live and meet together an unbroken family at the close of the war, or of my term[.] I will forgive you this time for not writing oftener, but somehow I do not like to wait two weeks or more, for a letter from you when we are in camp, and the mails come regular evry day, please write as often as you can, you know that I will write as often as I can find anything to write about. I have told you in my last letters to tell me all about your visit down on the prairie, and if you are all well I guess that you will. Alice says that she and Ida gets their pictorials and she thinks that they are very pretty. I hope that they will be worth the money to them. I know that they will like them, and I am satisfied with the investment. As you have received all of the money that I have sent to you, I will send you some more ($11.00) in this letter, and I hope that you will use it, if you need it for, sickness or anything else to make you comfortable, because I shall send all that I can spare to you, and if we both live to join each others in our little family circle again may we both be "ten fold" paid for all the sacrifices and deprivations that we undergo while far from each others presence, and I want that you, and the children should enjoy yourselves while you can. I have a plenty of company such as it is, but then it is not like being in the the presense of one's family and friends, shut out from the presense of the female portion of the earth, from the loving smiles and kind words, that helps to lighten our way through life, as well as the prattle of the dear little ones. God bless and protect them. I felt like droping a silent tear when I read that my little darling boy was sick, but I hope that he is well ere this. You wrote that you was down to Preston at the Union meeting. I heard about the meeting by one of Co. A's boys who was there, he says that it was quite a gathering, and that the copperheads were pretty quiet there now, he says that he saw Leonora and Eph. Wheeler there, and a good many others. Who did you go down there with, do you hear from Emery often, I wish that you would write about him. I see in some of the papers that the Indians had been down near where he was this spring, but that they had not done much damage yet, and I hope that they will not do a great deal.

Alice wanted to know if I ever saw so many negroes as there is in the Pictorials. I see more evry day, and they look just as bad as any that there is in the papers, regular darkeys from the plantation, of all colors from the sable black down to the white slaves of the south, "big bucks," wenches and nigger babies, with their thick curly wool and "long heels," thick lips and wide noses, of evry feature natural to the race, but they are to be pittied, for they are agoing to have a hard time of it for a few years at the least, but I hope that African Slavery will be ended and the blacks taken out of the country, this country was made for white men to till, and evry man to be his own master but enough of this. I was glad to hear that Mr. Westfall had given the folks down on the prairie a sermon but I suppose that it is to hard for them to believe that "the wages of sin is death," <u>for all men</u>, oh! no! nor that "Eternal life is the gift of God," <u>for all men</u>, "but only for a few," and "great I" is to be one of those few. I thank God that I can think for myself. I hope that he will continue to preach the <u>gospel</u> to them. I hope that you will have a chance to go to meeting often. I hear that Wesley Hazleton is in Chatfield have you ever heard from or seen him, he has taken a farm there, do you hear anything from Dan.

Now I must stop for to night for it is near 12 o'clock, and we have to get up at daylight, perhaps I will write a few lines in the morning but I will bid you all a good night, and go to bed, you must excuse my bad writing.

{ Good night "<u>Nerva</u>" }
{ Good night Alice }   May God keep and
  A { kiss } for all
{ Good night Ida }   protect you through life
{ Good night Edgar }   and at last may we all
meet in heaven. Good bye to night.   D. B. Griffin.

Tuesday morning,

I am well, with the exception of the teeth ache, and the piles trouble me some, once in a while, but I keep about my duty. We have cool mornings and warm days, but it is not any warmer here than it is in Minn. It is a beautiful morning. I have no news to write, we were not attacted <u>this</u> morning, but we look for it evry day. I will stop for I have got to go to work before long so I will bid you all good bye write as often as you can for I am uneasy when I don't hear from you evry week.

D. B. Griffin.

Letter Number 80

Triune Tenn. May 25th 1863

My Dear "Nerva."

As I feel rather lonesome this evening I will commence a letter to you. I have not been very well for a few days past. I had a touch of the diareah, and that set left me with the piles, so bad that I could hardly walk, set down nor lay down for three days, but I am a good deal better yesterday and to day, so I recon that I shall be all right again in a day or two. We have not had any fight here yet and it is the impresion of the boys that the rebels are a falling back from our front to go down and fight "Grant," but if all the reports are true, they will have to commence before long, or else they will have a hard bone to pick, but I will not surmise any of the results that are to take place on the Miss. but we know that our forces have done well, down there of late, and I hope that they will meet with great success and end with the taking of Vicksburgh, and the whole of the Miss. river, and it is almost as good now. We have been a building new forts and breastworks and strengthening the old ones for the last week, and it seems as though it would be almost impossible for us to be driven out of them, if we should ever be attacted here, but I have my doubts about the rebels visiting us here. We have an other change of Generals in our Division, Gen Schofield[4] has gone to Missouri, he superceeds Gen Curtiss[5], Gen Brennan[6] has taken the command of this Div. The Div. had placed a good deal of confidince in Schofield as a Gen. and were loth to part with him, but I hope the change will not be for the worse. Gen. Brennen appears to be very strict

---

[4] Union Gen. John McAlister Schofield, commanding the Army of the Frontier in Missouri, later the XXIII Corps in the Atlanta Campaign, and in 1888 rose to Commanding General of the U. S. Army.

[5] Union Gen. Samuel Ryan Curtiss, who resigned his U. S. congressional seat from Iowa to lead a state regiment, rising to Commander of the Army of the Southwest, and eventually placed in charge of the Departments of Missouri, Kansas, and the Northwest.

[6] Union Gen. John Milton Brannan, Brigade Commander, and later Chief of Artillery, for the Army of the Cumberland.

and carefull, and he does not intend to be taken unawares by the enemy. We do not see into the movements of the army of the Potomac, so we let them work, nor do we know what keeps us still so long a time here.

I have not got any letters from you nor any one else since I last wrote, so I have not got any thing to write to you about, as I hope that you get all the news in the papers that I do. We have a good deal of reading matter in camp of all kinds. We have had our Co record printed and I sent one of them to you, they cost $1.50 apiece, if you get it safe you would not sell it for that I know, you can get it framed or keep it as it is now. I sent you $11.00 in the last letter I will not send you any in this one. I am very anxious to hear from you so as to know how Edgar gets along[.] I hope that he is a getting well, I do not know how I should feel, to hear that any of you were dead, and I hope that you will not have to tell me of any such news. I hope that you will all get along well, and live, and that I shall live to meet you all alive and well. I have not received any letter from Em. perhaps he never received mine, you must write about him in your letters and about our folks to I like to hear from all of the folks as often as I can. Mr. Cutting is not very well, the rest of the boys are well, there has not been a death in the regiment since we came to this camp, to my knowledge, and that is a saying a good deal, while the Tenn. reg. looses some ten a week, they have buried over 75 men since we came here, and a great many of them are sick now. I have not any more to write untill I get a letter from you, and I must get one before long, or else I shall be more lonesome still, my bedfellow is out on picket to night, so I have got to sleep all "alone," don't you care, how does your garden look? did you plant the cotton seed? how much of a garden have you got? Is the children agoing to school this summer? do you hear from the third reg? &c. I will close for this time, and bid you all a good bye again, write often, please do "Nerva," accept these few lines with my best wishes, and a { kiss } for all. Good bye, from

D. B. Griffin

Letter Number 81

In Camp near Triune Tenn. Sunday morning May 31st 1863

Dear Wife and Children,

I will write a few lines to you this morning. I am not as well as I wish that I was this morning, but I am a good better than I have been during the week. I have lost over ten lbs in the last week, but I feel about well this morning, but I am weak. I got a letter from you last Monday just after I sent one off to you, so I thought that I would wait a few days before I wrote again, but I did not intend to wait quite so long. I wrote a long letter to sister Mariah since and one of my eyes was quite sore two or three days, and it rained for the last two days, but the sun shines bright this morning, and the air is pure and cool. We have not much stir in camp for a week, but the news from Vicksburgh, is watched with a good deal of interest from day to day, the most of us think that Grant will succeed in taking the place, he has done well so far as heard from, but the news comes slow[.] You can see all the news from here in the Weekly Union better than I can write it. The Cavelry went out in front yesterday, and saw a few of the rebels, having a little brush with them, killing two or three, our reg. was ordered out to support them, but had not gone far before they were ordered back. We are ordered out under arms evry morning at day light. Our new Gen. is not liked very well so far, he is not the man for the Volenteers, he puts on to much style, and goes to much upon formalities to suit us, but perhaps he will make a good fighting man, but he will never get the confidence of the boys that Thomas, McCook, or Schofield did while they were with us[.] I hardly think that we are agoing to have any fight of importance here now, but I think that we will move somewhere before long, and probably ahead.

Our reg. is gone out for a regimental review this forenoon, and then they will not have anything more to do to day unless something turns up. The mail has got in but not much news from Vicksburgh. Grant appears to hold his own, and a little more, but we are a having a hard fight there but I hope and pray that he will succeed in taking the place. But "Nerva" I got a letter from you dated the 23d and a good long one too, which done me more good than all the rest of the news we got. I felt a little ashamed of myself for not writing to you before, but you will see the reason. I cannot blame you, nor did I mean to <u>scold</u> you for not writing oftener. I think that you have your hands full to take care of your own sick and all the other sick in Spring Valley, but I was glad to learn that Edgar was well again, but you must take care of yourself and not wear yourself out, before you rest yourself. I have a plenty of time to write when we are laying still in camp, but when we are on duty or the march, we do not get much time, and it is hard work to write about nothing. We draw bakers bread now, it is very good bread[.] I had some potatoes and fresh beef and bread for dinner. I have not eaten anything but a little bread and coffee for a week before. We have a plenty to eat drink and wear. It was a getting very dry here, but the rain yesterday and the day before has raised the streams and springs some, we dug a well for our company and got good water. Can you get your cow pastured all summer, I hope that you can, for it will be a great help to you to have her where you can find her at night. I hope that the children will have a good school this summer and that they will learn fast, who keeps the school? I am glad that you have a plenty of reading these times. I shall like to set down with you, if I live to get home, and look over my old letters. I could connect them with all the places that I have passed through, and hundreds of incidents not worth while to write about. I hope that my expectations will be realized. I wish that I was there this spring so as to help you make your garden, do you have more than one lot for a garden? there has been some green peas and strawberies in camp, but they are all gone before this time the peach crop bids fair to be heavy in this quarter, and I expect that we will have to stay down here untill our time is up, so there is no use of our setting any time to be at home, but they will not keep us long after peace is declared. You seem to be willing not to have me come home untill I come home for good. I am glad that you are, for it would cost a good deal, and not do us much good, for Father seems to see to you, and keep things straight for you, just as well as though I came home to do it myself, so I will not worry myself about the affairs at all. I know what you meant when you spoke about Henry and Mariah's "children" you must not think that the Griffin's are all right because some of them are "lucky," perhaps Sarah has not stayed over with Mariah without some reason. I wrote a long letter to her, and I have asked her a good many questions, about her "children" and evrything else that I could think off[.] I told her to write one to you or to me, if I get one I will send it to you. I am a looking for a letter from Samuel evry day, and he said that he would send me some papers but I have not got any yet. I have not heard any thing from Em. yet. You wanted to know where the boys got their dresses to put on when they dance, they make them out of some old tent or blanket, and borrow some of the "wenches," they fit them as well as a "shirt does a bean pole," the flag is the same that I got at Louisville. We did not have any skirmish then, nor since, and the papers report that the rebel army is a falling back in our front all the time, we shall know before long. I hope that I can come home by another fall and then I will see about getting a dress for you and the children, the boys will soon begin to count the months, that they have got to stay in the service. I expect that they will go off very slow the last year, but we will try to be patient and do out duty to our country, while we do stay in the service, and let the future take care of itself. Mr. Cutting has been quite unwell, but is better now, Pete and the Case boys, Elicut, James Thornton, Wallace Clark, Sergeant Gaskill and the other boys from around there are well. What Warner do you refer to when you speak of Mr. Warners reading the paper, &c. Sergeant Wallace of our Co. used to be well acquainted with the Kingsley boys of Spring Valley. It is a very warm afternoon and it feels like having showers before long.

I cannot think of much more to write this time, I did not intend to write as much as I have when I commenced, but when I got your's I found something to write about. The regiment is just agoing out on dress prarade. We have got a Brass Band organized again, so we have a plenty of good music now. The 9th Ohio and the 35th Ohio both have a band. Our band is a playing now so I must go out and hear them, they do not play as well as a good many, for some of them never played upon an instrament untill about four weeks ago, but they are improving very fast.

Monday Morning June 1st

I feel quite well this morning, it rained hard last night, but it is clear this morning, and the birds are singing briskly, and the Sun is just a coming up. I was over in Co. A. last Eve. and I took up the Chatfield Democrat, and the first piece I read was a lie, and the whole paper was made up of lies, it was the editorial in regard to Valandigham's[7] arrest, he says that he had been arrested, tried and sentenced, "for no one knew what," strange he did not know for what, when evry paper in the Southern Confederacy knew. I wish that I could wield the pen. I would direct a few lines to him the boys say that he ought to be "hung," but as my sheet is about full I will close by bidding you all a good bye this morning.

Good bye one and all from your friend D. B. Griffin.

Letter Number 82

In Camp near Triune Tenn.   June 3d 1863

My Dear Wife and Companion,

As I received a letter from you to day, I will try to write a few lines in answer although I do not know what to write. I feel quite well to day. I left off going to the doctor Sunday morning. Monday morning we all had to go out on a Division review the first one we ever had, in our Division, we all had to have our knapsacks, haversacks and canteens on, besides having our gun and accoutrements on. We were out some four hours and I got

---

[7] Democratic Congressman from Ohio, Clement Laird Vallandigham, a prominent antiwar "Copperhead," convicted of treason and exiled to the Confederacy. He vigorously opposed Lincoln's 1864 reelection and, later, his Reconstruction policies.

very tired, the review went off very well, at night we had orders to be ready to march in the morning at six o'clock with one day's ration, we were up and ready, but it rained hard in the morning, so we did not start quite so early. Our reg. went out about twelve miles for the purpose of moving in a union family, we had a hard road to go on, through a cedar swamp, and over hills and rocks, but we got there all safe, and we got a few loads of corn and the familie's goods, and came back on a better road, but I did not walk but about four miles. I got so tired and the "piles" bothered me so that I got into a wagon and rode the rest of the way, and I was very tired last night, but, I rested well through the night, but this morning I had the tooth ache some and I had it drawn out, so I guess that I will come out straight by and by. When we got back to camp last night we had orders to be ready to march by tomorrow morning, so we have been drawing rations and one thing or ~~nother~~ other all day. Where we are going nor which way we cannot tell yet, we may not go at all, there has two more Briggades come here yesterday from Franklin, they had quite a fight at Franklin yesterday but the rebels were repulsed with quite a loss in killed and wounded and prisoners. We do not think there is much of a force of rebels very near us, now. The rest of our Division is a coming in now, so it ~~like~~ looks a little like old times to see soldiers a marching along. We will be very apt to advance in a day or two at least, and no knowing when I shall get another chance to write to you, but I will write as often as I can, if I am well, so you must not worry if you should not have a letter from me again very soon, your letter was dated May 26[.] I see that you thought that I was a scholding you in my letters, but it was not intended for any such a thing. I see that the trouble is in my not getting your letters so I will not say anything again[.] I asked you a few questions and you merely say that you have written to me before about it for instance I asked you about W. Hasleton and you say that he was as Fathers last winter and you wrote about it at the time. I never got any such letter, you say that you wrote all about your visit down upon the prairie, you wrote a letter when you were at fathers, stating that you had been to Beamans and Jery's and was agoing to go to Boynyton's and over that way, and in the next you said that you had been there, but did not say one word about how they were, what they were about &c, if you have I never have received your letters. I knew by your letter that you were down to Preston, but I merely asked you <u>who</u> you got a chance to go with, not that I was "jealous," but just to know who your friends were, and as it seemed a long time to me not to get any letters from you I thought that I would talk a little about it in my letters, but I did not think that you would take it that I was a scholding you, <u>Nerva</u>[.]

Now I will leave it to Mary if I was a "<u>scholding</u>" or not, I will not say any more, but I <u>do</u> like to hear all that I can from you, you must not think it hard in me if I should ask you a few questions, will you. Now you must not take this as all scholding to, for I do not know what other way I should let you know what I want to, if I could talk to you I could tell you in different language. It rained hard last night, but it is quite warm to day. I saw a few pieces of good wheat yesterday, but it is generaly very thin, it begins to turn some now, but the corn is not very forward here this spring[.] I picked a few rasberies yesterday, the Blackberies are begining to turn there is any amount of them this year, as well as peaches apples &c. We continue to get good news from Vicksburg, but they are a fighting hard, there. I hope that we will not get into any such a fight, if it can be helped, but if it is necessary let it come we are trained for it. If you want any more money before we are payed off again, I will send you some, but I have spent some more than I expected to, and I want to keep some by me so I will not send any more just yet unless you want it bad. If I cannot stand it to march all day I shall go to some hospital or convalescent camp for I find that a person gets along just as well, if he don't try to do the best he can, but still I shall not shirk, there has a number of the boys told me not to try to march along with the reg. when I am in my condition, but I tell them I shall go as far as I can before I stop, or leave the reg. I cannot think of much to write to night for I wrote you a long letter Sunday four of the boys went to the hospital yesterday because they could not stand it to march, and I guess if I had been here I should gone[.]

Sergeant Cutting went to the Hospital, he is pretty slim, I was weighed yesterday and I weighed 155 so you see that I am not quite so fleshy as I have been, but I feel quite well to day and if we do not have to march I shall get along first rate. I am not homesick nor do I intend to be, for that is a bad thing to have in the army[.] Was Alice very sick and have the other children had the same disease. I would like to see you all evry day, but I expect to have to wait untill the term of enlistment is out, you seem to think that perhaps they can keep us longer, but as I have told you before they cannot unless they pass a law to that effect, it will be a little over a year more now, we have been here $\frac{1}{4}$ of a year, and it is a short time to us, time does not seem so long to us as it did when we first came south, soldiering has become a second nature. But I will stop now by bidding you all a good bye again, and I hope and pray that we may all live to enjoy the comforts of home once more. May God bless and protect us all in his mercy.

Good bye   My Dear "Nerva" with a kiss for all
   Good bye   "   "   Alice
   Good bye   "   "   Ida   { Kiss }
   Good bye   "   "   Edgar
from your Dear Husband
and father in the army of the Cumberland
Corp. D. B. Griffin

P. S. Thursday morning.   I feel quite well this morning. I have got to go on picket this morning. We have not got any orders to move as yet, and some think that we will not go from here as they have got to leave two reg here, to guard the place, but I do not want to stay. I will let you know, soon good bye,

D. B. Griffin

Letter Number 83

Camp near Triune Tenn. June 8th 1863

Dear Wife and Children,

As I have an oportunity to write a few lines to you this morning, I will do so. I am about the same as I was when I last wrote, not exactly ~~well~~ sick nor either am I entirely well. The morning that I wrote, I expected to go out on picket, but the order was changed and I did not go. We had a grand review in the afternoon, there was twenty three regiments out besides the Batteries about 15,000 men, it was ~~an imposing~~ grand sight I tell you now. I wish that you could have seen us as we marched around in front of the Gen. (Granger)[8] each regimental band striking up some lively tune as they passed him. We all had our knapsacks on, and I got quite tired. While we were there we heard heavy Canonading in the direction of Franklin, and when we came back to camp we received orders to get our supper just as soon as we could and take one days ration and 40 extra rounds of cartrages and a blanket, and march to Franklin that night (15 miles) and a hard night's march we had of it to. It was just dark when we started, and for a while we were in the woods where you could not see anything, but we managed to get through after a good ~~dealing~~ of falling and stumbling over stumps and roots. I fell over one stump but did not hurt me any, after we had got a few miles it commenced raining, with a good deal of lightning, which had the effect of ~~macking~~ makeing it look darker, and the road was very rough and slippery, and we had to go very slow. I hardly think there was a man in our Brigade (four regiments) but what were down in the mud or stumbled over the rocks and stumps before morning. We got to Franklin just at the break of day, wet, muddy, and tired. I stood it through with the rest of them, but I could not held out ~~mu~~ much longer. We were taken in to a beautiful door yard where all was green, with grass and shade trees and were told to rest ourselves as fast as we could, we all lay down and

---

[8] Union Gen. Gordon Granger, a Division Commander under Gen. Rosecrans in his Army of the Cumberland.

were soon asleep. We found that the rebel cavelry under Forrest[9] made a raid on the place in the afternon, capturing a few of the pickets, robing the stores, and several other depredations, as well as cutting of the railroad and telegraph between there and Nashville and were about to take the fortifications as our Cavelry got there they had quite a skirmish with them, killing some and taking 16 prisoners which we brought back with us. We lay there all day a waiting for an attack from the rebels but they dare not come in again our Cavelry had a little skirmish with them in the fore part of the day but it did not amount to much. We lay there all day, and at night it rained and I got into a barn, and slept good all night. Franklin does not look much as it did when we went through there one year ago, there is not a fence left, not any thing a growing, and a good many of the houses empty. We started back to Triune about one o'clock, arriving in camp about sundown but I rode back in an ambulance. Yesterday the Tennessee Cavelry had quite a little skirmish here with the rebs. we got a few wounded and a few taken prisoners, and there was some of the rebs. killed and wounded, there appeared to be a reconoiter on the part of the rebs. along the whole line, to see whether we were here or not, and they found us a waiting for them at evry point[.] We are under marching orders now, that is to be ready to march at any moment, but when we go I cannot tell, the reg. is out a drilling this forenoon, but I did not go out, it is quite cool this morning, we had a little rain last night, but not much. I think that we are agoing to have good weather for a while now[.] I do not get any news any more than what you will see in the "Union." I will wait untill after the mail comes in, and perhaps I shall get some news to write about.

Afternoon

Well, the mail has come in but there is nothing exciting in the papers. We are looking with a good deal of anxiety for the fall

---

[9] CSA Gen. Nathan Bedford Forrest, often in independent command as a cavalry raider, capturing or destroying significant amounts of Union men and supplies.

of Vixburgh just now. We think that if that falls it will weaken the rebelion a good deal, but wheather it will end it this fall or not, is rather doubtfull. I do not expect to go home before my time is out, so look ahead with hope. But I got a letter from my dear "Nerva," dated June 2nd and was much pleased with it to. I was glad to know that you had a chance to go to meeting if the Methodist and Baptist are jealous of your Company. I guess that they would ride with almost anyone if they had no one to look out for them to ride any more than you and Mary has, it shows how large their souls are. I hope that some of them will be obliged to let their husbands and friends go into the army, and leave them to take care of themselves, it is the very ones that will talk the most, that would take the advantage of a woman in the absence of her husband, but Nerva do not mind their talk, go to meeting when you can and with Mr. Westfall if you can, if he is a good Universalist, he will protect you, and if I should live to come home I hope that I shall be able to repay him for all his trouble. As to Mary's being kissed and hugged, I should do the same thing, if I could see her or you either and I should not care what the folks sayed about it either. As to my placing sentinels up there to watch him, I had rather place them out here in front of the enemy where there is some danger of an attack from them ~~enemy~~ for I do not believe that any one would try to injure me or my family in my absence, if so they are worse than the southern traitor.

Yes I wish that I could have been there and heard him preach the sermon, but as I am not I will be content where I am, untill I am free again, and then if nothing hapens we will enjoy ourselves in going to metings and other places together. I have not got any clothes to send home this spring for I have not drawn any more than I actualy needed, the company stoored some clothes in Nashville, and I put in one of my blankets with them. It would look rather queer to see Edgar in pants and boots and hat. I cannot see him only as the little babe I left in Eliza's arms, the night I came away, if I am gone three years you will not know me, nor I you. I am sorry that your eyes are sore. I know how to pity you for one of my eyes have troubled me for a couple weeks or more, and now they are both quite weak, one of them is very red to day, and I cannot look upon my paper but a little while at a time, but I think that ~~that~~ they will get over it. I hope that yours will not get any worse off than they are[.] I cannot think of much more to write this time, how does the children get along with their school this summer, have they got a good one. I would like to see you all to day, but here I am away down in Tenn. and a fair prospect of going still further south "away down in dixie," but perhaps not. I wish that I could stop writing to you, and go to <u>talking</u> with you, and then I could find enough to talk about for awhile I guess, but I have been all day in writing this, and there is not anything to write about either, but I will close now by saying good bye to you all, and hope for the best to come this from your husband and father in the army of the Cumberland,

to Nerva and the babe's.

Corp. D. B. Griffin Co F 2nd Minn.

Letter Number 84

In camp near Triune Tenn.   June 14th 1863

Dear "Nerva" and "babies,"

I will try to write a few lines to you this morning. I feel quite well this morning to what I have been this ~~morn~~ week past. I went on picket once but came in quite ~~well~~ sick, but I took some medicen, and lay still, and I feel a good deal better this morning, but I shall not go upon duty again untill I am strong enough to go it. We have not had any news here of any account since my last. The rebel cavelry made a dash or two upon our pickets, within the last week, and there was quite a smart skirmish last Thursday with them, they fired a few shell into our lines, but without any damage, we took a few prisoners and Wounded some, and we lost a few. I cannot hear a strait story about the fight so I will not attempt to describe it, you will see some sketches of it in the Union. We have got a very heavy body of troops at this point. I do not know how many, but I think there is about thirty thousand men. We received orders last night about eleven o'clock to have two days rations in our haversacks and be ready to march at a moments notice, but it is now eight o'clock, and we have not got any marching orders yet, there is to be a general inspections to day, but I do not have to go out, with them. We have had some rain, and the nights are quite cool, but it is very warm during the day. We do not hear any different news from Vicksburgh yet but all eyes and <u>hearts</u> look there for something decisive. I hope that Gen Grant will conquer them at last, but he has got a "hard hand to beat." If he does not take the place this time, there is no hopes of our getting out of the war before our time of enlistment is out, about 13 months more as I will be mustered out the same time the regiment is, <u>(so count fast,)</u> if we do not have to do any more for the next six months, than what we have done in the last six, we will not be hurt much. We have been in this camp nearly three months and a half, or nearly one third of a year, and it hardly seems more than so many weeks to us, the time goes off so fast. I hope that the time will <u>soon</u> come when we will be permitted to meet <u>each</u> <u>other</u> at our <u>homes</u> in Minnesota, and if we live it will soon roll around.

I received a letter from you yesterday dated June 6th and was well pleased with it as I always am with a letter from "<u>Nerva</u>," and to hear that my little family is well, and enjoying themselves as well as they can[.] I hope that there will no cloud pass over your hopes, and that they will be fully realized in a short time, and that I shall return to you, to spend the remainder of my days in the presence of my family, but I see by your letters that there is a <u>man</u> coming up to fill <u>my place</u> one of these days, whose name is Edgar Lincoln. I think that he would look like someone's else boy, more than he would a <u>boy</u> of mine if I should see him going around the streets with a <u>hat</u> and "<u>boots</u>" on. I am glad that he is well, and I hope that he will grow up a good boy and be a blessing to his mother and sisters. I do not know why you cannot hear from Em. if he does go on an expidition for they will keep open the communication with the State most likely. I hope that he will come through all right, as well as myself, and I guess that we will. I am glad that "grisy" makes a good cow for you, what do you do with rosy this summer, and what does fathers folks do with the Oxen, are they doing well. I wish that they could earn a little Brakeing for you, if they could, is Allen a breaking any this summer. I wish I was there to work with him. I am sory that you had your cotton plants picked off. I do not think of much more to write this time, the band is aplaying a fine tune now, and the companies are out on inspection, and I am a getting dinner. I am getting some soup. I will close, good bye

D. B. G.

Letter Number 85

In camp near Triune Tenn.   June 20th 1863

My Dear Wife and children,

I feel as though I must write a few lines to you this afternoon, but I have not got any news to tell you for it is a very quiet time with us here, there has not been any movement of the troops here since I last wrote to you, and things remain about the same at Vicksburg but it seems as though the rebels had made a stir among the men on the Potomac[10], and I am glad of it, for it will wake them up a little, and give them something to do, but I have confidence to believe that Gen. Hooker will give them all that they ask for in his way. I hope that they will not get back very safe again but the papers are very still upon the movements of the army, but as near as we can judge evry thing is a working well, and I hope that it will end well, and hasten the close of the war. I received a letter yesterday from Samuel and two to day, one from you and Alice, and one from Sister Mariah, and I was glad to hear from you all, but none so well as from my own "Nerva," and the <u>babies</u>[.] I was glad to hear that

---

[10] This would mark the beginning of CSA Gen. Lee's northward push into Pennsylvania, paralleled initially by Union Gen. Hooker, then by his replacement Gen. George Gordon Meade, culminating in the July 1-3, 1863 Battle of Gettysburg.

you are all well, and are a getting along so finely this summer. I hope that you will have good luck, and that I shall be permitted to go home and find you all hapy, before winter, but I expect to have to stay another year, if we do not it will be a "hapy disapointment" won't it "Nerva?"

I have rather been on the gain since I wrote to you but I am not very stout yet, my appitite is note very good yet, but I guess that I shall get along without going to the Hospital if we stay in camp, but I shall not try to march any yet, you must not worry about me to much for if I should get any worse, I will let you know as soon as I can write or get any one to write, but I hope that I will not have to do so. Where does Mary Vandervaust live, you wrote that Mary got a letter from her. I hope that you and Mary will not get all the Women jealous of you as well as the Methodist down on the prairie, you had better look out, or you will have some of them in your hair before you know it.

I expect that if I was at home that I should laugh some to see the boys out a drilling under Jerry, but as to my being put into office with them if I was there would not be so well for I think if I serve my time out in the army, that they can let me alone the remainder of my life[.] I would be willing to help them all that I could and that is all. I am glad that the children have a good school this summer, and I hope that they will learn fast and well while they have a good chance. We have not had any very hot weather as yet, we have some very heavy showers, and the air keeps pure and cool. I hope that you will not suffer any up there for the want of rain, for we shall want all that you can raise to spare. I will send both of the letters and you must try to write Mariah a few lines if you can, I guess that she is a getting along very well, she seems to have almost evry thing but the "baby." I shall write to her before long. I will see if I can find any one in the Tenn. Reg. from that part of the state, if I can find out anything I will let you know, and you can tell the woman so, but it is hard to find any one in a reg. unless I know the name of the town they live in. Capt Barnes has gone to Wisconsin on a furlough perhaps he will come there, he is not very well, there is not a great deal of sickness in the reg now, we are in hopes that we will move before long for we are tired of being in one camp so long. I cannot think of any thing to write to day so I will close for this time, and bid you all good bye, from your Husband and Father

D. B. Griffin.

To Nerva
     Alice
     Ida and
     Edgar

The Tullahoma Campaign to Winchester, Tennessee

Letters 86–94 (June 30–August 13, 1863)

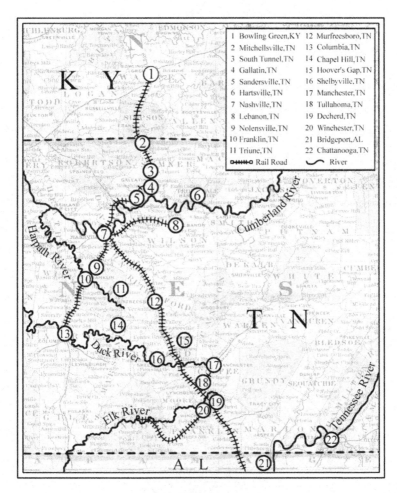

1 Bowling Green,KY	12 Murfreesboro,TN
2 Mitchellsville,TN	13 Columbia,TN
3 South Tunnel,TN	14 Chapel Hill,TN
4 Gallatin,TN	15 Hoover's Gap,TN
5 Sandersville,TN	16 Shelbyville,TN
6 Hartsville,TN	17 Manchester,TN
7 Nashville,TN	18 Tullahoma,TN
8 Lebanon,TN	19 Decherd,TN
9 Nolensville,TN	20 Winchester,TN
10 Franklin,TN	21 Bridgeport,AL
11 Triune,TN	22 Chattanooga,TN
⊶⊶⊶ Rail Road	⌒ River

Finally on the march again, Gen. Thomas's entire XIV Corps heads south, skirmishing almost daily with Confederate troops, suffering some losses, but capturing or killing many rebels as they push toward Chattanooga. At Tullahoma, they discover that Gen. Bragg has again evacuated his estimated fifty thousand men. After relating an interesting tale of Confederates being captured, Brainard describes everyone wading across Elk River, steadying themselves with a stretched rope. Upon learning of the Union victory at Gettysburg, their artillery fires a twenty-four-round salute, repeated the following day when news of the surrender of Vicksburg arrives, lifting the hopes of the men for an end of the war and of slavery. Griffin reports that daily hard rains continue, making any movement difficult for either army. As always, he creates a light banter with his wife and children about all he and they are experiencing. With the weather clearing and warming, Brainard reports that the troops are continuing south to Winchester, Tennessee, where they will establish a base camp for the next four weeks. News and encouragement from home continue to be exchanged with money matters and political opinions from camp. Brainard also responds to false rumors about the 2nd Minnesota being "cut to pieces" and writes a touching self-description of what he does when he receives a letter from home. Following an official review by Army Commander Gen. Rosecrans, Brainard reports they have been ordered to prepare to march, probably down to Georgia.

KING CORN.

Letter Number 86

In camp 6 miles from Tallehoma Tenn.   June 30th 1863

Dear Wife and children, as I have a chance to write a few lines to you this afternoon I will do so. I am well again and as tough as ever. We received orders in the morning of the 23d to march at 7 o'clock with two days rations, we got ready but did not start before 9 o'clock, we took every thing along with us and went about 15 miles towards Murfresboro[.] I rode in the Ambalance part of the day, the next day (24th) we marched acrost to the Shelbyville pike, and part of our regiment were skirmishing with the enemy in the afternoon, but no one was hurt although some of the men got bullitt holes through their coats, 25th we went acrost on to the Manchester pike, and camped near the same place where we got the watermellons last year, here our whole army choir[1] got together. 26 There was heavy skirmishing in the advance through Hovers gap, but our reg. was in the reserve and did not get in to it, we lost a few men, and took a number of prisoners and killed about 100. I was not with the company for I was not able to march, I was along with the team and it was sent back to Murfresboro for rations, we drove all night. 27th Went on towards Manchester, without any resistance to speak of, took a few prisoners in Manchester, drove all day and untill 11 o'clock at night when we camped in Manchester near the fair grounds that we camped in last year. I was very tired and sleepy for I had not had one night to sleep since we started, so I lay down without my supper and slept till day light, we got our rations the next day, 28th and had orders to go into camp at noon, but the order was countermanded and we went towards Tallahoma. I was ordered to report to the surgeon of the regiment, if I was not able to march, but I told them that I did not want to leave the regiment as long as I could keep from it, so I took my gun and started with the reg. We did not go but about 6 miles that day, the ninth Ohio in the advance, they had a considerable of

---

[1] He means "corps," here and through the remainder of his letters.

291

skirmishing for about one mile but no one was hurt, we went into camp on a large creek, where we are now. Yesterday 29th we were ordered out to reconoiter in the advance, we were in the advance Co. I and H. were thrown out as skirmishingers. We saw a number of the rebels, and we kept up a sharp fireing all day, but only one man in our reg. was touched, and he only received a small scratch on the arm. We fired two rounds at them from a battery but with what effect I have not learned, they soon answered with three rounds from one of their guns, only killing one horse for a doctor in the 35 Ohio, but the splinters and leaves flew around our heads but no one was hurt. It rained hard all the afternoon, and we were very wet, we were relieved just at sundown by the 1st Brigade and we came back to camp and dried ourselves and got our supper, and you must know that we was hungry for we had not eaten since morning, and to day I learn that there was a few men killed in our Division but I do not know how many, our boys shot a courier that came rideing up to them mortally wounding him. 30th We have been in camp all day and it has been very warm, it is the first day but what ~~we~~ it has rained hard since we started except the first day, and the roads are quite bad, so we have had to leave all our knapsacks behind us, and we have not got a change of clothes with us, and we do not know when we will get them, but we will try and keep as clean as we can under the circumstances. I have gained in health and strength evry day since we started so that I feel quite well and hearty to day. We do not think that we will have much fighting this side of Chattanoga, but I do not know, I hope not. I expect that we will go on in the morning. I have not much other news to write and no more paper and this I borrowed, so you must excuse me for not writing before, for this is the first time that I have to write a word. I have not got any letter from you since we started, you must not worry if you should not hear from me so often for I expect that we will be on the move for a while now, and be kept pretty busy, so we will keep up good cheer and look for the best. I hope that you will have good health through the summer[.] I cannot think of any thing more so I will bid you all a good bye, and a kiss for all, may God keep and protect you all, is the wish of your husband and father

D. B. Griffin

Letter Number 87

In camp on the South bank of Elk river Tenn.   July 6th 1863

Ever Dear and Affectionate Wife,

I have at last got a chance to write a few lines to you. I am well to day, and have stood the march well so far, and I am a good deal better than I was when we started from Triune. I wrote a few lines to you, with a pencil, stating how we got along up to the 30th of June, we stayed in the camp that night, and the next morning, July 1st I went out on picket, but had not been out long before the regiment received orders to march, and We were relieved of picket, and came into camp, and the boys handed two letters to me, and they were both from "My Nerva," and right glad was I to hear from you, but was sorry to hear that you and the children had been sick again, but was glad that you were a getting better when you wrote. I hope and pray that you will <u>not</u> be sick much, if <u>any</u>, while I am away from you, for it must be so lonesome to you all the time. I hardly had time to read the letters before we started for Tallahoma, which place we reached a little past 12 o'clock, without fireing a gun or seeing a rebel, for Gen. Bragg had evacuated the place in the morning after two o'clock, it was a sudden movement on their side, for they were fortifying and receiving reinforcements up to 9 o'clock of the evening before, there was from 35 to 50,000 troops in the place, but they did not see fit to stand and give us a fight on their own ground, but ran, as usual.

The place was entirely destitute of evry thing in the shape of any living thing except about 2 dozen of the inhabitants, the rebels took what little they had with them, except about 5 large siege pieces 3 field pieces, some amunition and some corn meal, which is all the bread kind that the rebel soldiers get, they were intending to have what wheat there was through here but they had cut it for our army to feed their mules with and for us to slleep on, there is no field that escapes our hands, if left.

We camped ~~on~~ in Tallahoma that night around the house that Gen. Bragg had his head quarters in the morning. Gen Rosecrans took the same house for his head quarters that night, the Cavelry brought in a good many prisoners during the afternoon, they drop out on purpose to be taken, they say that they will not fight any more, for they do not get half enough to eat, nor wear. The Tennessee rebels say that they will not cross the Tennessee river to fight, if they have got to fight, they will fight in Tenn. so they are coming into our lines by squads and giving themselves up, we take a good many, two of the boys in Co H. brought in ten on the 2nd, 2 of our boys were in the advance, without any gun, they were at a spring getting some water when they saw two rebels coming towards them, they thought that they had got to go down into dixie sure, but they hid in some bushes near by, and when the rebs came up, they set down their guns besides a water tank on the rail road, and went down to the spring, our boys crept up and got their guns, and told them to surrender which they did forthwith, our boys then started back with their prisoners when they saw two more crossing a field, one of them guards the prisoners, and the other one goes out and orders the other two to halt and surrender which they did, and the two boys brought the four prisoners into camp, so you see that they do not show much fight. On the morning of the 2nd we started at daylight and we marched out of the town with our colors flying and the band playing, there was a great many troops in the place, for they were marching in to the town all night long. We marched through a swampy country, and in the woods about 7 miles to Elk river, which was very much swollen by the rains, the rebels had burned the bridge, so we had to ford it, it was waist deep and ran very swift, one Division crossed over that night, there was said to be a few drownded in crossing over. I went down and had a good swim, it was the greatest swim I ever saw, for there was more than one thousand boys in the water at once. We camped in the woods that night, in the morning of the 3d it rained hard untill noon but as we did march we managed to keep dry. We commenced crossing the river in the afternoon, it took all the afternoon for the Brigade to cross over, there was two large ropes stretched across for them to hold on to but as most of boys striped themselves and tied evry thing up in a blanket and had their gun and bundle on their shoulder it was hard work for some of them to get over, at all, one boy in the 4th Ky. was drownded, we all got over safe. I kept my clothes on, and had no trouble in crossing over, we went into camp about1/2 mile from where we crossed, and I slept sound all night, the next day 4th of July it rained hard in the forenoon, but we moved about three miles in the afternoon through a swamp and it was bad getting along, we got to this place, and as we were getting rather short of rations, the Gen. said he would not go any farther untill we got some rations, so we went into camp in an open field, where we have got a plain view of the Tennessee mountains, which are about ten miles from us, after we got into camp the Gen had an order from Gen Rosecrans, to fire a salute, in honor of the victory gained on the Potomac, or in Penn.[2] Gen. Mead had taken the command of the army of the Potomac, and after three days of hard fighting, had completely routed an defeated Gen. Lee's army, and the papers that we received to day agrees with the report, our Battery fired 24 rounds, and it speaks louder than an old anvill, I tell you. I stood off about 20 rods and the shocks would fairly make the ground tremble, and then there is five or six Brass bands here and they kept a playing with them untill late in the night, and thus passed away the 4th of July 1863, the 5th we stayed in camp all day. I tried to get a sheet of paper to write a letter to you, but I could not get any, but some of the teams came up last night with some of the knapsacks. I have got hold of some to day, it rained yesterday afternoon about as hard as I ever saw it rain, and then it rained most all night last night, but it is very hot and sultry to day, and I think that it is agoing to rain some

---

[2] The July 1-3, 1863 Battle of Gettysburg.

more, the roads are very bad and the creeks are high, and we do not know how long we shall stay here. We get some meat and a few potatoes in the country, but there is not much, we have had enough to eat so far, but some of the regiments have not got any thing to eat, but the supply train will be up to night. We are within 8 miles of Winchester, and 6 of Dechard, so you see we are back to where we were last fall, the federals are 8 miles below Winchester, the rebels are said to be at Bridgeport on the Tenn. river where they intend to make another <u>stand</u> it is reported that our Cavelry is in possession of Chattanoga, but I do not know how true the report is. "Nerva" if the reports prove to be all true, there is some hopes of our spending the next fourth of July at home if we live and we are well, and may God grant that we may. I hope that I can get some better news to write to you the next time I get a chance, to write. I think if our army follows up the enemy now, as we have got them started, this war will soon end, and we be permitted to return to our homes in peace, may God grant it, is <u>my</u> prayer, all that keeps us back now is the weather and roads, for we are unable to get our suplies but the cars will run through in a day or two, and them we will be all right. I <u>wish</u> that I could talk to you instead of writing to you and perhaps I will before long but I do not expect to for a while yet let <u>us</u> look ahead and hope, the boys have all stood it well so far only one man has been left behind, and there is not a man on the sick list in camp, and the rest of the regiment is about the same[.] I shall look for a letter from you evry day now, and I will write to you as often as I can get a chance so good bye once more from

D. B. Griffin.

P. S.   I cannot say much about your letters for I have not got room. I am glad that you got a chance to go up to the camp meeting, and that you saw some of your old schoolmates there[.] I hope that he will come and see you. Kiss all the <u>babies</u> for me, tell them that pa would give a good deal to see them, all, and I hope that I shall before many months.

Letter Number 88

In Camp on Elk river Tenn   July 8th 1863

My Dear Wife Children and friends,

I will write a few lines to you this morning. We are still in the same camp that we came into on the 4th although we are a going to move camp a short distance to day, in order to get a better camping place, for it is a bad camping place where we are. It has rained hard evry day and night since we have been here, in fact this is the sixteenth day that it has rained, and it is impossible for the army to move any further untill the roads are fixed and some bridges made so that we can get suplies through to us, we have been pretty short of rations, but we have not suffered any as yet, but some of the regiments have been pretty hungry but we have got rations acrosst the river, and we are all right now, if it had not been for the rain, this army would have been hard after Bragg all of the time, but I guess that Bragg's army is hurt some by the rain as well as ours. I have no news ~~from~~ to write from here this time, for there has not been anything done since I last wrote to you, on account of the heavy rains, but we are cheered withe the news both from Grant's and Mead's army, last night we received the news that Gen. Mead had given the rebels fits in Penn. that he had taken 20,000 prisoners and 120 pieces of artillery, there was 35 rounds fired in honor of the victory, and this morning we got the news of the falling of Vicksburgh[3], and the same number of rounds was fired this morning, but we have not got the particulars of the fight yet. But it is good news, ain't it "Nerva."? We do rejoice some, for it does seem as though there was some chance of the war being ended before one year more, which will be the end of the three years, for two years ago to day Co. F. was sworne into the service of the U. S. so if we live we will be in Minn. one year from this time, any how, and if the war should end, we will be there before, so I hope that it

---

[3] July 4, 1863 marked the end of Union Gen. Grant's seven-month campaign against Vicksburg, Mississippi, culminating in a seven-week siege and the surrender of CSA Gen. Pemberton and his 30,000 men.

will end this fall, don't you "Nerva"?, and then we can go home to our families and friends before another cold winter sets in, but we will wait patiently for the time to come around. We do not expect any fight before we get to the Tenn. river at a place called Bridgeport, and I hope that we can move on before Bragg gets any reinforcements from Lee's or ~~Grant's~~ Pemberton's[4] army, if we have good success here, I cannot see where the rebel army is agoing to make another stand, if they do make one. I think that Dix[5] will keep watch of Richmond, and Banks of Port Hudson. We may expect good news evry day now, for our army has got started and with great success so far, and I hope that it will go on from Victory to Victory, untill there will not be a rebel left on the American soil, nor any chance for a rebelion to start in the US, as long as the world stands, and I hope that slavery will soon end in the bargain, for that is the bone of contention between the North and South, and it is a disgrace to any nation to hold slaves in the shape that the Southern Chivalry holds them, if you read the papers you will see some of the acts of the Slaveholders in the South, it is to awful to relate, is it not?

I have had to stop three or four times since I comneenced writing. We have moved our camp about one mile and have got into a nice shady place, and have got it all fixed and cleaned up nice, my tent is under a hickory tree, where it will be in the shade most all day. I am well, and in good spirits, as I intend to keep. I do not want to get a furlough nor go to the Hospital if I can help it, not that I do not want to see you, but because I do not want to go and leave you again, if I should come home, for the second parting would be worse than the first, and for one I would rather stay away a little longer, and if I live to get home,

---

[4] CSA Gen. John Clifford Pemberton, of Pennsylvania Quaker heritage but married to a Virginian, sided with the Confederacy and appears to have been promoted beyond his command capabilities.

[5] John Adams Dix, a U. S. Senator from New York and Lincoln's first Secretary of the Treasury, famous for his declaration: "If anyone attempts to haul down the American flag, shoot him on the spot!" As a Union Major General he held several territorial commands in the Eastern Theater.

I can stay there with my Wife and children, and friends, and in the society of men and <u>women</u>, especialy the latter, for we do not see a woman to speak to, except now and then a Black woman. I expect that I should make bad work of it if I undertook to talk to one, but I think that I should say <u>something</u> to <u>one</u> <u>woman</u> if I could see "<u>her</u>," and I guess that I should make some slip's of the tongue, that "<u>she</u>" would overlook them for a while untill I could learn to talk like other folks in "America[.]"

The country that we have passed through on our march here is very rough and mountainous, and not very productive, the wheat crop is good. I think that I have never saw any better wheat grow, but the rebels, nor the citizens will not get much good of it for we strip the country of all forage and provisions as fast as we go along, so if the rebel army should come back through here, they will not find much to live upon, but I do not think that they will come back, I think that we are a makeing our last journey through Tenn. after the rebels, the next time we go through I think that we will be a going <u>home</u>, "Home, Home, <u>Sweet</u> Home," what a sound that word has got to <u>my</u> ears. I cannot write any more to night, it rained all night last night and a little this morning, but it has come off very hot this afternoon. I do not think that it has cleared off for good yet, do you have much rain in Minnesota this summer. I hope that you are all well again, write as often as you can, and I will do the same, look forward in hopes. This from your Husband who hopes soon to be with you in Minn, so good bye, all this time.

D. B. Griffin.

Letter Number 89

Camp Winford, Tennessee,   July 12th 1863

My Dear Wife and Children,

I will write a few lines to you to day. I am well at present, and was glad to learn, by your letter of the 1st, which I received last night, that you were all well again, and a getting along first rate, and that you had got some rain there at last. I hope that it did not come to late to help the crops in Minnesota, for it you will need all that you can raise, to keep us through another winter and have some for us when we get home, in a year from now, if not before. I do not think that we will have to march much more for a while, at least, for we are agoing to go from here tomorrow either to Winchester or Dechard, to guard the rail-road, if so we will not have to fight much for a while unless it is with the Gurilles of the South. We have got a plenty of ration's now, and the black-berries are getting ripe, and they are very plenty about here, we have not had any green corn yet, and I have not seen any field that had tassled yet, although we had aplenty of corn by this time last year, but it was a very late Spring here and wet. I have not seen any peaches that were fit to eat yet, we get some apples to stew, and now and then a mess of new potatoes, but I should liked first rate to have been there and help you eat your ~~new~~ green-peas, for I have not had a mess since I came from home, but as I cannot be there, you can eat them and think of me, and plant a good lot of them another spring for "me and you," for I expect to be there next summer "any how" if not this fall. I wrote a letter to you on the eighth, and I told you all the news in that that I had heard off, but the news is all confirmed so far. Lee has lost about one half of his army in Penn. and at the last accounts we have of him he was at the Potomac, and it was very high, and his bridges were burned and he was a trying to cross over on flat boats, but that we had got a large army in his rear, that had cut off his communication with Richmond, and that Meade was a pressing him hard in the front. I hope that he will destroy the whole of Lee's army, so effectualy that they cannot organize a single regiment again. I think that it is the best thing that has ever happened to the North, to have Lees army march in to Penn., for it has had the effect to open the eyes of some of the "Peace" men of the North, and sat them to work for the

"Union," and their <u>country</u>. John Morgan[6] has crossed the Ohio river below Louisville, and was making for Indianapolis with about five thousand men, but that our men were close after him, and that the people of Indiana were coming to the rescue by thousands, and it was thought doubtful whether he would make his escape out of the state of Indiana or not, but we are not concerned about him in the least, we think that the troops in Ky. and Ia. will take care of him, for the present at least, and I <u>hope</u> that he will not be able to get back into Ky again with his <u>army</u>, if he does himself.

And there is <u>glorious</u> news from Vicksburg. Gen. Grant had captured the place with twenty thousand men, and evry thing in the place, he went into it on the fourth of July. I think that it must have been a great celebration for his army, and a day of <u>Liberty</u> to Pemberton's army, for it must been like a prison to them, only think of it one third of the men in the Hospitals, and unfit for duty, and all of them on very short rations, what a rejoicing there must have been to get out of the place, alive, for they had been shut in for two long months, and they were in the face of the cannon all the time and were liable to be shot down if they showed their heads outside of their hiding places, for a moment.

They have also had a fight at Hellena, in Ark[7], Gen Schofield routing Gen Price[8] from there taking some 1,200 prisoners and killing a good many, so you see that they are a getting "their

---

[6] CSA Gen. John Hunt Morgan, another famous cavalry raider of Union territories in the Western Theater, captured thousands of prisoners and destroyed millions of dollars' worth of equipment and supplies. Eventually captured in Ohio, he escaped prison there, returned to raiding, and was finally killed in 1864.

[7] The July 4, 1863 Battle of Helena, Arkansas was an attempt by CSA Gen. Price to relieve pressure on Vicksburg by attacking Grant's supply depot. Union forces successfully defended Fort Curtis, with significant losses suffered by the Confederates.

[8] CSA Gen. Sterling Price, who earned a mixed record of victories and defeats in the Western Theater.

rights," in good earnest this time, the accounts so far foot up about 70,000 prisoners taken from the rebels, that is quite a small army. Now if evry thing works well untill the first of August, our fighting will be about done, if not done. I am not the only one who thinks so either. Gen Thomas, our Choir Commander, gave the boys a short speech a few nights ago, he spoke well of this Division, and in his private conversation, said that he thought we would be mustered out of the service in three months, and that he thought that we would not have any more fighting to do here, for Gen. Bragg was agoing towards Atlanta, Georgia, and that if their armies east and west were whipped out, he could not get very heavy reinforcements any where, but that does not make it so, but we can live in good hopes at the least, and no man wishes that they can be at home this fall, any more than I do, but if I am needed here, it will not be but a short time to stay here at the most, so you must keep up good cheer and hope for the best, for the present, I will not say any more this time. We have had two days of fair weather, but we have just had a hard shower (12 o'clock) and it has spattered on my letter, there was an accident hapened this forenoon in Co. I. while one of the boys was a cleaning his gun, it went off, and the charge went through the ball of his foot, which will lay him up for a long while. I am glad that Alice and Ida have a good school, and I hope that they will improve it. I am also glad that they like their papers so well. We have not been payed off yet nor do we know when we are to be payed, they owe me four months pay. I am in no hurry to get it unless you want it, if you want any money let me know, and I will send you some. I must write a letter to Samuel before long for I have not answered his yet. I expect that Henry is at home now, how I wish I could see you all, and I hope and pray that the time will soon come that I shall be permitted to join you, and remain with you, the rest of my life, but I will bid you all a "Good bye," once more this from your Husband and friend

D. B. Griffin Co F. 2nd M.

Letter Number 90

In Camp near Winchester Tenn.   July 21st 1863

My Dear Wife and children,

As I have a few moments to spare this morning I will improve it in writing a few lines to you. I am as well this morning as I have been in a long while, and as we got fifty two dollars in "green backs" last night, I think that we can enjoy ourselves a few months longer, but I shall send you a twenty to day, and in a few days another twenty and as much more as I can spare, and I hope that you will enjoy yourselves in useing it as well as I do in sending it to you, if I send $50.00 to you I guess that you had better pay Mr. Boynton the interest on the land, for it will be rather uncertain about our getting payed off again before the interest is due. I have not written to you for a little over a week, for I wanted to send some money to you, and we were expecting pay before, but I have not got much news to write about, nor I have not got much to write about this morning. We moved our camp on the 18th we are camped within one mile of Winchester, and near the same camp ground that we were on eleven months ago, near the big springs, we camped in a large open field with nothing in it but black berries and a few small bushes, on Sunday we worked hard all day in cleaning up the ground and putting up shade's over our tents, and we finished them yesterday, we had a little shower in the night last night, and it is cool and nice this morning, we have had some very hot weather for the last week, but one thing is in our favor it is quite cool through the nights, so that we can sleep sound. I received a letter from you the same day that I wrote you before, but it was a back letter. I received a letter from Alfred Smith last week which was gladly accepted[.] I have answered it, and I hope that he will keep on a writing to me. I have not had a letter from any body else, there is not much news of late, any more than the particulars of the late fights in the east, and west, they have commenced again on Charleston and the news from there so far is very good. I hope that they will take that place if they have to burn evry house in it, for it is the hot bed of secession where Treason was hatched, and the rebellion set in motion, we look for the downfall of that place with a good deal of anxiety, and I hope that it will soon fall. We do not hear much from our front, but all is quiet just now, but I hope that it will not stay so a great while for I want to have them go through with it, and end this war, and let us go home to our friends and families. It seems as though they have a little trouble in a few of the Northern city's in drafting, but they will soon be put down, for the Government is in earnest, and I believe that it will put down all oppression and mob law at once, how does all the news take in Spring Valley. I hear that they had a large Celebration in Chatfield on the 4th. I hope that we will be there on the 4th next year, and I think that we will be there before that time, if alive, and well, if we are there we can have a celebration and a good one to, but I do not expect that we can all get home safe, but what boys there is left are well at present, and all enjoy themselves as best they can, but we had rather be on the move _forward_. I have been out a black berrieing two or three times, and as some one goes out evry day, we have all that we want to eat. I should like to have _you_ make a pie for me to day, for we do not get any pies made out of them. The Tennessee regiments are away from here, so I cannot find out any thing about that womans folks yet but if I get a chance to enquire I will do so. Capt. Barnes has come back to the regiment, he is quite well at present, he did not go to Minnesota the boys from the Valley are well. I do not think of any more to write this morning, so I will wait untill I get a letter from you to answer. I must stop for the mail will soon go out, kiss all the babies for me and tell them that I hope to see them and kiss them myself before many months, give my respects to all my friends, and accept my love for yourself, with a kiss. {Nerva}

D. B. Griffin Co F

Letter Number 91

In Camp near Winchester   Saturday Eve, July 25th/63

My Dear Wife and Children,

As I have just this moment heard that Col. Bishop is agoing to start for Chatfield in the morning, I thought that I would write a few lines to you and send some money in the letter, and give it to him to take to Minn, as it will be the safest way for me to do. I have sent you a twenty dollar bill since we was payed of, (the 20th) and now I will send you thirty dollars more ($30.00, in this, makeing in all fifty dollars, and I hope that it will do you as much good in useing it, as it does me in being able to send it to you. As I sayed in my last letter, I thought that you had better pay the interest on the land, or keep enough by you to pay it, as I did not know how soon we should get payed off again, but I can get some money almost any time, from the boys if you should get short of funds before we are payed off. I am well this evening, as I have been ever since we came here, we have good water and a plenty of rations, and not very heavy guard duty to do, we have drilled twice a day for the last three or four days, and it is very hot work, for it is very warm weather here, it has not rained any since we came here. Evry thing is very quiet here just at the present time, and it appears to be all around, except the John Morgan raid into Ind. and Ohio, and he is not a making out very well there, he has lost the most of his men, and it is doubtfull if he gets out of Ohio without being captured, what little news we do get appears to be ~~on~~ favorable to the cause of the Union army. We are a looking anxiously for the news from Charleston just now, we hope and believe that it will fall into our hands in a few days if it has not already been taken. You can see by the late mob riot in New York city, what the "Peace Democrats" would do if they could, but "Old Abe" is determined to carry through every means in his power, to end the rebellion, and I hope that evry man in Minn. will aid him in so doing. I see by the papers that quite a number of the leading "Vallandigham" papers in Ohio have droped him and are agoing in for the support of the

Administration, and there will be more before the fall elections come off, but we do not bother ourselves much upon political topics, let the men at home take care of that, let us end the war first and then we will attend to other matters afterwards. I have not had any letter from you since we came here, but I know that there is some on the road somewhere if you are well, and I <u>hope</u> that none of you are sick this summer and I hope that I shall be there before another summer if I live and am well, we have not only eleven months months more to stay in the service, and I believe that we will be at home in less time than that, if no great reverses occur to our army this fall, and I hope that all will go well with us, we have been very fortunate so far, in not being in any very severe engagements, the first Minn. reg. has lost heavily in the late fight with Lee. It is agetting quite late and I cannot think of any thing to write so I will stop for to night, it looks very much like rain, and there is heavy thunder in the west. You must write and let me know whether you get all of the money safe or not. I hope that you will, how is the Wheat crop there, does your wheat do any thing this summer. I will stop and bid you all a good night, and go to bed. I want to see you all very much, and I hope that I shall before long, so good bye one and all, from your husband and father, to Nerva and the babies, good bye.

Corp D. B. Griffin.

Sunday morning, 26.

I am as well as usual this morning, it did not rain but a very little last night, but it is pure cool morning, but I think that it will burn off hot before noon. I think that I will have to go on picket this morning, but the picket duty is not very hard here. I will send you a Cincinnati paper this morning by mail, this letter I will send by Col. Bishop, and in addition to the $30.00, I will send you $20.00 more which I have borrowed untill next pay day, for I think that I will not have another so good a chance to send home money, although I have never lost any through the mail, and I think that you will take as good care of it as I will here, it will not cost any interest. I have had enough by me all the time for spending money, and I have kept enough back this time, so you need not think that I go without, for I have enough.

All of the boys that are from around there are well as far as I know. I do not think that we will move away from here for a while yet, and perhaps we shall stay here a month or two, and by that time it will not be quite as warm weather as it is now. I have not received any letters from any one since I came here, but I know that they have not <u>all</u> forgot me, for I think that there is <u>some</u> letters on the road for me, from <u>you</u>, any how. I will write as often as I can find any thing to write about, and oftener if I do not get any news, so that you may know how I am a getting along, and where we are[.] I have not got to go on picket to day after all, and as it is sunday I will not have much to do. I would just like to step in and eat breakfast with you this morning, we are agoing to have some fresh beef and Coffee and crackers, (or <u>hard</u> bread) for our breakfast. I had some cheese yesterday for supper, but we have to pay 30 cts a lb for it, but evry thing else is high, on account of the cost of getting things through from the North, as all of the roads are in the <u>service</u> of the Government, but one good thing for us, we do not have to buy any thing unless we are a mind to. I cannot think of any more to write this morning so I will bid you all a good bye.

D. B. Griffin.

Sunday Evening July 26th 1863

After I had got the money and letter all ready this morning, I learned by Col. Bishop, that he was not agoing to go to Minnesota, he was going no farther than Galena Ill, if he could get leave of absence long enough, so I gave up the ~~Idea~~ idea of sending so much money to you this time[.] I will only send you a $20.00 in this letter, and a ten in my next, as I was to late this morning to send this away by the mail I waited untill after the mail came in thinking shure that there would be as much as <u>one</u> letter for me, but no letter, it is to bad ain't it "Nerva"? but they will be received with joy when they do come I'll assure you. It has not rained any to day, but it has kept ~~showery~~ cloudy all day, with a little thunder around, there is not much news in the papers to day and I have none to write so I will stop for this time, you must excuse me for not sending you more money this time, but I will not risk more than a XX at once in the mail, and I hope that you will receive it all safe and sound, write as often as you can, and let me know all that is agoing on in the Valley, and evry thing else that you can think of no matter what it is, and I will write as often as I can find any thing to write about, kiss all of the babies for me and take a good one yourself, { Kiss. } from your friend and husband, hoping that I shall see you before many months in health and good cheer.

Corp. D. B. Griffin Co F.
P. M. Griffin
A. J. Griffin
I. May Griffin
E. L. Griffin

Monday morning.

It was rumored in camp last night that John Morgan and 700 more of his men were captured. I hope that it is true. I am well this morning, it rained a little last night, no other news this morning, good bye.

D. B. G.

Letter Number 92

In camp near Winchester Tenn   Aug 1st 1863

My Dear Wife and Children,

I received a letter from you last night dated July 23, and you may feel assured that I was glad to hear from you, and hear that you were all well, but was sorry to hear that some one had reported that the 2n Minn. was all cut to pieces in their advance on Tullahoma, but it is not so for we did not lose a man, as you have learned in my other letters. But it must be hard for you to hear such reports, and then not to receive any letters from me for so long a time. I felt bad because I did not get any from you before, but I have not any thing to worry me, to what you have ~you~, to worry you, for I know that if you are sick, or need any help, you are amongst friends, who will see that you are provided for, and I know if you do not get any letters from me for two or three weeks, and in the mean time have such reports as that reach you, that it would be impossible for you, or any one who has got <u>near</u> and <u>dear</u> friend in the army, to help worrying or feeling bad, if they have got a spark of love for the absent ones. You wrote that you were proud of me as well as all the rest of our folks were. But "<u>Nerva</u>," I <u>was</u> proud of <u>you</u> when I read your letter last night, to see you after all your trials and sacrifices, in the last two years, ~to see you~, instead of asking me to come home if I could, or any thing of that sort, that would tend to make us homesick or discouraged, rejoicing ~and~ over, and cheering us on to victory and the defence of our country and ~or~ our flag. "Nerva" if I ever felt like shedding tears of joy, it was then, and you may <u>bet</u> that my eyes were not dry on the occasion. May God bless you and my <u>dear</u> <u>children</u>, and may I never do any thing that will lower me in your esteen, or in the minds of our friends, and I will try my utmost to be worthy of your esteem, so help me God.

I showed and read your letter to some of the boys, and they all pronounce it a <u>good</u> letter, just such a letter as evry <u>good</u> and true woman would and <u>ought</u> to write to their <u>husbands</u>, <u>sons</u> or <u>sweethearts</u>, who are in the army, if all of the <u>women</u> had written in the same way at the commencement of this war, ~wl~ we would have more men in the field to day, by thousands but if we live and come home, and know that the country is saved, and that we have done all that was required of us to do, we can have a clear concience, in knowing that we did not hold back, when our country needed us, but went at once to the defence of our country, and our <u>flag</u>, in knowing that we did not through the pursuasions of ~wifes~ wives, Mothers or sweethearts, get our discharges or shrink from the path of duty, when we were called upon to face the enemy in the field, but were always ready and waiting for the command, Forward, march[.] "Nerva" keep up good cheer a few months longer, look on the bright side of the world, and all will go well, bear up with the inconveniences of life alone, a few more weeks, and then if I am spaired to meet you at home, we will be blessed a hundred-fold, in knowing that we have done our duty as well as we could.

I am well today, and the health of the army is good as far as I know. I do not know when we will move from here, but it is very probable that we shall advance before long, there has a large body of Cavelry started for East Tenn, and I hope that the people of that part of the state, will soon be free from the oppression of the Traitors, of the slaveholders, for East Tennessee is as loyal as any of the Northern states, there is not a great many slaves in that part of the state, and the way they have suffered in the hands of the secesh, and how they long to be free, you will see by the Nashville papers. I do not think that we will go in there, but we are not supposed to know any thing. There is not much news from here, but it is said that there is a small force of rebels, back in Ky, but they will come out as slim as John Morgan did in Indiana and Ohio, we do not much trouble from that quarter.

Noon.

Well I have been to dinner, and I will tell you what we had for dinner I had some boiled beef, some vegetable soup and hard bread some ginger cakes and cheese. I should like to have some of Mothers cheese to eat, for it is better cheese than we get here, and we pay from thirty to fifty cents a lb, how much do they get a lb. for their cheese, this summer. I hope that they get payed for their work. If Father thinks that you had better sell the Oxen this fall, with Rosa and the steer, let him sell them for all that he can get, and take his pay for his trouble in takeing care of them, out of the money, and pay the rest of the money to Mr. Boynton, or pay up some of the other debts, for I will try to send you enough to live upon from here. If we could manage to pay $100.00 this fall for our land, I might get enough by the time I go home, to pay the whole amount and then we should have a home at least, but Nerva do as you and Father think best about the business. I have sent you twenty dollars in each of my two last letters, and I will send you ten dollars in this, which will make $50.00 this time, and I hope that you y will get it all safe. I have got enough left to keep me in spending money untill we get payed off again. You wanted to know what made the boys shoot the courier when he came up to them, they ordered him to halt two or three times and he did not heed the order, but turned to run, and snapped his pistol at the boys, then two of them fired at him, one of the bullets going right through his body, that is the way of war, it is what we came for. It is very warm to day, and looks very much like rain, it is a thundering off in the south, we have had some few showers in the last week. We did not get any mails for two or three days, on account of the railroad in Ky, but it came through yesterday, and I hope that it will not stop again while we are in the south. We have fixed up our camp some with boughs and with cedar fronts, but the 35th Ohio have fixed their camp up beautifully, they have got the fronts of their tents all fixed up with cedar boughs, with arched doors and windows and, they have put up boughs across the streest both in front and in the rear, the center one is arched very high and they have raised a high flag pole in the center, and a large flag is flying from it now, there is an artist here, that is a going to draw it off, and a photograph man is agoing to take a photagraph of it, it looks like a fairy garden, but they have worked hard to fix it up but it does not pay for we cannot tell how long we are agoing to stay in one place at a time, we are well shaded and that is good enough. We have to drill twice a day which does not hurt us one bit unless it is to hot weather, we are payed for soldiering. I guess that the Indian expidition has proved to be a failure this time at least, you will most likely see Em. there again this fall, on a furlough, but I think that I shall stay untill my time is out, before I go home unless the war ends beff before that time. I will send you a couple of papers in a day or two. I have had no letters from Vt. since the ones I sent to you. I shall look for one all the time. I do not think of any thing more to write this time. I will wait untill the mail comes in, perhaps there will be some news in that. Well the mail has come but as the telegraph is down between Nashville and Louisville, there is no news of interest there was no letters for me. I will send you two Cincinati papers, is there any agents there for the sale of the history of the war. I have read some in the first Vol, it cost is $3.50 a vol. I can get it and have it sent to you if you want that I should when we get our pay again. I do not think of anything more to write this time, I will try to write as often as once a week. I love to when I get your letters look in and see a piece of paper with different hand writing, I know that Alice has written a few lines to her father. I expect that I should hardly know my "great" "little" girls and boy when I get home again, but I hope that they will be good children and if we are all well, it will not be but a short time before I shall see you all again. I do not know but that I ought to write a letter to Fathers folks but I expect that they read all your letters and so they know how I am and where I am, kiss the babies for me, do not credit any of the reports that you hear about the 2n Minn reg. I will try to keep you posted, give my best respects to our folks and friends, good bye, to Nerva, from

D. B. Griffin

Letter Number 93

Camp Thomas near Winchester Tenn   Aug 6th 1863

Ever dear and affectionate Wife and children,

I will try to write a few lines to you to day, in order to let you know how I am and what we are a doing, as I have not got any news to write about. I am well to day, and I have been well for a long time, and I hope that I shall remain in good health the rest of my term of service. It is very hot to day, but as it is the President's Thanksgiving day we do not have any thing to do. There was a short sermon preached to us last evening and one this morning from an agent of the Sanitary Department, he spoke well this morning, there was a plenty of music, for we had three full brass bands, besides vocal music, he is agoing to speak twice this afternoon, at 4, and at 6 o'clock. I received a letter from you last night dated the 28th of July, and was glad to hear that you were all well, and that you were a getting along well, but it seems as though that you do not get all of my letters, or else you forget to mention any thing about them, one in particular, the one that had a few lines folded up in it, for "your own eyes." I think that I get nearly all of your letters of late, and I am glad to see you in such good heart in regard to the prospects in the future, keep up good cheer, and put your trust in God, and all will be for the best, let the old shanty rot down, or any thing else, untill I return, and then we will fix up something to live in, in some shape or other, I guess. I shall be thankfull if I return to the bosom of my family safe and sound, then we can begin life anew. I did not mean anything "<u>bad</u>" when I spoke about talking to the women, if I do talk southern "right smat," and "recon a heap." I "guess" that I shall know how to talk, and understand "Yankee," especially if I can hear a <u>Yankee Woman</u> talk for a while at first.

I received a letter from Mariah two or three days ago, which I will send to you in this. I have answered it, and I talked pretty plain to her for writing as she did about the draft, she thinks it is a wicked thing to call out men to defend her flag and her country, and she seems to think that ~~it is~~ all they want is get away the men and money. I told her what you wrote to me, and I told her that it was no worse for her to let her man go and fight for the Union than it was for thousands of others. I will send her a paper that has got Gen Logans[9] speech in it, and I will also send one to you. It is the best speech that I have ever

---

[9] Union Gen. John Alexander Logan, who lead the XV Corps of the Army of the Tennessee from Vicksburg to the Carolinas. After the war he returned to the U. S. House and Senate, again representing Illinois, and helped found the Grand Army of the Republic (GAR) as well as establish Decoration (now Memorial) Day as a national holiday.

seen on the topics of the day, it is just the <u>thoughts</u> of evry true soldier in the south-west, he tells you just what we want and what we are a fighting for, and what we will have, in the plainest way that I have ever seen, read it and let others read it, do you get any of the papers that I have sent to you, and have you got all of the money ($50.000) that I have sent to you this payment. "Nerva" it does me good to get letters from <u>you</u> and the <u>little</u> ones. I know that I <u>loved</u> you all when with you, but little did I know how much untill I had been deprived of your presence, and the longer we are separated and the farther we are apart, the stronger is that cord of love that binds us together, may it continue to strengthen untill no power on earth shall be able to break asunder. I wish that you could see me sometime when I receive a letter from you, hasten to my tent, and open the seal, that was closed with your hands, and draw forth the little missives of love from you and the children. God bless you all, you would think that I was foolish I expect, for I cannot always keep back the silent tear that steals down my cheek, but they are tears of love and joy to hear from the loved ones at home, if only a few words, and if any one gives me more joy than another, it is the ones with a little missive in them from Alice, have them write to me often, show them how to write, and what to say, I want to see you all very much, but I shall have to wait a few more months.

Afternoon.

I got my dinner, and then we had about as hard a thunder shower for about 30 minutes, as we ever get, the water came down in torrents, and Co. A, D & C were in the water knee deep as they are camped in low ground, but they have dug a ditch and drained it off some, they had great sport in the water for a while, the mail came in but there is not much news to day. I hear it reported that this army choir has been ordered to Georgia, but I do not know how true it is, whenever you see any account of Gen. Thomas'es choir, Gen. Brannam's Division, or

Gen Vandever's brigade, you may know that the 2n Minn is somewhere around. I do not think of much more to write this time. I had heard of the marrage of George Spaulding before, but I did not know how they were married[.] I hope that they will live hapy, but I fear that it will not be so. George was rather wild while in the army, as well as he was before, but still he may steady down now and make amends for his past conduct. It is curious that the people of the Valley are so warlike in their feelings, that they have to fight about a <u>dog</u>. I think that they had better take a musket and fight for their country, and then if they get wounded, it will be an honor to them, instead of shame. Do all of the pictorials come through straight, I get to see some of them, but I hope to live to look them over with you in days to come. I thought that you took the New Covenant, if you want to take it just send me the address and I will send for it for you, or if there is any other paper that you would like to take just say the word, I shall try and keep you in reading matter, if I can.

Cannot you get a plenty of letter paper there, if not I can send some to you from here. I think that the Merchants must be a making money there by the way they <u>keep</u> <u>their</u> <u>goods</u> <u>sold</u> <u>off</u>, but perhaps it is better for the citizens. I was sorry to hear that Dwight Nichols does not get any better, what appears to be his disease? are you not agoing to make another visit up on the prairie "<u>home.</u>" I should like to be there to make a visit with you, I think that we could have a good visit. But now I must stop and get my supper and go to meeting, if I can, it is a good deal cooler this afternoon than it was before. I should think that you had had some cold weather there by your tell, but I guess that the frost did not do much damage on our place. I hope that your corn will get ripe, and good. I have written to you about selling the Oxen, and the other creatures, we will wait untill near spring before we say anything about buying any more, you and Father can do just as you think best, any way that you do I will be perfectly satisfied. Now I will close by bidding you <u>all</u> a good bye,

Good bye "My" "Nerva" }
Good bye   Alice} { kiss }
Good bye   Ida}
Good bye   Edgar}
From   Brainard
D. B. Griffin

Letter Number 94

Camp Thomas, Winchester Tenn.   Aug. 13th 1863

My Dear Wife and Children,

As it is one week ago to day since I wrote to you, I will write a few lines to you, although I have not any news to write about. On the 6th I wrote to you that we had a speech in the morning, and was expecting one in the evening. We had a speech from Dr. Boynton, Father of Major Boynton of the 35 Ohio. His subject was about our foreign relations he spoke ~~for~~ about two hours, to a large crowd, as nearly the whole Division was there. He spoke well, and to the point, he thought that as soon as this rebellion was crushed, we could tend to "Johny Crapau" and "John Bull," and make them hunt their hole's. We had not anything else transpire untill the eleventh, day before yesterday, when this Division was reviewed by Gen. Rosecrans in person. As he rode down the lines he had a kind word with the boys in every regiment, and shook hands with each commander, he is a very pleasent man. It is the first time that we have ever been reviewed by the Commanding General. We received orders four or five days ago, to have our things packed up ready to march at a moments notice, but we have not received any further orders yet, so you can see how we are situated, liable to move at any time, or moment, but that need not make any difference about your writing to me, for the mail comes to us when we are on the march, if we are on or near the rail road. I do not know which way we will go, but we will make towards Chattanoga, most likely. It is very hot weather here, but we do not have much to do, here. We have the least duty to do now, that we have ever had since we have been in the service. I have been on picket only once since we came to this camp, and I will not be on for a week to come, so we cannot complain if we do not have evry thing just as we would wish. I have been a little under the weather for the last few days, but I feel prety well to day. I have done my camp duty regularly all the time, but my bowels have been a little out of order, and that sets me into the piles, otherways I feel well enough.

Afternoon

Well I have been to dinner, I had some boiled ~~rice~~ rice and fried beef. It is a clouding up, and it thunders all around us, so I guess that we will have some showers before night. I received your letter of the 2nd last night, and I see that you were all well, but I see that you do not get letters from me, ~~as~~ in as short a time as I do from you, but I expect that you will get them all some time. I thought that I always headed my letters by putting the name of the place where we were at the time when I wrote. I hope that you will have good luck in saving your grain, for you need it all. I hope that I shall be alive and at home before another harvest[.] I believe that I am as anxious to be with you all, as you are to have me there, and I believe that I shall live to see you all again, the time is fast flying away, a few more months at the farerthest, and we (those that are alive) will have a chance to go home ~~H~~ to our families and friends. I see that Alice and <u>Edgar</u> both write to me, but I do not see any from Ida, but Alice says that she was on the lounge asleep, and I guess that she did not wake up soon enough. I am glad that they go to Sunday school, and I hope that they will grow up and be good girls. Sergeant Gaskill[10] is as well as usuael, he received a letter from Spring Valley yesterday, all of the rest of the boys are well, Cutting has got a discharge and gone home I expect. I have not received any letter from Samuel, of late. I do not think of any thing more to write this time, so I will close this time, and bid you all good bye, hoping that a few more weeks will fetch me around in Spring Valley with Nerva and the babies. Good bye, from

Corp. D. B. Griffin.

---

[10] James F. Gaskill, a Spring Valley friend, Co. B, 2nd Minnesota Regiment of Volunteers.

On Toward Chattanooga, Tennessee and Chickamauga Creek, Georgia

Letters 95–100 (August 18–September 11, 1863)

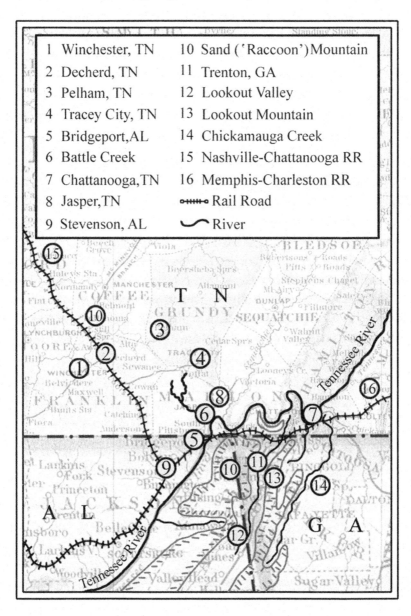

1 Winchester, TN
2 Decherd, TN
3 Pelham, TN
4 Tracey City, TN
5 Bridgeport, AL
6 Battle Creek
7 Chattanooga, TN
8 Jasper, TN
9 Stevenson, AL
10 Sand ('Raccoon') Mountain
11 Trenton, GA
12 Lookout Valley
13 Lookout Mountain
14 Chickamauga Creek
15 Nashville-Chattanooga RR
16 Memphis-Charleston RR
◦━┅━◦ Rail Road
〰 River

This last set of Brainard's letters chronicles the corps as it crosses, with great difficulty, the Cumberland Mountains, the Tennessee River, and a series of steep ridges bearing southeast of Chattanooga, toward what will become the setting for the Battle of Chickamauga and Brainard's death. He describes the torturous ascents and descents, the waiting required as such a mass of men and equipment traversed those slopes, the view from the top, and his constant longing for home. Learning from Minerva of the probably imminent collapse of their abandoned "shanty," he laments and looks forward to starting over upon his return. Arriving at the Tennessee River, Brainard's company, Co. F, is assigned the task of constructing log rafts to enable the crossing of the brigades—men and equipment—which is successfully accomplished. Minerva's grandfather's death elicits many questions and comments about their extended family and friends. A large saltpeter cave, open coal beds, and ironworks are described in passing. With Gen. Bragg's evacuation of Chattanooga, Gen. Rosecrans establishes himself there and orders the remainder of his army's pursuit of the escaping Confederates. An initial skirmish of the impending battle draws the elements of both forces closer to the valley of Chickamauga Creek, where they will meet in mortal combat on September 19–20, but Brainard's final words, penned on September 13 ("We have received orders to have three days rations in our haversacks, and be ready to march at a moments notice") don't take us that far.

LIBERTY—UNION.

Letter Number 95

In camp on the top of the Cumberland Mt.   Aug 18th/63

My Dear Wife and Children,

As we have got into camp in good season I will write a few lines to you, so as ~~H~~ to let you know where I am and what we are a doing. We did not have any thing transpire in camp after I wrote my last letter, untill last Sunday morning. We had polieced up our camp and I had gone out on picket, but I had not been on picket more than $\frac{1}{2}$ of an hour when we received orders to march forthwith. We went back to camp, and found them all "up and doing," ready to march. I packed up my things in double quick time and was with them in time. We started from camp about eleven o'clock, and marched about one mile, when we had one of the hardest thunder showers that I have seen in the South, the lightning struck the trees all around us and then <u>such</u> thunder, it would just shake the ground, and the rain fell in torrents for just about one hour, but as the most of us had our rubber blankets on, and we stood still, we did not get wet but a very little. We then went on through Dechard, on the road to Pelham, but as it was very slipery and wet, and bad for the teams to get along, we did not go more than five miles before we camped, we pitched our "dog tents" and got some green corn, and had a good supper, as it was the first full meal of green corn that I had had this summer, there had been a little in camp, but there was so many troops around Winchester that it was hard work to get it, unless you went a good ways from camp to get it, and I do not like to go far away from camp any time. The next morning we were up at two aclock, and were ready to march at daylight, we did not go but about three miles to the foot of the Mt, and as the teams belonging to a division ahead of us had not got up the we went into camp about noon and lay at the foot of the Cumberland Mt's. This morning we started with our knapsacks and gun and accoutrements, ~~to~~ on, to climb the Mt, the "hill" is about 2 $\frac{1}{2}$ miles long, and it is very steep a good part of the way, but we got up all safe and sound but it was rather trying work for the legs, and back. We were resting ourselves on the top, when the mail came to us, and I got two letters from "Nerva," but I did not have time to read them before the bugle called to forward, and the Band struck up a lively tune, and I just wished that you could have stood there with us, for we were on the top of the Cumberland Mountain, and there was the most beautifull landscape view that I have ever seen, there was wide valleys on either side of us, and they ran off as far as the eye could reach, and it is they were all dotted up with farms and villages, the village of Winchester, which is quite a large place, looked as though it was nearly under our feet, and you could see nearly evry house in it, and also other vilages, in the Valley, we did not have a long look for we had to move on, we have only came about five or six miles to day, we came into camp at eleven o'clock. We are camped near a place called Tracy City, there is a plenty of water near by, and as there is no water for a number of miles further, we will not go any farther to night, the teams have not got up yet, (3 o'clock)[.]

I am well and have stood the march so far first rate, and I guess that I can stand it as well as any of them yet, if I keep well, and I intend to. Capt. Barnes sent in his resignation, and it was accepted and he started for home last Saturday as a <u>citizen</u>, his health was not good, he told me that he should go to Spring Valley in three or four weeks, if he was well enough, and that he should go and see you, if he did, you need not be afraid to ask him any question's about us that you want too if you see him. I do not know for sure where we are agoing to from here but towards Chattanoga. I expect that we shall go to battle creek to-morrow.

Your letters were dated on the 8th and 12th. I was glad to hear that you were all well, but I was sorry that you were disappointed about going up to Fathers, as you had got your mind made up to go, but that should not have made you have the "blues" as you said, for it was probably all for the best. I have written to you all about the oxen &c, in my last letters, which I hope you have got before this time, and I hope that you have received the rest of the money too. I have sent fifty dollars in all, you will probably tell me when you get it all. I could not tell by your letters whether you had got more than one 20 dollars, or not. I guess that you will do about as well with the money as I ~~should~~ would if I should keep it here, but I do not want it. I have been a getting my front tooth filled, the one that the filling came out off, and both of them filled up by my gums. I would have liked to been there and helped you eat some of your prairie chickens, for I am fond of them, the chickens and pigs have "played out" in this country, as well as almost every thing else, there is not many peaches ~~nor~~ or apples around here, for there has been soldiers here ahead of us, but there is corn and we eat it to, but I expect that you have got a plenty of it there by this time.

I guess that the harvesting will be done there before the conscripts are taken away from there if there is <u>any</u> taken away. I see by the papers that the Indians have been driven out of Minnesota, and that Little Crow was killed and his son taken prisoner. I guess that Em. will have a chance to come home on another furlough this fall, but I can stay here in the south for ten months more if they need me, and then I shall give some one else my chance in the army. I cannot think of any more to write this time. I hope that you will not <u>schold</u> yourself for not writing any better letters, for I am shure that I prize them highly, and I do not think that I shall schold you for writing anything, and I hope that you will not have the sick head ache nor the blues, any more, for a long time if ever again.

I see by Jim. Thornton's letters that Jery's wife has got a girl, so it seems that your suppositions were about right last fall. I hope that Jery will get his <u>health</u> again. They have heard from Russell Rexford, he is in Ohio somewhere. I have not heard from Henry yet[.] I hope that I shall get a letter from there before long, if not I shall have to write to them, do you get any thing from them? I hope that your wheat will get saved good, and all of the other crops, so that you will have enough to <u>eat</u> <u>drink</u> and <u>wear</u> and I mean that you shall have enough, if what little money I get will do it. I do little jobs now and then, and get money enough to spend in one way and another. I am agoing out about ½ mile from here where there is a place to look off on the valley on the east side of the mountain, and if it is not to late when I get back I will tell you if there is any thing to see. I do not know when I can send this letter off. Alice's and Edgar's letter was thankfully received, although I could not <u>read</u> Edgar's letter, but I think that he will improve some if he keeps on a few years longer.

The mail call has just sounded and I have got a chance to send this off. I am not agoing out from camp, yours in great hast,

D. B. Griffin

Letter Number 96

In Camp at the mouth of Battle creek   Aug. 27/63

My Dear Wife and children,

I will once more write a short letter to you. I am well this morning, as I have been since I last wrote to you.(the 18) We were then on the top of the mountain. We started from there the next morning, and our regiment was the rear guard of the Brigade, so we had a slow tiresome march of it, for we were behind all of the teams and they went slow, for it was very hot, we kept on top of the mountain for ten miles or over, and then we had one of the worst hills to go down that I ever saw, in any of my travels, you can judge a little about it, for it was about 2,000 feet high and it was not over one mile from the top to of the mountain to the bottom of the valley, but the raad crooked and turned around so much, that it was about two miles from by the road. We got into camp a little after dark, we camped in the "Cove" (as the inhabitants call it,) on a creek called Sweton's creek. It was one of the most picturest places that I have ever seen, imagine, a level valley about ½ to 1 mile wide and about four miles wide long, surrounded by twelve high mountain peak's, that are from 2,000 to 2,500 feet high, all covered with heavy timber, and the valley dotted with here and there a corn field, which is about all that is on the land now. I saw some of the largest growth of corn here that I ever saw. I stood by the side of one stalk and placed the but of my gun on my shoulder, and the ~~muz~~ muzzle of it was just as high as the ear of corn on it, some of the stalks were all of twenty feet high. We lay here two nights. There is ~~an~~ a man in this cove, that has been shut up in a little log house, or pen, about eight feet wide and fourteen feet long, without either door or window ~~it~~ in it and only a small place between two logs large enough to hand in his vituals to him, and here he has been shut up for fifteen years, he is a manaic, he keeps himself clean, he has not been let out but once in the time, and then it took a dozen men to put him in again, he imagines that evry one is his enemy, and he pitches in to them, the doctor of the ninth Ohio put his face up to close to the hole to talk to him, and he fetched him a wipe, he looks very pale, but his eye looks wild, he is an oldish man with a <u>small</u> family of only <u>21</u> children, but they looked as well in the house as any one about here, there is some of the boys in our army, and all of the rest are grown up men and women. On the 21st we received orders in the morning to fix up our camp, in regular style, for it was probable that we should stay there for a number of days, so we went to work and fixed our tents up and made us beds, when, at ten o'clock, the order came to be ready to march at twelve o'clock, so we pulled up stakes and packed up our knapsacks, and got our dinners in a hurry and were ready at the call of the bugle. We marched thirteen miles, to the Tennessee river at the mouth of Battle creek, about four mles from Bridgeport and thirteen from Stephenson Ala, it is about four miles to Ala, and five to the Geo. line, and about thirty miles to Chattanoga by rail road, but it is not near so far across the mountain's. The rebels have their pickets on the other side of the river and our pickets on this side, the boys talk to ~~one~~ each other across the river evry day, and there has a number of the "rebs" deserted and come across to us. They all say that they are sick and tired of the war, and that they want to get back under the protection of the stars and stripes, there is men deserting them evry day, and if they leave Chattanoga, hundreds and thousands of them will leave them if they can get away. Our Brigade is camped here between the mountain's, the other two Brigades are camped up the river about two ~~months~~

miles from here, near a place called Jasper. It has been very hot weather for the last two weeks, but it is quite cool nights, and very foggy in the morning's, but the health of the regiment is good, and we are all ready for orders to go ahead. On the 24th I was detailed to go to Stephenson for rations, so I was up and ready by daylight, but the train did not get under way before eight o'clock. We got there and loaded up the train (127 waggons) by dark, there was about 80 men of us, we came back about four miles and camped in the woods. Stephenson is where the Nashville and Chattanoga rail road joins the Memphis and Charleston road, it is not a very large place, there is a few stores (or has been) and a couple tarverns, and a couple large depot buildings, but most of the buildings are old rickety things, like the most of the houses throughout the south, the most of the farms along the road are deserted, and have gone up to weeds and bushes. We are camped on an old field, where the "rag weed," is higher than our heads, in some places, it is on the same ground Major Gen. McCook[1] was camped on one year ago, there is a small fort, and some earth works thrown up here. We do not have much to do here, we have not drilled any here. I do not know when we will go from here, but as near as we can learn, we shall go by the first of next month. There has been some canonading off towards our left for two or three days, but I have not heard the particulars. We shall most probably move on towards Chattanoga, and we may have a fight before we get there, but it is the opinion of a good many, that the rebels will not make much of a stand there, but that they will go to Atlanta.

It is the report that Fort Sumter and Wagner is taken, but we have not had it confirmed yet. I hope that it is true, for I think if Charleston is taken, that it will go a good ways towards ending the war in the South[.]

I received a letter from you last night, dated the 18th, and was glad to hear that you were all well, and that you had been up to

---

[1] Probably Union Gen. Alexander M. McCook, brother of the Robert L. McCook reported killed in letter 48.

Fathers once more, and that you found evry thing in good shape on the farm except the old <u>shanty</u>, and it seems that it is getting rather lame, and about to fall, it has stood it pretty well I think, but I hate to see it fall, for we have passed many a hapy day under its roof, but if I live to get home, I think that we can soon rig up something for a shelter, but that does not worry me at all. I wish that I had all of the locust seed sown, and all a growing nice, they will soon make a good wind-break for us. I am glad that you have got rid of the cattle, for now you will not be bothered with them this winter, have you got any hay cut for your cow this winter. I am glad that you have heard from Dan. I have not heard a word from Samuel or Henry for some time. I see that you had not got all of the money when you wrote, but I hope that you have got it all before this time, we have got two months more due us the last day of this month, and ten months more will soon roll around, when I hope that we shall be permitted to meet each other again, the boys from there are well, Sergeant Gaskill is well. I do not think of anything more to write, and as my dinner is about ready I will tell you what we are agoing to have for dinner, it is some boiled beef, and some rice soup, thickened with crackers. We have all the corn to eat that we want, ~~to get~~, there is not many apples or peaches around here, we do not get many papers since we came here, so it is rather dull, times just now. Gen. Rosecrans went past here yesterday he has gone up the river some where, to view the lines in front. Now I will close by bidding you all a good bye once more. Good bye "Nerva" and the babies, from your husband and friend,

D. B. Griffin.

Letter Number 97

In Camp, on the south bank of the Tenn. river   Aug 31st/63

My Dear Wife "Nerva" and the babies,

As I have a few spare moments this afternoon, I will improve them by writing a few lines to you. I am well, as usual, but I feel some tired, for we have been prety busy for the last four days. On the 28th Co. F. was detailed to build a raft, so that we could cross the river, so we tore down a number of old vacant log houses and pinned them together, and made a raft fifty feet long and sixteen wide, and we finished it enough, so that we took over two companies of the 35 Ohio, on the afternoon of the 29th. They advanced back from the river some two miles, but did not find any rebels, as they had left, (as usual,) the night before. Yesterday the whole Brigade crossed over, (or nearly all of it) except the teams, and I was left in charge of the rations and camp equipage, expecting to take it down to Bridgeport to cross, but the order was countermanded, and we took it across on the raft last night after dark, and when we got it on this side of the river and got our stuff piled up, it was one o'clock, and we went into camp some ¾ of a mile from the river in the woods. I lay down and ~~slept~~ sleep a little, but I was up again at daylight and got our breakfast, and I was some hungry (for I did not get a chance, last night to get my supper,) and then we went down to the river and brought the things all up to camp, and then we went to work and fixed up our tents, and beds, and got our dinners. We had some potatoes, and green corn, coffee and "hard tack" for dinner, and I eat a hearty dinner, and I feel first rate now. The Battery is crossing over to day, and also the 1st Brigade, and we will probably lay here untill evry thing is over. It is the report in camp that Chattanoga was evacuated by Bragg, and that our men were in the place, and I do not doubt it much, for we were getting them pretty well shut up, and they would either have to fight or <u>run</u> away, and as the latter mode of warfare was Bragg's favorite mode, they have again taken to the foot race, and gone <u>towards</u> "the last ditch," but where that is I do not know, and it is uncertain whether Gen. Bragg himself knows, but it is said that he has gone to Atlanta Geo, where we shall follow him to, when we move again. It is some fifty miles from here. We are ordered to take 25 days rations with us, and the officers have to leave their tents behind them, and we are not allowed but one change of clothes in our knapsacks, in addition to our blankets and tents, and to have two days rations in our haversacks, so you can see that we have got some marching to do, and I do not care how quick it is done, so that it will help to shorten the war. We have very good news from both the east, and west[2], that Fort Sumter, and Wagner were in our possession, and that Gen Gillmore[3] had commenced shelling Charleston, and it is most likely that it will soon fall, if it has not already done so, and that Gen. Meade had defeated Lee again, but the news is so uncertain that we cannot decide on it for a number of days to come, but I hope that it will all prove true, if it does I shall have some hopes of getting home by next "July" at least. I do not build any "castles in the air" and then I will not be disapointed, but evry thing look's favorable towards a speedy tirmination of the war. I see by the papers that the Indian Expidition is on its return home, after having a hard fought, campaign, loosing 3 killed and a few wounded, and killing a few of the red skins, but perhaps it is as well as they can do under the circumstances. You will most probably see, or hear from Em. before long, he will probably be at home this fall.

I have heard by the way of some of ~~some~~ the boys, that the State has issued an order to have all of the soldiers clothing that has been sent home by the soldiers, turned over to the State for the use of the State. You need not tell any one that I have sent any home, but if they search for them, and take them away, make them give you a receipt for them the over coat is worth as much as a new one, ($9.50) and so is the dress coat, ($7.50), that is what I will have to pay for ~~any more~~ others if I draw any more, but I do not see how they can take our clothes away from us just because we are ordered to box them up and leave them or send them home, but they may not look for them there, but if they take them let me know, for I want one of the over-coats if I come home, and I can draw another almost any time.

---

[2] All of the following news proves to be untrue.
[3] Union Gen. Quincy Adams Gillmore. Fort Sumter does not surrender however, until April 14, 1865.

329

It is not quite as hot weather now as we have had, but it is quite warm through the day, and cool at night, we are not troubled much with the flies or musquaitoes now, so we can sleep first rate night or day, but I do not sleep near as much as I used to at home. I am generaly up as soon as any one in camp, and I have to divide all of the rations in the company whenever we draw them, but I had rather have something to do than to lay and sleep and do nothing all of the time. I cannot think of any more to write just now, so I will stop untill after supper any how.

Supper is over. I had a little <u>change</u> for supper, instead of "<u>corn</u>, <u>potatoes</u> & <u>coffee and</u> <u>crackers</u>" I had some "<u>crackers</u> <u>and</u> <u>coffee</u>, <u>potatoes and corn</u>"[.] There has not any mail come in to day, so there is nothing new to talk about, and as it is a getting so dark that I cannot follow the lines, I will have ~~the~~ to close for to night and bid you all a good night with a kiss for you all, { kiss }

D. B. G.

Sept 1st

there is no news this morning. I am well the mail call has blown and I must send this off. So good bye one and all.

D. B. Griffin

Letter Number 98

Camp of the 2nd Minn.   Sept 4th 1863

Ever Dear Wife and children,

I will again address a few lines to you this afternoon. I am well to day, and as hearty as ever. I sent you a letter on the first, but as we have moved our camp about three miles since, and I received a kind letter from you last night, I will write a little more to day. We moved our camp on the afternoon of the first, about three miles towards Chattanoga on the rail-road. Our camp is in a piece of timber which has been a camp of the rebels, one year ago, but it is not a very good place, for there is not a great plenty of water near here, but I understand that we are agoing to move again in the morning, but I have not heard how far, our boys have been all around the country for five or six miles ahead, after apples, potatoes, peaches, chickens, and anything that they can get, there is not a great supply of such stuf, but there is a little at almost evry place, and the country is quite thickly setled among the mountains, and a good many of the inhabitants are Northern people, but as the boys are loth to believe in their loyalty, the innocent have to suffer with the guilty. I have not been out yet, but I have had all of the stuf that I wanted to eat. My bed-fellow (James Brennan) has gone out to day. I went down to the river this morning, and had a fine wash, it is about a mile to the river. We are within one mile of the line of Georgia and Alabama, where they corner on to Tennessee, it is most likely that the next camp that we make will be in the State of Georgia. The whole army is a crossing the river as fast as they can get over upon rafts, canoes and pontons and if Gen. Bragg does not evacuate Chattanoga before long, (as we have learnt that he has not,) "Old Rosy," will be very apt to give him another call, but it is thought by a good many that he is a removeing evry thing to Atlanta, such is the reports of the deserters, and Contrabands, and other reports are that they are fortifying very strong, and that Gen. Hardee[4] is a coming with reinforcements from the Vicksburgh army, if so we may head them off. Gen Burnside[5] is said to be a moving down on our left, if so we will soon get them prety well hemed in. We look anxiously to the fall of Charleston, but the news we comes very slow, but it is encouraging so far, but I expect that you get more news than I do, and that you read all of it too.

---

[4] CSA Gen. William Joseph Hardee, author of *Hardee's Tactics* which was used by both sides, and a Corps Commander at Shiloh, Perryville, and Murfreesboro. Hardee does not actually arrive until November's Battle of Chattanooga.

[5] Union Gen. Ambrose Burnside was able to liberate Knoxville and reopen the Cumberland Gap to Union movement.

Dear "Nerva," I see by your letter that another one of <u>our</u> friends has gone to his last resting place. But it was not any thing strange to hear of your Grandfather's[6] sudden death, for that is the way that my Grandfather[7] died, and he was not so old by eight years as your's was. He told me when I came away that he should never see me again, and alas how true, he has passed through a great many hardships and trials, he lived to see all of his brothers and sisters go before him, he was the last of his family. I believe that he has gone to that rest, which was prepared by our Lord and Savior. May we all live to a good old age, and at last we <u>shall</u> meet him in heaven. How does Grandmother seem to stand it this summer, and how did she take his death. I hope and pray that the rest of us will be permitted to meet each other upon this earth, and I believe that we shall.

I do not know of what denomination the Sanitary Agent was, he did not preach a religious sermon, but spoke of home, and the general topics of the day. I do not know where he was from.

I think that Mariah's man is a little <u>snakeish</u>. I have not got any letter from either her or Samuel, since I sent them to you. I was glad to hear that you had received all of the money, and that you had payed some of it towards the farm, if you get your pay for the Oxen and cattle, I think that it would be best to pay it all of it towards the place, and look to me for your spending money. I will send you all that I can spare, and you must know that it does not take much to keep me, for I do not need it. I am not as much in debt when pay day comes, as most of the boys are who do not send home <u>one</u> <u>cent</u> of their pay, and I am just as well clothed and fed as they are, it is all spent foolishly for <u>whisky</u> or nicknacks, that is of no benefit to them in the least. If you should need any money before before we are payed again, just let me know, and I will get some for you, if there is any to be had. I am glad that your Wheat and corn is

---

[6] Minerva's paternal grandfather, Daniel Almon Griffin, and her step-grandmother, Rhoda, living in Chittenden, Vermont.
[7] Ebenezer E. Thompson, mentioned in letter 48.

doing so well, this summer, you will have enough to keep yourselves a chewing for another year, and perhaps have some to spare, are you a fatting any pig this fall?

I sent for the pictorials for one year, and the Nashville Union, six months, and when the time runs out, I will send it longer to you. I have not got any money to spare just now, or else I would send the Covenant to you, I will send it the first chance that I get. I hope that Jennett and Mary Cook, and all of the girls who have Volunteered to work on the farms, while we are ~~on the~~ fighting for the preservation of the union, will find some good "Union Man" and join ~~farms~~ their fortunes and hearts together and walk through life hand in hand. If they should get a soldier, they would know how to <u>cook</u> and <u>wash</u>, and they could work together by changeing works. I hope that they will all be hapy and do well, has Alfred Smith got a letter from me, that you know of.

Evening.

Well, I have been to supper, and have listened to the playing of the band, they play some nice tunes, the 35 Ohio Band is a playing now, there has been troops passing here all of the afternoon, it looks a little like war again. We are agoing about eight miles to morrow, I hear, and that we are to march at daylight. The mail came in this afternoon but there is no news of importantce. I will send some morning glories seeds to Alice and Ida, there is two kinds[.] I pickett them in a corn field this forenoon. James has got back from foraging, he went out about six miles, he got some sweet potatoes and Apples, &c, they got them at a secesh house, which belonged to a hard shell Babtest preacher, they dug his potatoes and got his apples, and then yoked up his oxen and hitched them on to a waggon and brought them all into camp. I expect that he will make a <u>good</u> prayer for them to night, they passed by the poor folks and took of the rich, but there is so many soldiers about here that there will not be anything left in the country, the corn is almost to large to eat but it will soon be good for the mules, and we will get it all any how. It seems hard to have evry thing in the world taken from you, but such is the fate of war. I cannot take things as some do, so I had rather not go out at all. I can not stand and see the women beg of them not to take the last thing they have, but they have blowed the call to bring in the mail so I must close in haste and bid you all a good bye, so Good bye one and all, with a { kiss } from your husband and father

D. B. Griffin

Letter Number 99

In Camp at the foot of Coon Mountain Geo.   Sept 7th/63

My Dear Wife

I will write a few lines to you this evening in order to let you know where we are, and how we get along. I am well as usual, and stand the march first rate. We started from camp on the morning of the 5th. I was on guard that day. We started from camp at six o'clock, and marched about 5 miles[.] We was all day on the road as we were expecting to go up the mountain that day, but the teams that were ahead of us did not get up, we went into camp in the State of Georgia, at a place called "Nicol Jack." There is a saltpeter cave and works ~~here~~ at that place, which the rebels had been at work in, the cave is a large one, it has been explored for a number of miles. The way they make Saltpeter, is this, they dig the dirt out of the cave, and put it in large leeches, and leech it, and then boil the lye down in large kettles, the works are all destroyed now. The next day we went up a long mountain, it was a very steep hill, but it was not as rough as the one we went up at Decherd, the hill was nearly three miles long, there is a number of coal beds in this mountain, here I saw a coal bed for the first time. We camped on the top of the mountain, on the line of Alabama and Geo, a part of the regiment being in Geo. and a part in Ala. I received a letter from Mariah, there, which I will send to you. I guess that they did not like my <u>kind</u> letter to them but I shall not take back a word that I have said to them[.] I shall write them another letter the first chance I get, but I shall not say much to them, for fear that they will not write any more to me. To day we have marched about ten miles over a rather rough road, and <u>down</u> a long steep hill, but it was not as long as the one that we went up, we were a good while right on a ridge, not more than 20 or thirty feet wide in a good many places, and we could look down both sides untill ~~evrry~~ evry thing looked blue below[.] We are camped at the foot of the mountain to night. It has been very hot and dusty all of the time, and the water is very scarce on the road, but there is a plenty of water here. We are within ten miles of Chattanoga, and about four miles from a place called Trenton, which place we are said to be a going to if we can, for the rebels are there[.] We have got orders to have three days rations in our haversacks, and forty rounds of cartriges in our catridge boxes, so you se we may get into a skirmish before long. There has been some Canonading this evening in the direction of Chattanoga, the place is not evacuated as yet. I have not time to write much to night as the mail is agoing out at eight o clock, and I did not commence untill about dark to write. You need not be afraid to say anything that you want to in your letters to me for no one sees them unless I show them[.] I will write as often as I can untill after the campaign is over yours in much haste. May God bless and protect us all, is the wish of your husband. Good bye, from

D. B. Griffin

Letter Number 100

In Camp at the foot of Lookout Mt, Geo.   Sept 11th, 1863

My Dear Wife and children,

As I have a few moments to spare this afternoon I will improve them by writing a few lines to you. We are upon the march again after Bragg, as that celebrated individual has skedaddled once more. As I had written to you in my former letters that it was thought he would leave Chattanoga, without any fight. He has left the place and has gone south to find another <u>ditch</u>.

Our army went into the place on the ninth without meeting with any resistance. Gen Rosecranz established his head quarters there on the tenth. We lay in the last camp ready to march at a moments notice untill yesterday morning, when we were called up at three o'clock, and started at daylight. We went nearly South all day, and not far from the state line of Ala, in what is called "Lookout Valley." It is a very rich fertile valley, from two to three miles wide, with high mountains on each side. We marched about thirteen miles, the country is not very thickly setled, we passed through Trenton a small place in the valley. It is the county seat of Dade Co. There is a couple of churches, stores and taverns, and a number of old dillapedated buildings. There is two large buildings nearly finished by the Confederate Government which were intended for Iron furnaces, but that is stopped now, and there is hardly any <u>man</u> at home, but it is nothing strange to see a woman and eight or ten children around an old house, that does not look fit to keep a horse in, and the children are <u>all</u> of a size and age. I saw one family of 7 and the oldest was not over 8 years old. It appears to be a sure crop here in the south, they are very poorly clothed and do not have a great deal to eat, they are to be pitied[.]

We camped in a fine grove of oax trees at the foot of Lookout Mt. which is a high range of Mt. between Chattanoga and Ala. We were on a fine creek, where we all took a good wash, and went to <u>bed</u>, and slept as well on a bed of gravel stone as we would on a feather bed. We were aroused up this morning about daylight, and got ready to march but did not get away before 9 o'clock, and as there is a good many troops ahead of us and we have got to climb over Lookout Mt, we have not come over three miles to day, we are in camp to night at the foot of the hill, the place is called Johnson's crook, the rebels have comenced a large furnace here, there is a plenty of Iron ore here, and they were a making great calculations for the future[.]

I cannot write any more to night for it is a getting too dark to write, so good night.

Sunday the 13th

Well, Nerva I will try and finish this letter to day. Just as I stopped the other night we had orders to march in a half an hour, so we had to pack up again and start. It was reported that the rebels had made an attack on Negley's Division[8], and that we had got to go over the Mt. and help them. We went about two miles to the foot of the Mt. but as the road up the Mt was so much blocked up with teams and it was so dark, that we were drawn up in a line and stacked arms, and told to rest for we should likely have to wait a couple of hours, so we unslung our knapsack's, and lay down on the ground, with our knapsack's for our pillow's, and as we did not get any further orders, we lay untill daylight, when we were woke up and told to make us a cup of coffee, for we would start in a half an hour. We were all ready in time to fall in at the sound of the bugle. We had to climb the steepest Mt ~~of~~ that I have seen, it is about two miles long and very steep and winding, but we got up all safe before seven o'clock, after taking a short rest we went on going on the top of the Mt. for about two miles when we commenced desending, and you had better believe that it made a fellows knees weak before he got down to the bottom, and it was awful hot, but I have not heard of any one being sun struck. We found that Negley had been attackted by a heavy force and as he had not force enough to fight them he fell back some three miles, our loss in killed and wounded, was about 150, which mostly fell into the hands of the enemy, the loss of the enemy not known, but it was considerable, about sixty prisoners fell into our hands[.] We came into camp about ten o'clock and lay here untill about two, when we were ordered to make a reconnoicense. We went out four miles but ~~the~~ found no rebels as they had all left in the forenoon, and gone south,

---

[8] Union Gen. James Scott Negley, a Division Commander of Gen. George Thomas's XIV Corps. His Division was in the lead of that Corps' assignment to attack what was thought to be the rear of CSA Gen. Braxton Bragg's Army of Tennessee as it evacuated Chattanooga. Facing superior Confederate fire from Bragg's main force, however, Negley withdrew to await the arrival of Thomas and the support of the other three Divisions.

but if evry thing works well it is thought that they will be cut off below here, by Gen McCook[9], and we shall be very apt to ~~to~~ follow them up in the rear, so that they will not get much of their train away with them. I hope that it will work. We found where they buried a number of their men, but they did not bury our men, we brought five or six in with us. We came back to camp about seven o'clock tired and dusty as it is very dusty and dry, the dust lays about six inches deep, and as we march along, there is a cloud arises all the time, but it is not so bad as it would be if we were not used to it. Our teams are all back yet but we expect them in now. We all stand the march first rate, and are willing to march a good while longer if it will end the war, and secure a permanent peace for the country, the news as far as we can hear is good, evrything appears to be a working for our good, and I cannot see how the rebs. can hold out much longer, but they are ashamed to own that they are whiped by the Yankees, but we think they are whiped, and badly too. I do not think of much more to write[.] We are in Lookout valley, which is a very rich valley, there is a plenty of corn for the teams, and there is a considerable foraging done among the men, for we are on half rations but we have had a plenty to eat so far. I am agoing to have some boiled and fried beef, some chicken and some sweet potatoes, now I will wait untill after dinner, and then write some more.

I received your letter of the 1st on the 9th and was glad to hear that you were all well, and that you were enjoying yourselves in drying fruit and makeing preserves. I hope that you will have the pleasure of my company when you eat some of them. It seems that you have had a frost rather early for Minnesota even. I hope that it did not spoil all of the corn for you, nor your sorghum either, for I may want some of it, if I should live to get home, and I hope I shall. How much do you

---

[9] Union Gen. Alexander McCook's XX Corps was sent south of Thomas's XIV Corps to strike the head of Bragg's retreating forces. Instead, they will swing back to participate in what will become the Battle of Chickamauga Creek.

have to pay for your wood, do you have any trouble in getting it, and in getting it cut up into stove wood. I hope that Mr DeGroot will have good luck if he goes up a hunting, but he may have to watch the Indians a little and look out for his own scalp. I have seen the account of the Indians war, and I do not think that they have had much of a fight after all, but I suppose that they have done all that was asked of them to do. I hope that Em. will be at home so that he will get you fixed up for winter a little. I should like to be there at the same time, but I do not see any way for me just now, and I guess that I shall stick to it nine months more. I think that Alice does very well in writing to me[.] I think that she does very well if she gets fifteen verses to recite at sabath school. I hope that they will all be good children, and learn well. I suppose that they all grow fast, so that I should hardly know them. We have received orders to have three days rations in our haversacks, and be ready to march at a moments notice, so I cannot tell where I shall be the next time I write to you. I will try and keep you posted while we are on the march. I am well, Sergeant Gaskill is well, and all of the boys. I will bid you all a good bye.

D. B. Griffin

We are not agoing to march to night, and I am glad of it.

Endings—Chattanooga, Tennessee, to Spring Valley, Minnesota

Letters From His Captain and Friends
(September 30–November 3, 1863)

Three letters were saved by Minerva Griffin. The first is from Captain Loomis of Co. F, 2nd Minnesota Volunteers, written from Chattanooga, informing her of her husband's death eleven days earlier. The second is from the often-mentioned Sergeant Gaskill, at the prompting of Gaskill's father, a Spring Valley resident with Minerva, which gives a fuller description of the event. The third letter, from a friend of Brainard's in Co. A, is probably a response to Sergeant Gaskill's inquiries. They are not uniform in the details they relate.

Mumford & Co., Cin.

A wreath of Glory for
every Patriot's brow.

Letters From Comrades - 1

Chattanoga Tenn   Sept 30th 1863

Mrs David B Griffin

Madam

It becomes my painful duty to inform you that your husband, formerly a member of my company, was killed in the desperate battle which took place near here on the 19th & 20th of this month. But he fell as becomes a soldier while in the discharge of his duty.

The final statements of his accounts with the Government have been sent as required to the Adjutant General at Washington.

His clothing was all lost upon the Battle field, but I enclose you 10.55 the amount of Money found upon his person

Respectfully

Your Obt Svt

D. B. Loomis Capt
Co F 2nd Minn Vol

Letters From Comrades – 2

Camp of the 2nd Minn. Vols.

Chattanooga Tenn.   Oct 25th/63

Mrs. Griffin

Reeceived my father's letter with a note from you enclosed yesterday and I will do anything that I can to assist you in your affliction with the greatest of pleasure. I went over to Co. F this morning & made what inquiries I could concerning Mr Griffin.

There is but one man here at present that belongs to the Co. they are all upon the other side of the River doing some work, the man said that there was the Captain's book & he gave it to me & I will have it sent to you the first mail that leaves   He also said that the wallet & flag were in Mr Griffin's knapsack together with his clothes & fell into the hands of the rebels. We all lost our knapsacks & everything excepting what was on our backs

All of our dead were buried by the rebels as we were forced from the field & had to leave all of our killed & wounded in their hands but flags of truce were sent out every day for nearly two weeks by our men and they reported that they were all buried as well as though we had done it ourselves.

Mr. Griffin was killed in the first days fight he was shot in the head the ball struck him directly in the forehead & came out the back of the head. He was killed instantly & never spoke after he was struck.

He was beloved by all that knew him & his memory will long be cherished in the hearts of his comrades.

As soon as Co. F comes back to the Regiment I will see Mr. Breman & make further inquiries. It is no trouble to me at all to do these little things & if there is anything more that I can do I will do it with pleasure

Yours &c

J L Gaskill

Letters From Comrades – 3

Chatfield Min. Nov. 3/63

Mrs. D. B. Griffin,

Respected Lady,

A gentleman called here last evening to learn the fate of Mr Griffin of Co. F 2d. Minn. Vols. and as I was absent, left word for me to write you in regard to him.

I am sorry to be obliged to tell you that your husband was one of those brave men who gave their lives for their Country's cause on the memorable battle field of Chickamauga Sunday Sep. 20th 1863

Before closing this allow me to add a word of tribute to the memory of my late comrade & friend, coming among us a comparative stranger, none learned to know but to love him. By uprightness & integrity of character & cheerful devotion to duty, he won from all admiration for the soldier & regard for the man.

In addition you may have the satisfaction of knowing that he never turned his back to the foe but died for his countries good, A brave soldier covered with glory.

With heartfelt sympathy for the death of one so noble & good,

I am very Respectfully

C. A. Edwards
Co. A. 2d. Minn. Vols.

Epilogue

The story of David Brainard Griffin's death is known from the official records and from at least three letters that Minerva received from his companions. He was killed by a shot through his forehead in the opening minutes of the battle on September 19, as the brigade moved east along Reed's Bridge Road and was mistakenly ordered to secure that crossing from additional Confederate incursion. Because the brigade was eventually forced to withdraw by overwhelming forces, mainly under Gen. Bedford Forrest's command, Brainard's body and effects were abandoned, to be buried that night by a detail of rebels. His body was subsequently removed to a mass grave of unknowns at Chattanooga National Cemetery.

What of his family? Minerva continued to work their farm with the help of her brothers, Allen and Dan. It took her three months to prove her prior marital status and the parentage of their children in order to receive a military pension totaling eight dollars per month. Despite that—or perhaps because of that—she became quite active in the Women's Relief Corps, dedicated to rendering assistance to the widows and orphans left by the Civil War. In 1868, she married Warren D. Andrews, who had served in Company A of the 2nd Minnesota and was undoubtedly known to Brainard in Company F. By 1870, the family migrated south to Le Roy in neighboring Mower County, moving again five years later up to Spring Valley. There, she died in 1895 at the age of sixty-five and lies buried between the two stones that memorialize her Civil War husbands.

Alice Jane married Manuel Beardsley Hutcheson, a maternal cousin of Laura Ingalls Wilder, in 1873. They settled in Whittier, California, and remained childless. She died a widow in 1928 and is buried next to her husband.

Ida May married Jacob LeFevre in 1880, eventually establishing a farm in Granger, Washington, where they raised five sons and a daughter. One of those sons became my maternal grandfather and my mentor–image of an educator. Ida May lived until 1943, a year after I was born, and is my connection to the American Civil War.

Edgar Lincoln, last in this branch of the family bearing the Griffin name, tragically died after ingesting poison hemlock in 1870 at the tender age of nine. He is buried beside his mother and stepfather.

The letters survive because they were lovingly saved by Minerva and passed down through Ida May's line. A copy of them was made available to me while I was still teaching, and I used them to introduce my students, on a very personal level, to this period of great conflict in our history. I here use them again to introduce a wider interested audience to David Brainard Griffin, a remarkable recorder of his thoughts, emotions, and experiences during two years of service in the 2nd Minnesota Regiment of Volunteers.

Appendixes

Appendix I – Significant Family

David "Brainard" Griffin, 1831–1863

Son of Orlo Bronson Griffin and Hannah Kellogg Thompson

Brother of Henry, Mariah, Mary, Samuel, Sarah, and Sylvia

Settled in Beaver Township, Fillmore County, Minnesota, 1857

Philinda "Minerva" Griffin, 1830–1895

Daughter of Almon Daniel Griffin and Mary "Polly" Chase

Wife of Brainard, his second cousin, and mother of his three children

Sister of Catherine (mother of orphaned children Eliza and Helen Churchill), Allen, Daniel, Mary, and Henry

Alice Jane Griffin, 1854–1928

Daughter of Brainard and Minerva

Ida May Griffin, 1856–1943

Daughter of Brainard and Minerva

Married the author's mother's grandfather, Jacob LeFevre, 1880

Edgar Lincoln Griffin, 1861–1870

Son of Brainard and Minerva

Almon and Mary "Polly" Griffin

Minerva's parents, and grandparents of Alice, Ida May, and Edgar Lincoln

Settled in Beaver Township, Fillmore County, Minnesota, 1859

Caretakers of grandchildren Eliza, Helen and Horace Churchill

Horatio "Allen" Griffin

Minerva's brother, farmed with his father

Provided significant help on the homestead in Brainard's absence

Mary Elizabeth (Griffin) Durand

Minerva's sister, and wife of William "Emery" Durand

Shared her house in Spring Valley with Minerva and children, 1862–1863

Corp. William "Emery" or "Em" Durand, Co. E, 7th Minnesota

Husband of Mary Elizabeth Griffin

Helped quell Sioux uprisings in Minnesota during the Civil War

Mustered out in July 1865

Appendix 2 – Significant Friends

Pvt. Warren D. Andrews, Co. A, 2nd Minnesota Regiment of Volunteers

Not mentioned in letters, but discharged from hospital care, July 1865

Returned to Spring Valley, married Minerva Griffin, 1868

Pvt. Wesley Baldwin, Co. F, 2nd Minnesota

Discharged as disabled, March 1863, and returned to Hamilton

Capt. Charles H. Barnes, Co. A, 2nd Minnesota

A Spring Valley friend

Resigned his commission in August 1862

Corp. James Brennan, Co. F, 2nd Minnesota

One of Brainard's tent-mates

Discharged at term of service, July 1864

Sgt. "Limon" (listed as Herman G.) Case, Co. A, 2nd Minnesota

A Chatfield friend and brother of Norman Case

Reenlisted in December 1863 and mustered out in July 1865

Corp. Norman Case, Co. A, 2nd Minnesota

A Chatfield friend and brother of "Limon" Case

Killed at Chickamauga, September 20, 1863

Mr. Chipman

Neighbor to the Griffins who shared work with Brainard

Minerva's hired hand during the first year of Brainard's absence

Sgt. Hiram B. Cutting ("Mr. Cutting"), Co. A, 2nd Minnesota

A Chatfield friend

Discharged as disabled in July 1863

Corp. Tom Douglass, Co. C, 3rd Minnesota

A Fillmore County friend

Mustered out in September 1865

Sgt. James F. Gaskill, Co. B, 2nd Minnesota

A Spring Valley friend

Letter writer to Minerva after Chickamauga

Lt. Charles H. Haven, Co. A, 2nd Minnesota

A Chatfield friend

Died at Nashville in March 1862

"Jery/Jerry"—A mystery at this point, as never referred to with a last name

Seems to be Brainard's best friend, probably from Beaver Township, and probably also in Co. F, 2nd Minnesota (not found on any official list).

Ida May Griffin LeFevre's letter seems to connect him to James Nichols, but they are often mentioned in the same letters as being in different places.

On questionable medical leave from July to October 1862, when a Minnesota physician's "certificate of disability" finally removes him from the "Absent Without Leave" category on the muster role, according to Brainard.

Pvt. James Nichols, Co. C, 3rd Minnesota

A Fillmore County friend

Discharged at expiration of service in November 1864

Mr. Andrew Peters

General Store Postmaster of Alba in Beaver Township

A close family friend

Pvt. Charles H. Phillips, Co. A, 2nd Minnesota

A Beaver Township friend

Transferred to a Marine brigade

Pvt. Edwin Rexford, Co. C, 3rd Minnesota

A Chatfield friend

Captured at Murfreesboro and paroled

Discharged at expiration of term of service in November 1864

Ellicutt Rundell, Unknown Company, 3rd Minnesota

A Chatfield friend

Captured at Murfreesboro and paroled

Corp. Charles F. Russell, Co. F, 3rd Minnesota

A Fillmore County friend

Mustered out in September 1865

Corp. George Rutherford, Co. F, 2nd Minnesota

A Fillmore County friend

Wounded at Kenesaw Mountain and discharged as disabled in January 1865

Pvt. George S. Spaulding, Co. A, 2nd Minnesota

A Fillmore County friend

Discharged as disabled in May 1862

Pvt. James Thornton, Co. F, 2nd Minnesota

A Fillmore County friend

Wounded at both Chickamauga and Kenesaw Mountain

Appendix 3 – Resources

- Bishop, Judson W., *The Story of a Regiment, Being a Narrative of the Service of the Second Regiment, Minnesota Veteran Volunteer Infantry, In the Civil War of 1861 to 1865, 1890.*

- Bowman, John S., *Who Was Who in the Civil War,* 2002.

- Kennedy, Frances H., *The Civil War Battlefield Guide,* 1998.

- McPherson, James M., *Battle Cry of Freedom,* 1988.

- Minnesota Board of Commissioners, *Minnesota in the Civil and Indian Wars, 1861-1865,* 1890

- Woodworth, Steven E., *Chickamauga, A Battlefield Guide,* 1999.

CPSIA information can be obtained at www.ICGtesting.com
Printed in the USA
BVOW04*2344020916

460912BV00005B/14/P